Sub-creating Middle-earth.
Constructions of Authorship
and the Works of J.R.R. Tolkien

Judith Klinger (ed.)

Sub-creating Middle-earth

Constructions of Authorship
and the Works of J.R.R. Tolkien

2012

Cormarë Series No. 27

Series Editors: Peter Buchs • Thomas Honegger • Andrew Moglestue • Johanna Schön

Guest Series Editor responsible for this volume: Stephanie Luther

Library of Congress Cataloging-in-Publication Data

Sub-creating Middle-earth.
Constructions of Authorship and the Works of J.R.R. Tolkien
edited by Judith Klinger
ISBN 978-3-905703-27-6

Subject headings:
Tolkien, J.R.R. (John Ronald Reuel), 1892-1973
sub-creation
authorship
The Silmarillion
The Lord of the Rings
The Hobbit

Cormarë Series No. 27

First published 2012

© Walking Tree Publishers, Zurich and Jena, 2012

All rights reserved. No portion of this book may be reproduced, by any process or technique, without the express written consent of the publisher

Cover illustration *The Red Book* by Anke Eißmann.
Reproduced by permission of the artist. Copyright Anke Eißmann 2007.

Set in Adobe Garamond Pro and Shannon by Walking Tree Publishers
Printed by Lightning Source in the United Kingdom and United States

Board of Advisors

Academic Advisors

Douglas A. Anderson (independent scholar)

Dieter Bachmann (Universität Zürich)

Patrick Curry (independent scholar)

Michael D.C. Drout (Wheaton College)

Vincent Ferré (Université de Paris-Est Créteil UPEC)

Verlyn Flieger (University of Maryland)

Thomas Fornet-Ponse (Rheinische Friedrich-Wilhelms-Universität Bonn)

Christopher Garbowski (University of Lublin, Poland)

Mark T. Hooker (Indiana University)

Andrew James Johnston (Freie Universität Berlin)

Rainer Nagel (Johannes Gutenberg-Universität Mainz)

Helmut W. Pesch (independent scholar)

Tom Shippey (University of Winchester)

Allan Turner (Friedrich-Schiller-Universität Jena)

Frank Weinreich (independent scholar)

General Readers

Johan Boots

Jean Chausse

Friedhelm Schneidewind

Isaac Juan Tomas

Patrick Van den hole

Johan Vanhecke (Letterenhuis, Antwerp)

Contents

Judith Klinger
Introduction   xi

Dirk Vanderbeke & Allan Turner
The One or the Many? Authorship, Voice and Corpus   1

Martin Simonson
Tolkien's Triple Balance:
A Redemptive Model of Heroism for the Twentieth Century   21

Judith Klinger
Tolkien's 'Strange Powers of the Mind':
Dreams, Visionary History and Authorship   43

Margaret Hiley
(Re)Authoring History: Tolkien and Postcolonialism   107

Patrick A. Brückner
One Author to Rule Them All   127

Cécile Cristofari
The Chronicle Without an Author:
History, Myth and Narration in Tolkien's Legendarium   173

Index   193

Guest Series Editor's Preface

Throughout the history of literature, questions concerning the authorship of a text have been of interest to writers and scholars of literature alike.

As a scholar of Old English and Middle English literature(s), J.R.R. Tolkien was most likely familiar with the diverse perceptions of the concept of 'the author' from the early Middle Ages until the 'Modernity' of his own times.

One question which almost inevitably emerges is how he incorporated these ideas of authorship into his works, especially into the work which many consider his primary one, *The Lord of the Rings*. Who is the 'author' of this story set in the Secondary World Tolkien intended to create? Another group of questions following and still closely related to first one would consider the author Tolkien himself. Where, for example, can we position Tolkien in the literary tradition? Can he already be called 'modern' in a literary sense?

The authors in this volume took a look at these and other problems (and some even try to solve them) from different points of view. The result is a diversified insight into the matter 'authorship in Tolkien' which I hope the reader will enjoy as much as I enjoyed reading and editing it.

Stephanie Luther
Jena, October 2012

Judith Klinger

Introduction

With the worldwide success of *The Lord of the Rings*, J.R.R. Tolkien – poet, philologist, sometimes hailed as the 'father of modern fantasy' – became a focus of widespread fascination. The lasting impact of his books, his "utter single-mindedness" (Shippey 308) that shaped an expansive body of literary works, and his lifelong dedication to the history of Middle-earth have drawn increasing attention to the man behind the tales and, consequently, to Tolkien's biography. Although Tolkien "never subscribed to the cult of the Great Author" (Shippey 314) and strongly voiced his opinion that "investigation of an author's biography [...] is an entirely vain and false approach to his works" (*L* 414; cf. *L* 288), this approach follows not only the common practice of literary criticism in the 20th century. It also reflects a desire to anchor reading experiences and journeys of the imagination in a reality beyond the text. While biographers thus seek to disclose the origins of the writer's exceptional creativity, literary critics employ biographical information as the key to unlock meaning within the literary works. Both necessarily generate conceptions of the author whose life and mind complement and explain his texts.

Among the many portrayals of the author J.R.R. Tolkien, the vivid image drawn by Humphrey Carpenter, based on a single encounter in 1967, stands out:

> He says that he has to clear up an apparent contradiction in a passage of *The Lord of the Rings* [...]. He explains it all in great detail, talking about his book not as a work of fiction but as a chronicle of actual events; he seems to see himself not as an author who has made a slight error that must now be corrected or explained away, but as a historian who must cast light on an obscurity in a historical document. [...] He has a strange voice, deep but without resonance, entirely English but with some quality in it that I cannot define, as if he had come from another age or civilisation. (Carpenter 15)

Tolkien's profound engagement with the world of his imagination elicits a striking image: "It is rather as if some strange spirit had taken on the guise of an elderly professor" (Carpenter 17).

By contrast, Tom Shippey's influential study *J.R.R. Tolkien: Author of the Century* insists that Tolkien was deeply involved with the pivotal issues and experiences of his own time. Introducing Tolkien as a "combat veteran", Shippey argues for the contemporary relevance of his works and refutes a dismissive view of Tolkien's writing – and the fantasy genre as a whole – as a vehicle of escapism and thus denial of reality (cf. Shippey viii f.).

Yet the reality in question may embrace more than present-day concerns. "Tolkien tapping away on his typewriter keys," writes David Day, "as the wandering soul of his hobbit hero moves and dances to its pulse is not unlike the shaman tapping his drum": an image carefully moulded to distinguish Tolkien as "the heir of an ancient story-telling tradition that used the common symbolic language of myth" (Day 12).

The above-mentioned books cannot be reduced to these statements, of course, but the diverging portrayals highlight – rather like snapshots – how the author Tolkien is framed within time. Whether he engages primarily with contemporary reality, with traditional languages of myth, or an imagined history has immediate bearing on the perceived meaning and relevance of his texts. His specific authority, too, derives from the diverse roles assigned to him by critics and biographers. As "historian" of Middle-earth, "shaman" or "combat veteran", he may speak with authority about varying subject matters and does so in different (literary) languages.

What becomes apparent here is that the preferred image of the author cannot be separated from the approach to, and the perception of, his works. Author and text, placed in an ongoing dialogue, complement each other. Viewed from this angle, the desire to engage with a closer reality beyond the literary work inevitably generates further texts with their own set of quests and heroes. The author Tolkien may then emerge as an inspired individual and skilled creator of an imaginary world, as commentator and critic of his own times, or rather – in Humphrey Carpenter's account – as a chronicler of contexts, conditions and events beyond his immediate control.

Yet portrayals of the author (introduced here in the most cursory fashion), form but one thread in the larger web of authorial presence both in- and outside the literary texts. This presence extends from Tolkien's self-perception as author to the (explicit or implicit) concepts and practice of authorship within his works, to the 'implied author'[1] and the surrounding assumptions that govern readers' perceptions of literature.[2]

Tolkien's essay *On Fairy-stories* is the text critics most frequently consult to illuminate his understanding of authorship and art. It represents, in the words of Verlyn Flieger and Douglas Anderson, "the theoretical basis for his fiction" and "his most explicit analysis of his own art" (Flieger and Anderson 9). It is here that Tolkien develops the concept of sub-creation (the human faculty conferred by the divine creator), intertwined with his reflections on Faërie and "the Elvish craft, Enchantment" (*OFS* 143), as well as the "Cauldron of Story", "where so many potent things lie simmering agelong on the fire" (*OFS* 125, 127). To this Cauldron however, cooks come rather like a subsidiary force, and they come in plenty: not one but many contribute to the "soup" that "has always been boiling" (*OFS* 125). This image closely approaches a postmodern perception of literature, which questions the author's importance as the governing source of meaning: "a text consists of multiple writings, issuing from several cultures and entering into dialogue with each other," writes Roland Barthes (148).

Turning to Tolkien's literary works, various author figures emerge and are in turn named creators of the presented narrative – from Ælfwine to the hobbit authors in *The Lord of the Rings*. Some texts are attributed to a team of annalists, writers or poets, whereas others seem to speak with the authorless voice of History itself.

Following these diverse threads, we may envision the author Tolkien as a "strange spirit" or a man of his century, negotiating the brink between realities – between 'primary' and 'secondary' world, between sub-creation and re-construction – as the "soup" of story is once again stirred and replenished. Our diverging perceptions may locate him somewhere between original intentions and a vast body of

---

1 'Implied author' refers to the image of an author emerging from the text, defined by characteristics of style, ideology, etc. Thus the 'implied author' is at once a projection of an intratextual authority above the narrator and subject to the reader's re-construction.
2 In brief, the set of assumptions about the creation, circulation and reception of texts constitute what Michel Foucault labels the 'author-function' (Foucault 124f.).

texts that speak in many voices about the ramifying history of Middle-earth, even while addressing a 20th-century audience.

Yet an author may well engage with a complex set of realities that shape and modify authorship in turn. That Tolkien's works interweave mythologies, literary traditions and ideas from diverse historical and cultural contexts, involving not only their content matter but also their specific forms of expression, their vocabularies and imageries, has been amply demonstrated. Moreover, his texts reveal a clear awareness that the understanding and practice of authorship is itself subject to historical change.[3] It seems reasonable, then, to assume that the notions of authorship wrapped up in these tales cannot be traced to a single, unifying concept (or a single biographical reality).

The purpose of this collection, therefore, is not to present a unified image of Tolkien the author, or of authorship within Tolkien's works. Rather it addresses the diverse manifestations of authorial presence and the textual realisations of authorship within different – literary, philosophical and historical – contexts. The pluralism of perspectives here employed certainly does not – and cannot – exhaust the subject, yet it illuminates a most profitable field of study and opens up new avenues of inquiry.

In "The One or the Many? Authorship, Voice and Corpus", Dirk Vanderbeke and Allan Turner address the tension inherent to a mythology composed by a single author and examine the specific strategies that characterise Tolkien's 'mythopoeia' against the background of myth revival since the 19th century. Martin Simonson, in "Tolkien's Triple Balance: A Redemptive Model of Heroism for the Twentieth Century", traces Tolkien's authorial presence in *The Lord of the Rings* to the uneasy combination of Christian and pagan elements that is however held in balance by a distinct awareness of contemporary concerns. My own contribution to the volume, "Tolkien's 'Strange Powers of the Mind': Dreams, Visionary History and Authorship", explores a specific remodeling of authorship within the texts, marked by visionary dreams that bridge the gap between history and Other Time.

---

3 Cf. Barthes 142f. and Foucault 125.

Margaret Hiley, in "(Re)Authoring History: Tolkien and Postcolonialism", relates "feigned history" and the incorporation of historical fragments into a new text to a postcolonial setting and the attendant change of authorship concepts. In "One Author to Rule Them All", Patrick Brückner critically reviews the construction of Tolkien as a modern author and confronts this conception with the pre-modern notions of genre and authorship arising from *The Lord of the Rings*. Finally, Cécile Cristofari compares Tolkien's works to medieval histories and chronicles in "The Chronicle Without an Author: History, Myth and Narration in Tolkien's Legendarium", and examines how the symbiosis of history and event generates a realistic 'secondary creation'.

In closing, I would like to express my profound gratitude to all contributors, and to those colleagues and friends who encouraged me to pursue the idea for this book and took part in greatly inspiring discussions. I am most grateful to the editors of Walking Tree Publishers for their generous support and deeply indebted to Thomas Honegger for invaluable encouragement and advice.

Judith Klinger
Berlin, 22 September 2012

Works cited

Barthes, Roland. "The Death of the Author." *Image – Music – Text*. Essays selected and translated by Stephen Heath. London: Fontana Press, 1977. 142-48.

Carpenter, Humphrey. *J. R. R. Tolkien. A Biography*. London: Harper Collins Publishers, 1977.

Day, David. *Tolkien's Ring*. Illustrated by Alan Lee. London: Pavilion Books Limited, 1999.

Flieger, Verlyn and Douglas A. Anderson. *Tolkien On Fairy-stories*. Expanded Edition with Commentary and Notes. London: Harper Collins Publishers, 2008.

Foucault, Michel. "What Is an Author?" *Language, Counter-Memory, Practice. Selected Essays and Interviews by Michel Foucault*. Ed. Donald F. Bouchard. Ithaca & New York: Cornell University Press, 1977. 113-38.

Shippey, Tom. *J. R. R. Tolkien. Author of the Century*. New York & Boston: Houghton Mifflin Company, 2002.

Tolkien, J. R. R. *The Letters of J. R. R. Tolkien*. A Selection edited by Humphrey Carpenter with the assistance of Christopher Tolkien. 1981. London: Houghton Mifflin, 1995.

---. "On Fairy-Stories." *The Monsters and the Critics and Other Essays*. Ed. Christopher Tolkien. 1983. London: Harper Collins, 1997. 109-161.

Dirk Vanderbeke & Allan Turner

The One or the Many?
Authorship, Voice and Corpus

Abstract

A myth, regardless of how many times it is retold and in how many different forms, is ultimately the product of a culture and not of an individual. In the case of a literary creation in the mythical mode, any impression of historical depth must be created by the author, as is well known in the case of Tolkien. We examine Tolkien's technique in comparison with some other re-writers of traditional tales in order to see whether, either inside or outside the fiction, it is possible to establish any real or putative 'original'. We also consider whether the posthumous corpus of texts in the form in which it has been edited by Christopher Tolkien actually equates to the textual structure of a real world mythology, as has been claimed.

The problem of authorship in Tolkien can be seen as a Chinese box of worms. On each level from the various versions of world history as performed in front of Ilúvatar to Bilbo's and Frodo's version of the War of the Ring, to the different sources implied or actually presented in the 'Silmarillion' corpus and other writings, to the fictitious translator or editor who reworked the tales into the form we now read, to Tolkien who transformed fairy-stories, myths and legends for his own ends, and finally to Christopher Tolkien editing the works of his father – an absent original is turned into something new, but not quite new.

Historically, Tolkien's endeavour can be located halfway between the Germanic and Irish projects of the 19th century with their revival of myth in the service of a nationalistic agenda (medievalism, Wagner, but also Lady Gregory and Yeats) and postmodern revisions of myth. The literary output of Lady Gregory and Yeats was intimately bound up with their programme of cultural and (in the case of Yeats) national politics, and made a significant contribution to a sense of identity upon which, at least in part, the Irish Free State could be founded. There is no indication of any such cultural or political programme in the work of Tolkien, who was after all a professional academic whose reputation for most of his life was restricted to Oxford and other centres of learning. He wrote largely in obscurity, reading his tales or lending his manuscripts only to a small group of like-minded scholars who shared similar tastes. It is even debatable how many of the numerous manuscripts he left behind at his death were actually intended for publication. It could be argued that the concept of what has become known as a "mythology for England" became less important as his 'Silmarillion' expanded into the world of *The Lord of the Rings*, while the planned frame narrative to connect the 'lost tales' with medieval and modern England, in spite of vaguely planned radical alterations (cf. Flieger 94f.), gradually faded from the scene. Or rather, the attempts to create a mythical pedigree for Englishness became displaced into the more concrete depiction of the Shire and its Hobbit inhabitants, which Shippey (81ff.) sees as a reference point through which modern readers can successfully engage with a pre-modern, heroic world. However, what links Tolkien to the revival of myth in the 19th and early 20th centuries is the evocation of a heroic past as a model to which people in the present need to aspire.

On the surface there is much less common ground between Tolkien and post-modernism. In particular, there is nothing of the playfulness which marks, for example, literary fireworks like John Barth's postmodern revisions of myth, e.g. *Giles Goat-Boy*, *Chimera*, "Menelaiad", "Anonymiad" or some chapters of *Tidewater Tales*. One can hardly imagine a text less capable of irony – not to speak of self-reflexive irony – than the 'Silmarillion' corpus, and whatever the tale in question may be, it is always presented with a seriousness bordering on the grim. However, there are also similarities, not the least being a radical departure from the sources and a willingness to treat some of the most renowned and almost sacred texts in world literature as a quarry for their own projects. In this respect, Tolkien's Nordic image of a 'cauldron of stories', to which "have continually been added new bits, dainty and undainty" (*OFS* 125), is closely matched by Barth's frequent references to the 'Ocean of Story', not only the Indian collection of tales from the 11th century by Somadeva but also the larger concept of a reservoir of tales.¹ In *Tidewater Tales*, for example, the protagonists sailing on Chesapeake Bay at the same time take "a cruise through the Ocean of Story" (90) on a ship named Story, and the body of water indeed turns into a reservoir from which not only stories can be recovered; in the course of their voyage the story-loving couple also meet some slightly displaced literary figures (e.g. Donald Quicksoat) who re-tell them their stories and what really happened after the final curtain.

John Barth compared his particular variety of authorship not to the work of a composer but to the performance of an arranger:

> At heart I'm an arranger still, whose chiefest literary pleasure is to take a received melody – an old narrative poem, a classical myth, a shopworn literary convention, a shard of my experience, a *New York Times Book Review* series – and, improvising like a jazzman within its constraints, re-orchestrate it to present purpose. (*Friday Book* 7)

In the arrangement, John Barth most decisively alters the tone of the tales he reworks in his novels, turning them into wild and occasionally rambunctious yarns within a rather complex postmodern framework. Fascinated by the oriental tradition in general and the idea of the *Arabian Nights* that storytelling is a necessity for survival, but adding his own flavour of a less threatening environment, Barth frequently replaces the 'camp fire' or hearth situation of oral story telling by the more intimate meeting of lovers, sharing food, tales and the bed. In consequence there is little inhibition, and the body functions that are part and parcel of mythology² play a significant role in his re-tellings.

---

1 The image is once more taken up by Rushdie in *Haroun and the Sea of Stories*, in particular in the Story "An Iff and a Butt": "So Iff the Water Genie told Haroun about the Ocean of the Streams of Story, and even though he was full of a sense of hopelessness and failure, the magic of the Ocean began to have an effect on Haroun. He looked into the water and saw that it was made up of a thousand thousand thousand and one different currents, each one a different colour, weaving in and out of one another like a liquid tapestry of breathtaking complexity; and Iff explained that these were the Streams of Story, that each coloured strand represented and contained a single tale [...]. And because the stories were held in a fluid form, they retained the ability to change, to become new versions of themselves, to join up with other stories and so become yet other stories; so that unlike a library of books, the Ocean of the Streams of Stories was much more than a storeroom of yarns. It was not dead but alive." (72).
2 As the origin and the very material of the universe in mythology is frequently the body of a giant, the role of all the aspects of a body's biology can hardly be overestimated.

But the myth itself is usually kept intact;[3] in the "Perseid" novella of *Chimera*, Cassiopeia is Andromeda's mother and Medusa was turned into a Gorgon when she overstepped the rules of propriety in Poseidon's temple. Thus the myth is there even though the narrative performance differs in many ways from earlier accounts, similar to the improvisation of a jazz musician who takes one of the many standards to rework it into something quite, but not totally new.

Mythopoeia and historicity

However, that is something altogether different from the creation of a mythology from zero, even though, as we shall argue, there is not really any zero to start from, since readers already have reference points in pre-existing myths or legends. Tolkien most naturally expressed his deepest feelings in mythological form; he once described himself as a person "whose instinct is to cloak such self-knowledge as he has, and such criticisms of life as he knows it, under mythical and legendary dress" (*L* 211). Using the musical analogy once more, an original melody is no longer really recognizable, but motifs and phrases are taken from all over the place and reworked into a new tune. However, the mood of the Tolkien tunes unvaryingly preserves a distinctive sombre tone – the tone he considers appropriate to myth. With some exaggeration and with tongue in cheek one might claim that all the different voices of mythology have been transformed to a single dominant style appropriate for the elegiac and slightly melancholy lays of Elvish origin, that all the Tolkien orchestra will ever play are dirges.

In more than one respect Tolkien's project of creating a new myth within a new world most closely resembles the analogous invention of a mythological past in the works of his contemporary Howard Philips Lovecraft, who

---

3 *Giles Goat-Boy* is an important exception, but then, the "adventures of a young man sired by a giant computer upon a hapless but compliant librarian and raised in the experimental goat-barn of a universal university" (viii) are simultaneously a parody and fulfilment of the quest of the wandering mythical hero: "He must leave his (usually adoptive) home and parents, the familiar daylight world of conscious reality and sundry ego-tokens; he must pass through the twilit territory of dreamish forms and porous categories; aided by guides, helpers, intuitions, tricks, and secrets, he must deal with initiatory riddles and ordeals, with irreal (but not unreal) monstrosities of the subconscious; he must attain at last the Princess, the Elixir: unmediated, noumenal knowledge in the dark, unconscious nameless centre, the bottom of things" (vi-vii).

was similarly successful in the forging of a new sub-genre which has by now achieved cult status among a devoted readership and also inspired a host of epigones. And, as in the case of Tolkien, there is no mistaking of the Lovecraft voice – far less literate, very repetitive and frequently turning to the nigh unintelligible utterances of his imaginary demon worshippers, but also enamoured with the names of fictional locations, pseudo-mythological creatures and ancient books hinting at even older knowledge. As both authors reorganized their sources to a degree which makes any explicit reference to existing myths impossible and, in addition, divorces the implicit recognition by a perceptive readership from the textual system of meaning production, an alternative body of tales and legends was required to make up for the lack of an authentic past and to add the veneer of historical and mythological depth to the respective narrations.

In the case of Lovecraft there are constant references to fictitious books of yore like Abdul Alhazred's *Necronomicon*, von Junzt's *Unaussprechliche Kulte* or Ludvig Prinn's *De Vermiis Mysteriis*. In *The Lord of the Rings* the supposedly ancient lore is recalled in the main text not only through direct reference, as by Elrond and Faramir, but also in the form of tales and lays, supported in the frame narrative of the Appendices (see Turner 2008) by histories and allusions to 'documents'. Even the *Silmarillion*, which is presented as the source of the mythological and historical background legends, has its embedded texts, such as the extract from the *Lay of Leithian* in 'Of Beren and Lúthien'. However, none of these texts aspires to the role of the true and original source, the *Ur-Text*; instead they rather offer different accounts and versions of some even earlier lore which has been lost in the course of history.[4]

The absence of an *Ur-Text* and its evocation as a means to add historical and mythological depth to the world of Tolkien's creation is discussed in Gergely Nagy's essay "The great chain of reading: (Inter-)textual relations and the

---

4 There are even some striking thematic similarities between Lovecraft and Tolkien. In *The Silmarillion*, "Manwë put forth Morgoth and shut him beyond the World in the Void that is without; and he cannot himself return again into the World, present and visible, while the Lords of the West are still enthroned. Yet the seeds that he had planted still grew and sprouted, bearing evil fruit, if any would tend them. For his will remained and guided his servants ..." (312). According to Lovecraft's Cthulhu Myth, there has been a cosmic battle in prehistoric times between the benevolent Elder Ones, now absent, and the evil Great Old Ones, who were overthrown and locked away in remote places but persistently try to return with the help of their depraved servants (cf. Derleth, ix-x).

technique of mythopoesis in the Túrin story". In particular, Nagy points out the analogy between *Beowulf* and *The Lord of the Rings* in their allusions to a "background of knowledge", adding depth to the narration and thus creating the illusion of a complete world with an equally complete past. Analyzing the various layers of narration, levels of intertextual references and the relationship between contextualisations, textual backgrounds and pseudo-texts, Nagy claims that "*[c]reating* a mythological system is done in essentially the same way as *inventing* one" (247). He comes back this point again later, arguing that "Tolkien's texts and the background mythological system they succeed in creating are essentially similar to real world mythological corpora and the way they invoke their mythological system because of the basically similar relation of text to myth" (252). According to his line of argument, the actual myth is told and retold in the various texts but it cannot be identified with any of them. All versions are legitimate retextualisations (cf. Nagy 250), but none is the myth itself, and thus he finally proposes "the handling of *myth as a pseudo-text*, with an indefinite number of retexts, which is a way to account for both the differing story versions and the complex textual tangle" (252). This is a problematic conclusion to the widely discussed topos of myth in Tolkien, as it turns the usual line of critical pursuit on its head. According to Nagy,

> [a] pseudo-text [...] is mainly a theoretical construct: it is a text we know never to have existed but to have been invented by the author. Needless to say, no real textual relation can exist between a text and a pseudo-text: its main function is to *create* one, to situate the author's text in a textual relation and thereby endow it with certain characteristics. (244)

This of course fits Tolkien's use of references to earlier variants quite well, and it seems as if Nagy now transfers the useful concept of the pseudo-text in the fictional secondary world to the discussion of myth in the primary world of our experience. But this brings some major problems, as in Tolkien's fiction indeed the references at some point are no longer to existing previous versions, while in the case of myth the chain of different versions does not break off, even though there is, of course, no original *Ur-Text* on which all the retellings are based, but only the complex web of interacting variants.

Thus the concept that there is ultimately no *Ur-Text*, no original version, in Tolkien as in the real world does not necessarily entail that the mythological systems are essentially the same. As long as we see the various retextualisations chiefly as a textual system, the similarities are indeed striking, but once we ask what possible meaning is conveyed by myth and what relation the tales have to their respective worlds the differences can no longer be ignored.

In Tolkien the allusion is frequently to a knowledge that does not exist anywhere and never did. However, as the world of Tolkien is derivative of his own scholarship about myth and medieval literature, the allusion may on one level be to an invented past via a non-existent source,[5] be it myth, tale or legend within Middle-earth, but on another level also to an existing source in our own past. Thus there are, in fact, two levels of absence involved, the absent original of some hypothetical source within the fictional world and the absent mythologies – Germanic, Greek, Finnish, etc. – that were dismembered by Tolkien and served up as the soup of Middle-earth sagas. In this respect, the bones out of which it has been boiled need to be addressed, even though *in absentia*, and in spite of the fact that Tolkien dismisses such an academic endeavour (cf. *OFS* 120).

This may seem to be a rather trivial point, but the fact that the fantastic elements of Tolkien's secondary world are familiar to everyone who ever cherished Nordic mythology – or even everyone who grew up with the usual exposure to fairy tales – indicates either a conscious decision by the author or a lack of imagination we would not like to attribute to Tolkien. After all, even a mediocre author like Lovecraft was able to invent some monsters and creatures that are not directly derivative of earlier myths and tales. In contrast (and ignoring the not entirely successful balrogs), Tolkien not only introduces dragons that look and act precisely as we would expect them to, he also puts them on a dragon hoard or infuses them with the desire for gold that is the most stereotypical feature of our scaly brethren ever since Sigurd and before Michael Ende turned the imagery on its head and invented the recently fashionable dragons of wisdom or luckdragons. Of course, one might argue that the adherence to traditional traits supported one of the primary objectives of Tolkien's production of fairy-stories, the secondary belief in the coherence and

---

5 In this context Nagy also mentions the medieval practice of inventing sources and backgrounds as, for example in Chaucer or Malory (cf. 240), and one may add the perhaps not fully serious reference to the fictitious predecessor Kyot in Wolfram's *Parzival* as another example.

internal plausibility of the secondary world, but then it also means that in the face of the cauldron of stories the author is strictly on the receiving end and dismisses the chance to add some dainty bits and morsels of his own to the steaming stew. Moreover, the author necessarily keeps one of his feet firmly in the primary world and its reference systems; in Tolkien's case this includes not only traditional myths and fairy-stories, but also the whole body of literature and philosophy, bits and pieces of which also turn up at unexpected places.

For example, the orcs are, of course, within the mythology of Middle-earth as narrated in *The Silmarillion*, the products of the sub-deity Melkor, the Middle-earth equivalent of Satan. This, however, bears strong parallels to medieval tales and legends according to which monsters were the offspring of the devil or the result of an original sin.[6] The orcs are sometimes called goblins, which may be derived either directly from folklore or indirectly via George MacDonald. But then there is, of course, also the home-made mythology of William Blake and his character Orc, addressed as "Blasphemous Demon, Antichrist, hater of Dignities, / Lover of wild rebellion, and transgressor of God's Law" (Blake, *America: A Prophecy*) but ultimately nevertheless a positive figure. Similarly, the image of a seven-walled city has a long pedigree from Herodotus's description of Ecbatana to Campanella's City of the Sun.

This 'double vision' which shifts between the topoi of the primary world and the legends of the secondary world has some impact on Nagy's argument. He suggests that the allusions to Túrin in *The Lord of the Rings* may be seen as a form of reference to an unknown hero of the past which requires the existence of other texts for its full comprehension. He writes that "not much of the actual story of Túrin can be gleaned from these, other than that he was a great hero" (241), but this is not quite the end of it. It is true that we may not at this stage know anything about the story of Túrin as told in other texts of the Tolkien corpus, but then the second passage he quotes will not remain contained within

---

6 In *Beowulf*, all ogres, elves, evil shades and giants are the kindred of Cain in consequence of his killing of Abel (cf. also *OFS* 13), and while Tolkien obviously had a more benevolent perspective on Elves, the genealogy of evil creatures as the descendants of a first perpetrator bears some resemblance to his conception. Moreover, some medieval demonologies argue that the devil and his demons are envious of God's creation but unable to create by themselves. According to the *Malleus Maleficarum* of Jacob Sprenger and Heinrich Institoris, this is the reason why demons act as *incubi* and *succubi*. They use semen 'borrowed' from a man to impregnate a woman under unfavourable constellations and so produce corrupted offspring.

the text. Inevitably, the claim that Shelob's hide has no soft spot and thus cannot be pierced by any hand "not though Elf or Dwarf should forge the steel or the hand of Beren or of Túrin wield it" (*LotR* 728) will not fail to evoke Siegfried or Sigurd piercing the soft belly of Fafnir with Gram/Balmung/Nothung, the sword reforged by the dwarf Regin/Mime, or Beowulf's fight with the dragon.[7] In consequence, and in contrast to Nagy's subsequent argument, it is neither necessary that the content of Túrin's story needs to be supplied in order to elucidate the allusion, nor would the allusion create depth by some feeling of incomprehension, as the paradigmatic source is readily available to any reader who has noticed by the time Shelob's lair is reached that Tolkien is heavily indebted to European medieval and traditional sources. Taking the situation at Shelob's lair as a point of departure, the reader is faced with an allusion in a text, allegedly written by Frodo (although only Sam could have provided the information)[8], vaguely referring to a dragon-slaying hero of their past but understandable to the reader by reference to a host of similar heroes from the mythology of his own world and culture.[9]

The generic dragon killer is perhaps more relevant for the present purposes than any specific sources, medieval or modern, which the individual reader may have chanced to read. Tolkien himself certainly admitted that a similarity to the Sigurd story could be seen, but added the typical caveat "by people who like that sort of thing, though it is not very useful" (*L* 150). This is an oblique re-statement of the point he made in *On Fairy-Stories* (119), that in his opinion the reduction of story motifs to archetypes is the task of folklorists, whereas literary critics should concentrate on exactly how an author uses a motif in its new unique context. But in the case of the mythological allusion,

---

7 The twofold allusion is complicated by the fact that the dragon-slaying Völsung is actually alluded to in *Beowulf* and his heroic deed is thus enfolded within the saga of the Geat.
8 The fact that neither Bilbo nor Frodo nor Sam can be identified with the narrator of *The Lord of the Rings*, because he sometimes steps outside the time-frame and refers to events that take place much later, does not alter the dilemma, as the question of where the allusion originated remains unsolved.
9 The dragon-slaying hero is also well known from a wide range of popular versions and representations, of which Andrew Lang's *Red Fairy Book* is only one. For English readers of Tolkien's generation it would also evoke images of St. George, the patron saint of England. Before the modern trend for pub chains with formulaic or ironic names, there were numerous inns called "The George and Dragon" with signs depicting the fight with the dragon. The original reference to Smaug growing fat through eating the "maidens of the valley" (removed from the 3rd edition of *The Hobbit*) surely owes more to legends like that of St. George than to either the *Völsunga saga* or *Beowulf*. To the already saturated broth one might also add Perseus, as a possible narrative predecessor to all of the later tales.

at first there actually is no 'how', as the tale itself is absent, a gap to be filled by the reader from his or her knowledge of any other mythological, literary, cinematographic, pictorial or even musical source. Only with the several versions offered in other works is a background provided, that indicates that there has always been an earlier version, but also re-enforces the first association with one or more mythological motifs of our world. The text remains a wanderer between worlds without any certain hearth and homestead it can ultimately return to. The reason for this ambiguous situation lies in yet another empty space in Tolkien's mythological corpus, this time in the missing (or at least fragmentary) frame narrative of the 'Silmarillion' legendarium. The long gestation period meant that not only did it grow by a process of accretion, but also its mythological significance changed as what was originally a closed-ended cycle became drawn into the extended history of *The Lord of the Rings*. What Tolkien was always trying in vain to achieve was a seamless and convincing transition into the present. On the one level, this was required by his medievalist's desire to provide a manuscript tradition calqued on that of the genuine medieval texts with which he worked, as well as to satisfy his sense of verisimilitude. On another, it appears to have been linked, as Christopher Tolkien's cautious comments suggest, with an ambition to create a 'supermyth' for north-western Europe. A lot has been written about Tolkien's supposed 'mythology for England', an aim which he admitted was "absurd" (*L* 144f.), but there is no doubt that throughout his works there is a recurrent tendency to provide putative 'originals' which will explain the apparently nonsensical fragments of folklore and legend, from the early nursery rhyme rewritings like 'The Cat and the Fiddle', which subsequently found its way into *The Lord of the Rings*, through the use in *The Hobbit* of dwarf names from the *Völuspá* which retrospectively turns that virtually meaningless list into "the last faded memento of something once great and important, an Odyssey of the dwarves" (Shippey 80), to the Elvish Tol Eressëa as the origin of culture heroes, ship burials, and medieval beliefs about an earthly paradise.

Tolkien tried out many different combinations with the proto-English traveller Eriol, the Anglo-Saxon Ælfwine and the regressive inherited dream device of *The Lost Road* and *The Notion Club Papers*, but they all remain fragmentary. This is not surprising, as he tried increasingly to make his invented world meet the standards of credibility of our own primary world. That was of course an impossible task, since a narrative that is one hundred percent congruent with reality as we understand it cannot also be a fictional text. In the end he fudged the issue with the conceit of the 'Red Book', leaving the manuscript tradition within the secondary world and keeping it a mystery how the texts came into the hands of an English 'editor' in the 20th century. The supermyth thus never actually came into existence and can be perceived only by the traces that it has left behind in the legendary motifs which belong to both worlds.[10] It is therefore no lack of imagination that caused Tolkien to feature northern European dragons rather than creating entirely new monsters, but rather a mythopoeic conception that was simply too vast to be realised.

Myth and metaphor

Our argument so far has assumed a model of authorship, whether for rewritings of traditional mythologies or for modern fictional creations in a mythical mode, in which we are to imagine a hollow centre, an ultimate void. The alternative view, that there was indeed a hypothetical first version, based on a real event or series of events, from which all later ones differ except in the tone and style to which they all aspire, leads to a new problem, the ontological status of the tales and their content.

One of the most significant points in this context is the role of the narrated past. In this respect, the status of the events as told and retold in the various versions of the myths is of course of crucial importance in the context of narration and the transmission of tales within the work of Tolkien. Nagy points at the significant aspect that within the textual world they are "not simply stories, but *history*" (247). This indicates that behind the different textualisations there has been an event. From this first an oral tradition developed which later coagulated into a

---

10 So in this sense Túrin *is* Sigurd, just as he is Kullervo of the *Kalevala*, since in this concept either of them might have originated with him, but at the same time he is neither. The identification with Sigurd at a very early stage of Tolkien's writing is proved by an entry in the *Qenya Lexicon* (95f.), where the gloss for Turambar includes "cp. Sigurðr". The editors identify Turambar 'Conqueror of Fate' as a calque on Tolkien's (possibly erroneous) interpretation of the name as *sigr* 'victory' + *urðr* 'fate, destiny'. But in the course of the elaboration of the tale over more than 40 years, the life of Túrin becomes part of a web of event and causation that bears no further resemblance to its original models, which is no doubt the reason for Tolkien's dismissive comment.

variety of versions in prose or verse. These, in turn, became part of a complex network of interconnected texts with internal references and allusions.

Of course, the original event is on a different ontological level than, let's say, some hypothetical historical action, event or process that may have been at the root of the tradition that later led to the myth of Perseus, Beowulf or Sigurd. Within the textual world of Tolkien one can neglect or dismiss many elements that need to be taken into account in real world myths. When it is told that Túrin or Bard kills a dragon, we are to understand that that is what they actually did. Thus, when Elrond, Sam or anyone else alludes to a heroic deed of some mythological past, the allusion is also to a historical event of bravery, which is retold in many different versions. The knowledge transmitted in these allusions is historical knowledge, albeit transformed and possibly distorted by time.

This, of course, is hardly the case in real world mythology. Whatever glorious feats of courage were performed in any prehistoric past, our knowledge of palaeontology tells us that they did not involve the slaying of dragons or similar monsters. Moreover, there could not possibly occur any situation in which someone, while fighting an oversized spider, compared this deed to some previous actual fight against a dragon as neither of these creatures has or had any existence in our world. However, this by no means indicates that myth merely presents us with the imaginative perspectives of a prerational imagination or that myth does not transmit any serious knowledge about the real world. In the course of the last century there has been an enormous amount of fascinating research into the possible meanings of myth, as for example in Jerome Lettvin's "The Gorgon's Eye" or Georgio de Santillana's and Hertha von Dechend's *Hamlet's Mill: An Essay Investigating the Origins of Human Knowledge and Its Transmission Through Myth*. But then the knowledge is transmitted not by any narrative about realistic actions, but by metaphorisations or allegorisations, i.e. the tale of Hamlet's Mill may offer some insight into cosmological processes and the petrifying eye of the Gorgon may carry aspects of an octopus, but also of Algol, the variable star in the Perseus constellation. This, of course, is not altogether new, and even in Plato's *Timaeus* myth is presented as a form through which knowledge of a very different kind can be transmitted, even though the ability to decode it may be lost at later times:

There is a story, which even you have preserved, that once upon a time Phaeton, the son of Helios, having yoked the steeds in his father's chariot, because he was not able to drive them in the path of his father, burnt up all that was upon the earth, and was himself destroyed by a thunderbolt. Now this has the form of a myth, but really signifies a declination of the bodies moving in the heavens around the earth, and a great conflagration of things upon the earth, which recurs after long intervals. (*Timaeus* 22c-d)[11]

The fact that myth can be interpreted in many ways is not merely derivative of myriad retellings, the multiple uses a myth has been put to ever since antiquity or even a modern or postmodern perspective, but a property it had since its very beginning, because it actually always meant several different things at one and the same time. On a different level, the legend of Siegfried and the Nibelungs in all probability offers knowledge about a historical event, albeit less about the feats of an individual hero but rather of an extended historical process which was mixed with elements of other Nordic myths and garbed in the narration about Siegfried's death, the Kings of Burgundy and their adversary Attila/Etzel.

The presentation: voice and tone

At this point it is necessary to return momentarily to the problem of voice as it has some impact on the discussion of different versions and variants of myths and tales in the Tolkien corpus. When we tune our ears to different accounts of a myth or a mythological motif in the primary world, we will hear a huge variety of different voices. No one could possibly mistake Homer's voice for Ovid's in the respective narrations of Odysseus' adventures – not even if the texts were translated into a third language. The *Völsunga saga* differs from the *Nibelungenlied* not only in content but also in style and tone, and the motif of a father having to sacrifice his daughter because she was the

---

[11] Tolkien acknowledges this aspect, "'nature myth' or allegory of the larger processes of nature", when he dismisses the (for him) simplistic and mistaken arguments of Max Müller, who assumes "that nothing actually exists corresponding to the 'gods' of mythology: no personalities, only astronomical or meteorological objects" (*OFS* 123). This aspect quite obviously plays little or no role in his own works, and it is possibly significant that in the course of the same argument he also plays down the role of humour in myth, when he claims that the *Thrymskvitha* "is certainly just a fairy-story" (*OFS* 124). It seems as if Tolkien models his concept either on a totally solemn and spiritual view of myth or even on his own writings, which for some readers lack any kind of humour. However, in the context of myth, spirituality, humour and even bawdiness are not necessarily mutually exclusive.

first to meet him after his return home sounds very different depending on whether we read it in the *Book of Judges* 11 or in the multiple fairy tales to which it has been adapted. As we have argued above, this is hardly the case in Tolkien's works where the tone of the different narrations is far less diverse than their content. Whoever tells the tale is invariably enamoured of names, be it places, persons or things, and the tone is always sombre and slightly melancholic – probably aspiring to an approximation of Elvish poetry in a non-Elvish language.

In contrast to a real-world mythology, Tolkien's narratives share a common underlying tone. This applies in particular to the 'Silmarillion' corpus, where in spite of the different text forms (annals, epic verse) and textures (the compressed chronicle style of the *Quenta* as against the more expansive, novelistic style of the *Narn*), the story is one of defeat and loss. *The Lord of the Rings*, in spite of the comic earthiness of the hobbits and the great moments of eucatastrophe, is also suffused with a sense of the imminent loss of something ancient and wonderful. The different parts of the long history may differ in events and characters (Elvish, hobbit or human) but not in the world view or in the gaze on the line of events within a history and possibly eschatology.

An interesting example occurs in the story of Númenor, which is significant in that it is definitely based on a primary world model, that of Atlantis. This is the one narrative where Tolkien at one point felt a need to distinguish between an Elvish (*The Fall of Númenor*), a Mannish (*The Drowning of Anadûnê*) and a mixed Dúnedainic (the *Akallabêth*) version. In each there is a difference of viewpoint based on knowledge of events, since the Mannish myth is characterised by ignorance concerning Elves and Valar, but the interpretation of the cataclysmic event and the tone in which it is expressed remain virtually the same; the tale of the Elves – who actually experienced the fall of Númenor and the bending of the seas – does not differ so very much from the narration of Men, for whom it is the equivalent to prehistory and thus might have been expected to have undergone radical narrative and stylistic transformations. The changes in names and temporary confusion over the Avalāi (*SD* 354) are only a minimal difference where one might expect new metaphorisations and, possibly, also a human perspective that includes a fascination with the seducer. Moreover, the view on the most important aspect of the tale, death vs. immortality, does not differ in the narrations of immortal Elves and mortal Men. One might argue that even in the two tales of Atlantis, both told by Plato and attributed to Critias, there is more difference than between the accounts of the Middle-earth equivalent – in *Critias* the destruction is the result of divine punishment for the islanders depravity while in *Timaeus* the catastrophe is simply caused by earthquakes and floods.[12]

Admittedly, the original versions in *The Book of Lost Tales* are in places markedly Ovidian, in spite of the Germanic and Finnish influences in some of the tales; it is primarily a literary mythology. The story of the Two Trees is very poetical, but it could appear to the modern reader as pure decoration. The story of Túrin, in spite of the motifs taken from Kullervo and Sigurd, has something of the feeling of a Greek tragedy about it. But a general tone prevails in all the narrations, the melancholy or even gloomy feeling of loss and decay informs the narrative style no matter whether it is Elves or Men who transmit the tales.

It can hardly be assumed that someone steeped in philology did not notice this predominantly monochromatic aspect in his own works. Therefore it must be at least to some extent the result of a conscious choice, for which two possible explanations may be put forward: an inordinate fondness on Tolkien's part for literature with this particular flavour, and the incomplete, fragmentary nature of the 'Silmarillion' corpus. The tone can certainly be compared with that of the literature to which Tolkien devoted a large part of his professional interest, the elegiac poetry of Old English, and particularly *Beowulf*, which he described as "full of dark and twilight, and laden with sorrow and regret" (*EW* 172). Within the fiction, the feigned authors are typically writing their accounts in Gondolin, the last outpost of the Elves against Morgoth, or else at

---

12 However, once this is stated, the question immediately raises its head whether Plato's account of Atlantis can be treated as a myth. The narrations of the Egyptian priest in *Critias* and *Timaeus* certainly aspire to the status of historical knowledge, and the fact that gods are presented as agents in the destruction of Atlantis does not necessarily change anything in this respect. The use of myth in a narration does not immediately turn the narration into myth itself. Moreover, as no other source for the fabled island has ever been found either in Greece or in Egypt, the probability is high that Atlantis is Plato's invention, and in this regard the similarity to Tolkien's literary productions is striking. The two accounts of Atlantis differ considerably and so we have to deal with two versions of a lost source, albeit both in the hand of the same author twice pretending merely to report what he has been told by one and the same person.

the Havens of Sirion after the fall of Gondolin, or on the shores of Middle-earth after escaping from the cataclysm of Númenor. They may imagine themselves to be the survivors of a civilisation in ruins, looking back with regret for what is lost. Even the compressed style of the *Quenta* and the *Annals* has about it something of the epitomes of Classical learning compiled in the last days of the western Roman Empire.

The nature of the 'Silmarillion' corpus, taking into consideration the form in which it has been published as *The History of Middle-earth*, is an issue that has not yet been addressed in depth by Tolkien criticism. Following Nagy with his idea of conflicting variants would lead to the conclusion that Tolkien is a modernist author. This could be supported by the specific status of the legends. If they are indeed the conflicting and possibly even incompatible accounts of historical events, the problem of how it is possible to access and recover the past becomes a significant aspect of the tales. Take the following quote in which we have merely changed a few nouns:

> All [the different versions of the story/history] construct mnemonic spaces to account for what has happened and to create a narrative order for the representation of that which is irrevocably gone. In the course of the [work] the subjective dimension, the role of imagination in the reconstruction of the past gains more and more dominance over the futile attempts to objectively represent historical reality. Finally, the underside of these various attempts to regain the lost past is brought to the fore. Images of decay pervade the [texts]. The bygone past is only present in the materiality of its decay: as ruin, dust, ash, or illegible mark. These materialities that signify nothing but the absence of the past have a twofold, somewhat paradoxical function: They are the sites that enable the playful imagination to fill in the gaps and to reconstruct what might have happened, and at the same time, as opaque monuments, they transcend and resist the historical as a space for the construction of meaningful narratives. (Albers)

The image created of a multi-voiced presentation of the historical past matches Nagy's account of the multiple versions and narrations about a heroic past as transmitted within the different texts of the Tolkien corpus. The past was unquestionably superior to the present which is marked by decline, but then the knowledge of the past is also almost lost and only recoverable through the remnants of ancient lore that are not always accurate and may differ in the various accounts. History has turned into myth. However, the quotation is not about Tolkien but about Faulkner's *Absalom, Absalom*, and this novel is almost paradigmatic as a modernist investigation into the evasiveness of history. Seen from this perspective, the pre-modern elements of the text cannot obscure the fact that Tolkien was a child of his time and thus could not escape the modern condition in his fiction.

However, a shift in perspective shows that this is exactly what Tolkien is not. Nagy's argument depends to a large part on accepting the independent status of all the texts; his complex model depends on the way in which the posthumous works were presented to the public rather than any demonstrable design of the author. This is legitimate in so far as they all exist in published form and are therefore available individually for literary criticism and analysis, but in their completeness they represent a corpus rather than a canon. The meticulously edited texts on the printed page should not let us forget Christopher Tolkien's comments that in many cases a particular version had apparently been abandoned by its author as his ideas changed, or had been almost annihilated by layers of subsequent amendments to the manuscript. If Tolkien had completed *The Silmarillion* to his satisfaction, to judge by his usual practice it is not unlikely that he would have decided on a 'canonical' form of the story, even if the narrative was not completely unified, following Christopher Tolkien's suggestions that his father came to the material as "a compilation, a compendious narrative" (*S* 8). He would have done this not least for the sake of "Secondary Belief". If this was the highest objective in Tolkien's production of his secondary world, and there are good reasons to believe that it was, at least from the late 1930s on, the tales would be constructed in such a way as not to disrupt the involvement of the audience, quite unlike Barth with his deliberate alienation effects and incongruity between the ancient and the modern. In this respect Tolkien would certainly appear as pre-modernist.

Ultimately we are facing a multi-levelled paradoxical situation which cannot simply be resolved but requires either an Alexander to cut through the knot or else the acceptance of inherent contradictions. On the one hand there are the multiple accounts, the various re-tellings of the legends of yore, indicating the multiplicity of traditions and narrators. On the other hand the stories in all their different versions are stylistically so similar that they suggest a common authorial voice behind each and every one of them.[13] On the one hand, the assumed historicity of the tales told in the lays and legends suggests that history is always a construction and that every re-telling is only a fiction, and that is a modernist concept. On the other hand, Tolkien's insistence on the importance of "Secondary Belief" challenges any notion of a deep epistemological doubt or despair that is an integral part of the modernist condition and the relativist perspective on history. And if we decided to accept these contradictory elements in the work as a form of creative playfulness, we would construct a post-modern Tolkien who would be completely unrecognisable to his readers and critics alike.

There is, of course, a way out of the dilemma, i.e. reject all texts that were not published by Tolkien himself as incomplete and thus unsuitable to take their full place in the corpus. All the variants would then be reduced to drafts and drafts only, and even *The Silmarillion* would remain a hypothetical entity, "unfinished, sent before [its] time into this breathing world, scarce half made up" (Shakespeare, *Richard III*, I.i.20-21). It would be the radical method of dealing with the authorial problems, with a knot so entangled that it looks like a Chinese box of lindworms – but where is the Sigurd, Túrin or Alexander who would dare to raise the sword?

Works cited

Albers, Phillip. "History – Memory – Decay. Deconstruction / Reconstruction of the Past in William Faulkner's *Absalom, Absalom!*" Abstract to "Geschichte – Gedächtnis – Zerfall. Dekonstruktion / Rekonstruktion der Vergangenheit in Willliam Faulkners *Absalom, Absalom!*" 19 February 2007 <http://web.fu-berlin.de/phin/phin18/p18t1.htm>

Barth, John. *The Friday Book*. New York: Putnam, 1984.

---. *Giles Goat-Boy*. 1966. New York: Doubleday / Anchor, 1987.

---. *Tidewater Tales*. London: Methuen, 1988.

Derleth, August. "The Cthulhu Mythos." *Tales of the Cthulhu Mythos*. Vol. 1. 1969. London: Panther, 1975. ix-xvi.

---

13 This objection is not completely removed for primary world criticism even if we assume a 'final redactor' within the fiction, whether Bilbo or anyone else.

Flieger, Verlyn. *Interrupted Music: The Making of Tolkien's Mythology*. Kent OH & London: Kent State University Press, 2005.

Lettvin, Jerome. "The Gorgon's Eye." *Astronomy of the Ancients*. Eds. Kenneth Brecher and Michael Feirtag. Cambridge MA & London: MIT Press, 1979. 133-151.

Nagy, Gergely. "The great chain of reading: (Inter-)textual relations and the technique of mythopoesis in the Túrin story." *Tolkien the Medievalist*. Ed. Jane Chance. London & New York: Routledge, 2003. 239-258.

Plato. *Timaeus*. Trans. B. Jowett. 2 March 2007 <http://www.ac-nice.fr/philo/textes/Plato-Works/25-Timaeus.htm>

Rushdie, Salman. *Haroun and the Sea of Stories*. London: Granta Books, 1990.

Santillana, Giorgio de, and Hertha von Dechend. *Hamlet's Mill. An Essay Investigating the Origins of Human Knowledge and Its Transmission Through Myth*. 1969. Boston: Nonpareil, 1999.

Shippey, Tom. *The Road to Middle-earth*. 3rd ed. London: HarperCollins, 2005.

Tolkien, J. R. R. *The Lord of the Rings*. 1954/55. 50th Anniversary Edition in one volume, London: HarperCollins, 2005.

---. *The Silmarillion*. Ed. Christopher Tolkien. London: Allen & Unwin, 1977.

---. *The Letters of J. R. R. Tolkien*. Eds. Humphrey Carpenter and Christopher Tolkien. London: Allen & Unwin, 1981.

---. "On Fairy-Stories". *The Monsters and the Critics*. Ed. Christopher Tolkien. 1983. Paperback ed. London: HarperCollins, 1997. 109-161.

---. "English and Welsh". *The Monsters and the Critics*. Ed. Christopher Tolkien. 1983. Paperback ed. London: HarperCollins, 1997. 162-197.

---. *Sauron Defeated*. Ed. Christopher Tolkien. London: HarperCollins, 1992.

---. "The Qenya Lexicon". Eds. Christopher Gilson, Carl F. Hostetter, Patrick Wynne and Arden R. Smith. *Parma Eldalamberon* 12 (1998): 29-106.

Turner, Allan. "Putting the Paratext in Context." Ed. Sarah Wells. *Tolkien 2005. The Ring Goes Ever On. Proceedings*. Two volumes. Volume One. Coventry: The Tolkien Society, 2008. 283-288.

About the authors

DIRK VANDERBEKE studied German and English Literature at the University of Frankfurt/Main. His doctoral thesis, W*orüber man nicht sprechen kann (Whereof One Cannot Speak)*, deals with aspects of the unrepresentable in philosophy, science and literature. His habilitation study, *Theoretische Welten und literarische Transformationen (Theoretical Worlds and Literary Transformations)* examines the recent debate about 'science and literature' and science's role(s) in contemporary literature. He has also published on a variety of topics, e.g. Joyce, Pynchon, science fiction, self-similarity and vampires. Dirk Vanderbeke has taught at several universities in Germany and the USA; he is currently holding the Chair for Modern English Literature at the Friedrich-Schiller-University Jena, Germany, and a permanent guest-professorship at the University of Zielona Góra, Poland.

ALLAN TURNER studied German, medieval studies and linguistics at the Universities of Reading and Cambridge. His doctoral dissertation in translation studies (Newcastle) investigates the problems of translating the philological elements in *The Lord of the Rings*. He is interested in stylistic aspects of Tolkien's works, and at present teaches English at the Friedrich-Schiller-University Jena, Germany.

Martin Simonson

Tolkien's Triple Balance: A Redemptive Model of Heroism for the Twentieth Century

Abstract

This paper attempts to disclose Tolkien's authorial presence in *The Lord of the Rings* by referring to a particular kind of triple balance that is frequently found in the text. The continuous mélange of Christian and pagan elements, together with the story's applicability to twentieth-century themes and concerns, makes the tale articulate an unorthodox and redemptive model of heroism for the contemporary readership which, as we shall see, is closely related to Tolkien's own inner tension.

Over the last few years, the disclosure of Christian elements in *The Lord of the Rings* has been central to a certain current in Tolkien criticism.[1] One of the main arguments for the validity of such a reading is commonly a reference to one of Tolkien's letters, in which the author states that his work is "a fundamentally religious and Catholic work, unconsciously so at first but consciously in the revision" (*L* 172). However, Tolkien is not as unequivocal on this matter as some of these critics play him out to be. In the first place, the word "fundamentally" leaves at least semantic room for other influences, and in another letter Tolkien states that "[Middle-earth] is a monotheistic world of natural theology", further explaining that "the 'Third Age' was not a Christian world" (*L* 220).

What does this leave us with? Is it, or is it not a Christian work according to the author? Tolkien himself is not clear on the matter. As in *Beowulf*, which is a work of a Christian about a pagan world, "the religious element is absorbed into the story and the symbolism", to quote Tolkien's words from the first letter referred to above (*L* 172). Now, Middle-earth means 'a land between seas', and the seas surrounding Tolkien's Middle-earth seem to be both Christian and pagan, because the idea of 'northern courage' permeates *The Lord of the*

---

1 See, for example, Pearce, Bruner and Ware, Smith, Birzer, Arthur, Wood, and Dickerson.

Rings like an insistent undertow that subverts the homogeneity of the soothing Christian waves, troubling the narrative waters to a considerable extent. This northern spirit, which Tolkien claimed to have "ever loved" (*L* 55), is an inheritance from pagan Norse culture and is, at least in Norse literature, mainly expressed by a resistance to the forces of destruction by showing unbreakable courage in spite of the certainty of defeat.

For a Christian, to show courage in the face of death becomes a matter of minor drama as long as the post-mortem celestial prize is taken for granted. In *The Lord of the Rings*, nothing of the kind can be dogmatically assumed – in fact, the stance portrayed in this work is sometimes deliberately crude and tinged by an element of despair which runs counter to the Christian attitude. This adds a good deal of poignancy to the question of how the characters approach their mortality and their duty as mortals.

At the same time, Tolkien is reluctant to let go of the Christian saving grace, and the northern courage is accordingly given an essentially Christian treatment. What I find particularly interesting about this is that the sequences in which the combination most forcefully emerges often address situations with which the twentieth-century reader could easily identify.

I believe that the apparent contradiction expressed by the blend of pagan and Christian views can be explained by this third layer of applicability, which refers to the twentieth-century spiritual wasteland that became a potent symbol of modernity in the wake of the Great War. As we all know, the First World War was followed by the rise of several totalitarian regimes in Europe, which paved the way for the Second World War. All of this was fresh in most people's memory when Tolkien's books were first published, and therefore probably became the parallel real-world scenario that the average contemporary reader found it conceptually easiest to relate the War of the Ring to. While Tolkien insists explicitly in the *Foreword* to the 1966 edition that there is no allegory to the Second World War in this tale, he admits *applicability* as a possibility, meaning that the text allows for certain readings even though the author does not consciously direct the reader's attention towards any given interpretation (*LotR* 10). At any rate, the relationship between Tolkien's tale and twentieth-century culture, literature, events and general concerns has been sufficiently elucidated by a wide range of scholars[2], and the validity of such a reading should no longer be an issue for debate.

However, in order to explain the presence of this third layer of applicability, the critic needs to take into account and acknowledge the author's presence in the text. I believe that if the tale has any applicability to the historical conflicts taking place in Europe in the first half of the twentieth century, it is probably found in the author's *desired* response to them, not to something that actually happened. To see this more clearly, we will have to jump boldly back and forth in time for a while (as Tolkien's own mind probably did continually, both as a linguist and as an imaginative writer). To begin with, we know from Tolkien himself that he had a "burning private grudge" against Hitler for messing up what he considered one of the most noble expressions of early English culture, "[r]uining, perverting, misapplying, and making forever accursed, that noble northern spirit, a supreme contribution to Europe, which I have ever loved, and tried to present in its true light. Nowhere, incidentally, was it nobler than in England, nor more early sanctified and Christianized" (*L* 55-6). To Tolkien, the northern spirit, when it is tempered by prudence instead of exaggerated by *ofermod*,[3] is perfectly compatible with Christianity. In this sense, the literary work expresses a particular model of heroism which in context – though only implicitly, and not even allegorically – can be seen as a severe corrective to Hitler's vulgar use of the "northern spirit" for propagandistic purposes.

---

2 C.S. Lewis, being also a veteran of the Great War, was the first reviewer to acknowledge the presence of imagery and themes of the First World War in the War of the Ring (13). Garth offers the most exhaustive study of the impact of this war on Tolkien. See also Brennan Croft. As for studies that disclose more general references to twentieth-century culture in Tolkien's work, see Veldman, Curry, Shippey (*Author*) and Honegger and Weinreich.

3 In *The Homecoming of Beorhtnoth*, Tolkien's Christian character Tídwald criticizes the *ofermod* – the overmastering pride, to use Tolkien's own translation of the term – showed by Beorhtnoth that led him and his men to a useless death on the battlefield in the Old English heroic poem *The Battle of Maldon*. At the same time, Tídwald's response to Beorhtnoth's destructive boldness is curiously ambiguous, expressing admiration for the leader's decision while at the same time deeming it too rash: "Too proud, too princely! But his pride's cheated / and his princedom has passed, so we'll praise his valour. / He let them cross the causeway, so keen was he / to give minstrels matter for mighty songs. / Needlessly noble" (*HBBS* 16). Tídwald's statement probably reflects Tolkien's own attitude towards the northern spirit, and the need to temper it if it is to be compatible with the Christian – and hence his own – creed.

As we have seen, Tolkien's model of heroism is based on the assumption that man cannot rely on Christian faith only – he has to act as if he would not be posthumously saved and defy the forces of destruction until his last breath, as the Norse heroes (among others, Beowulf) did. This strain is a substantial part of the process by which Tolkien creates narrative tension, because the very concept of *eucatastrophe*, which is crucial to any deeper understanding of *The Lord of the Rings*, depends on not taking the saving grace for granted. However, I believe that the idea of eucatastrophe is not merely a technical device used by a calculating author, totally detached from his text, but rather a direct consequence of a committed author's perceived need to lean on both approaches in order not to yield – spiritually or otherwise – to the laissez-faire attitude, so common in the years between the two World Wars, towards what he regarded as (and certainly were, in many cases) dangerous and destructive forces at work when *The Lord of the Rings* was written.

The reason why a deeply Catholic man like Tolkien should create a model of heroism which constantly questions one of the very cornerstones of his religion may thus be related to the fact that it reflected his own inner tension,[4] which in turn was accentuated by the events that took place in Europe in the first half of the twentieth century. *Beowulf*, the Old English epic which was a life-long source of inspiration for Tolkien (who found it imaginatively stimulating partly because of the fruitful combination of pagan and Christian elements that the story articulates), portrays exactly this kind of tension, in which hope and despair creatively mingle, having been written at a time when the two outlooks nurtured each other and blended naturally. The epoch in which Tolkien lived showed, in a way, the other end of the process, as Christian faith was losing ground to modern kinds of paganism.[5] However, the new secular myths (Mardones 141-42) that emerged in the decades following the Great War, such as Soviet communism, German nazism, Italian fascism or

---

4 Burns suggests that as a Christian specialist in Norse mythology, Celtic legends and Old English literature, Tolkien's ideological and religious allegiance may have been divided (178), and his diary shows that although he remained a Catholic for his whole life, he was prone to suffer from depressions and was not seldom overwhelmed by hopelessness (Carpenter 243).
5 Shippey, in "Heroes and Heroism: Tolkien's Problems, Tolkien's Solutions" (*Roots* 267-83), explains Tolkien's particular stance as regards the combination of pagan and Christian matters in his literature, but he does not offer any deeper analysis of how it can be related to the actual times Tolkien lived through before and during the composition of *The Lord of the Rings*.

American neoliberal capitalism, had nothing to do with the Norse creed and Tolkien found them more or less abominable.[6] In particular, as we have seen, was Tolkien disgusted with the fact that Hitler had profaned and disgraced what he called the "northern spirit". To write a tale portraying the northern spirit "in its true light", combining it with Christian virtues, would be to liberate this early feature of his own culture from Hitler's appropriation of it – in a sense, to redeem it.

Furthermore, Tolkien may have perceived that a potentially lax Christian response to these spiritually barren ideologies, turning the other cheek to the enemy when attacked, implied a certain dose of defeatism, which is an attitude that he detested. In Tolkien's best-known essay, *On Fairy-Stories* (1937), we find his response to the accusations of escapism supposedly present in imaginative literature, in which he relates the concept of evasion to a prisoner who is trying to escape: those who criticize the attitude of the prisoner who "thinks and talks of other topics than jailers and prison-walls [...] confound the escape of the prisoner with the flight of the deserter" (*OFS* 79). He emphatically adds: "To such thinking you have only to say 'the land you love is doomed' to excuse any treachery, indeed to glorify it" (*OFS* 79-80). The redundancy of this statement gives us a hint about Tolkien's strong personal convictions regarding one's duty when faced with an exterior menace, and with a characteristic applicability to the twentieth century, since he largely conceives the essay as a defence of the value of fairy-tales for the spiritually lost modern reader, implicitly (at times explicitly) attacking the post-war writers, critics, architects and politicians who considered the modernist approach to art and modernity the only valid one.[7] In the same essay, there is a particularly illuminating passage that shows the author's attitude towards modern art:

---

6 For Tolkien's personal opinions on these aspects of modernity, see letters no. 30, 45, 52, 77, 81, 83, and 100 (*L* 37, 55, 63-4, 89, 93-4, 96, 115).

7 As Tolkien predicted, the question of escapism was at the centre of most of the polemic debates regarding the literary value of *The Lord of the Rings*. Negative criticism, tending to view Tolkien's work as little more than a juvenile and escapist entertainment, reaches back to the 1950s and belongs mostly to representatives or inheritors of the school of New Criticism that arose with modernism – see, for example, the articles by Edmund Wilson (*The Nation*, April 4, 1956) and Philip Toynbee (*The Observer*, August 6, 1961). The influence is also present in the criticism of Manlove and Jackson. On the other hand, C. S. Lewis's early reviews and, more recently, the works of Curry, Flieger (*Time*), Shippey (*Author*), and Segura, among others, prove that the accusation of escapism in Tolkien's work is the result of a narrow critical outlook that wilfully excludes the applicability of the tales to modern times. For a summary of the different critical reactions to *The Lord of the Rings*, see Hammond (226-32).

> We may indeed be older now, in so far as we are heirs in enjoyment or in practice of many generations of ancestors in the arts. In this inheritance of wealth there may be a danger of boredom or of anxiety to be original, and that may lead to a distaste for fine drawing, delicate pattern, and 'pretty' colours, or else to mere manipulation and over-elaboration of old material, clever and heartless. But the true road of escape from such weariness is not to be found in the wilfully awkward, clumsy, or misshapen, not in making all things dark or unremittingly violent; nor in the mixing of colours on through subtlety to drabness, and the fantastical complication of shapes to the point of silliness and on towards delirium. Before we reach such states we need recovery. We should look at green again, and be startled anew (but not blinded) by blue and yellow and red [...] This recovery fairy-stories help us to make. (*OFS* 76-7)

If we apply this to written creation, Tolkien seems to say that some modern literature is unable to recover a fresh perception of reality due to its excessive formal experimentation and the attention to the negative details of modernity. He speaks of the need to avoid this apathetic attitude towards tradition and modernity, stating that fairy-tales, as he understands the term, may help us renew our perception of the world and see new possibilities. Reading *The Lord of the Rings*, a work that illustrates the ideas outlined in the essay, it is therefore possible to discern an attempt not only to redeem the idea of northern courage, but also to redeem modern literature that referred back to previous traditions by putting different literary genres in dialogue, such as Eliot's *The Waste Land*, Pound's *The Cantos*, or Joyce's *Ulysses* – canonized modernist works that tend to accept the negative aspects of modernity.[8]

T. S. Eliot had certainly also perceived the need to transmit the religious (and specifically Christian) sentiment to the spiritually impoverished modern civilization. In Brooks' words, Eliot attempted to reinvigorate the Christian terminology by resorting to a technique based on clashes between old and modern conceptions of reality, in order to create ironic contrasts that in the end turn out to be similarities: "the only method is to work by indirection. The Christian material is at the centre, but the poet never deals with it directly" (161).

At a first glance, this may seem similar to Tolkien's approach (apart from the use of irony), but the actual outcome is very much different. Eliot, a modernist,

---

8   For a full discussion of the relationship between high modernism and *The Lord of the Rings*, see Simonson (2008), *The Lord of the Rings and the Western Narrative Tradition*. See also Honegger.

feels a strong need to explicitly reflect the modern world to be able to convey his vision of contemporary life. Accordingly,

> [t]he gap between a modern secular experience, honestly accepted as the only starting point available to a poet who recognizes the obligation to reflect his time as it is, and traditional religious forms is not of the kind that a true poet can bridge by mere assertions of belief [...]. [In *The Waste Land*] Christianity not only co-exists with other [...] non-Christian aspects which are in no sense subjected to a religious 'message' or conclusion, but is seen to emerge from a development which is thoroughly and without prejudice contemporary. (Traversi 54)

Eliot's assumption was that the modern readership would recognize his "obligation to reflect his time as it is" (that is, marked by chaos, disillusionment and fragmentation), as if this concept of modernity were the only one available. However, the artificially constructed mythological framework that Eliot is obliged to design in order to reflect the modern times explicitly is too shaky to sustain any solid ideological or religious message, and as a result of the elitistic choice of references to previous tradition found in Eliot's work (and in the other modernist works we have referred to), instead of elucidating the conditions of modern life, the texts are often obscure and sometimes even impenetrable for the average reader.[9]

Tolkien looked for a different way to reintegrate the forgotten models of heroism in his literature[10]; a new road that would elude the fatal combination of "overelaboration of old material" and defeatism. Like T. S. Eliot, he was conscious that he could not propose a new evangelium completely in the 'old style' if he wished modern readers to relate to it. He felt, as Eliot did, that he must avoid all explicit reference to Christian dogma and propose a new myth, though deeply rooted in the European literary traditions. At the same time, as his words quoted above indicate, he probably believed that the modernist literature that attempted to do the same thing often failed because of the mentioned "overelaboration of old material" and defeatist acceptance of the negative conditions

---

9 Craig believes that the vision of modernity hailed by poets and critics like Eliot and F. R. Leavis as the only possible was not accepted by everybody, and that "the limited public response to *The Waste Land* is an indication that it is not the representative work of the present age" (212). Today, *The Waste Land*, *The Cantos* and *Ulysses* still occupy a central place in the modernist canon, but can hardly be said to stand on their own, depending as they do on scholarly publications and institutions in order to be properly understood or even read at all.
10 Honegger discusses how Tolkien's "mythical method" is related to high modernism.

of modern life. Tolkien's response to the contemporary reality was markedly different from Eliot's, and his literary alternative to the modernists' confusing self-referential network of ironic clashes between the old and new, only loosely held together by references to works of Classical Antiquity such as Homer's *Odyssey*, was a self-referential "secondary world"[11] with a proper mythology, in which the different narrative traditions were able to co-exist simultaneously and the past could interact with the present with a certain degree of fluency, in order to renew our vision of the world. If the readers were attracted by this vision and accepted it, as many have, the threads of references to different narrative and cultural traditions of the real world subtly shine through the fabric of the tapestry, giving rise to a vast scope of applicability that embraces different eras and events, fictional as well as historical, from Classical Antiquity up to the twentieth century.[12]

Many of the narrative traditions that Tolkien's work implicitly refers back to[13] display pagan and Christian models, given their historical context. As a result of the fluent interaction, these models often merge in the text, as in the sayings and doings of Gandalf, the leading spiritual authority of the Free Peoples who in the end turns out to be nothing less than a messenger of the Valar. But what is his message? Basically, that there is always hope for those who do not give up in the struggle for a just cause, and we can find a hint about what a just cause is in Gandalf's mysterious assertion that Boromir "escaped" before he died: "Galadriel told me that he was in peril. But he escaped in the end. I am glad. It was not in vain that the hobbits came with us, if only for Boromir's sake". (*LotR* 517)

Escape from what? And what did the hobbits have to do with it? One possible interpretation is that the answer is related to the same motivations that made Aragorn forgive Boromir after his treason: a mélange of Christian and pagan

---

11 Tolkien distinguishes between "Primary World" and "Secondary World", explaining the difference in the following terms: "the story maker [...] makes a Secondary World which your mind can enter. Inside it, what he relates is 'true': it accords with the laws of that world. You therefore believe it, while you are, as it were, inside. The moment disbelief arises, the spell is broken; the magic, or rather art, has failed. You are then out in the Primary World again, looking at the little abortive Secondary World from outside" (*OFS* 60).
12 A quick glance at the growing corpus of Tolkien criticism shows that the possibilities for different readings of the work are enormous.
13 For an in-depth study of genre-interaction in *The Lord of the Rings*, see Simonson *The Lord of the Rings and the Western Narrative Tradition*.

heroic ethics. Boromir's soul was saved due to his repentance, and the hobbits provided him with a just cause that helped him achieve heroic redemption in battle.

This paradoxical mélange – the need for a pagan courage in the face of impending disaster and death, without any clearly defined hope for posthumous rewards other than one's lasting reputation, and the Christian humility based on virtues such as hope, mercy, forgiveness, and generosity – marks Gandalf's message, and is a clear inheritance from *Beowulf*. The need to avoid defeatist stances and actively fight against evil without losing hope may of course be applied to situations from all eras, but in *The Lord of the Rings*, as I have argued, a third layer of applicability related to the events taking place in Europe in the first half of the twentieth century often infiltrates the treatment of the characters and events that integrate the pagan and Christian stances, creating a new, meta-narrative myth that integrates and reconciles apparently opposing forms of literature, ideologies and religious outlooks.

The particular applicability to this third layer can be found at several points in the narrative. The Shire of the first chapters, for instance, is a sort of synthesis – and consciously so[14] – of pre-war England, and the spirit (especially in hindsight) of the almost archetypically pastoral summer of 1914, in which the whole idea of a long and bloody war seemed absurd to most English people (Fussell 23-4), is very much present in the descriptions of the carefree hobbitesque idyll only disturbed by Gandalf's ominous warnings and by the sporadic presence of the Black Riders that anticipate a great, foreign war marked by a massive destruction. However, the triple balance does not take off seriously until the Fellowship reaches the Gates of Moria, where the analogues to the twentieth-century scenarios become slightly more conspicuous – among the possibilities of interpretation offered by the text is the applicability to the Great War and its aftermath. According to the British authorities, it was the hostile attitude and threatening presence of Germany, that culminated in 1914 with the attack on Belgium, that compelled Britain to take part in the conflict later known as the Great War. Once this happened, the whole continent was drawn into a spiral of violence – the mass

---

14 See Shippey, *Road* 102-03, and Tolkien *L* 235.

destruction of the First World War was succeeded by the imperialism of opportunistic totalitarian regimes that eventually paved the way for the even bigger conflict of the Second World War.

Something similar happens to the Fellowship of the Ring in Moria. While they know that they are probably heading for war sooner or later – that the waters outside the gates of Moria are only deceitfully still, so to speak – the *kraken* breaks the dead calm of the surface and the members of the Fellowship are forced to enter the mines hurriedly and plunge headlong into the dark and labyrinthic mines. This will give rise to the first open confrontation with the Enemy, and later to more confrontations, on a much bigger scale, with the totalitarian regimes of Saruman, first, and then Sauron. Before the War of the Ring is over, the hobbits will have experienced the feeling that the old world is gone – both because of what happens in the Mines, where Gandalf and the Balrog fall into the abyss, and the apocalyptic mass-destruction of the ensuing war.

Gandalf's words reinforce the analogue:

> 'Well, well!' said the wizard. 'The passage is blocked behind us now, and there is only one way out – on the other side of the mountains. I fear from the sounds that boulders have been piled up, and the trees uprooted and thrown across the gate. I am sorry; for the trees were beautiful, and had stood so long.' (*LotR* 326-27)

Is it possible to consider the uprooted trees an embodiment of a previous tradition that revered beauty and order, and the closed gates and boulders as symbols of irretrievable destruction and loss of such a culture – the collapsed ceiling that blocks any possibility of return a premature and hasty "good-bye to all that" (to use the title of Graves' well-known account of his experiences before, during and after the Great War)? I believe it is, or at least that the First World War and its aftermath are allowed some room in the back of the reader's mind. For this reason, it is interesting to notice that Gandalf's response to the fallen trees is not mourning for what is irretrievably lost, but a vigorous thrust ahead to defy the destructive forces, to make the best out of the given time without yielding to sorrow, despair, or indifference. When Boromir expresses his lack of faith in the road they must follow, and asks who will lead them through the "deadly dark", Gandalf answers: "I will. And Gimli shall walk with me. Follow my staff!" (*LotR* 327). Gimli, significantly, belongs to a race with roots in pagan folklore and myths,[15] and the fact that the two should walk together is consistent with the idea that combined Christian (Gandalf) and pagan (Gimli) virtues is the proper remedy for modern evil.

While Gimli cannot embody this mélange on his own,[16] Gandalf does so naturally, which becomes evident for the first time on the bridge of Khazad-dûm, where the Balrog, described as a shadow that wields a sword shrouded in red flames in one hand and a whip in the other, is challenged by the wizard, with a sword of white fire and a staff. The weapons as such tell us as a good deal about the type of duel that is being portrayed, opposing two types of authorities by means of traditional symbols – the punishment, as represented by the Balrog's whip, and the guidance and protection symbolized by Gandalf's staff[17] – apart from the association with the fire, that can be of divine or demonic origin (De Paco 259). The colour of their swords may also be significant: the red glow of rage and Hell illuminates the Balrog's sword, while the white radiance of Gandalf's blade, which furthermore has a name of its own,[18] recalls light and the forces of Good.[19]

Apart from the Christian symbolism, there are also pagan ingredients that add to the applicability of the scene. Day (36-8) highlights the similarity between the Balrog and Surt,[20] the guardian of the gates of Muspellheim (the giants' territory in Norse mythology) – the battle at the bridge being analogous to the fight between Surt and Frey, the god of the Sun and the rain, on the bridge Bifrost, that marks the onset of Ragnarök (the twilight of the gods). To this parallel we may add that in *The Lord of the Rings*, also, a horn sounds – Boromir

---

15 See Shippey, *Road* 61-3.
16 When the Balrog attacks, Gimli, overcome with superstitious fear, lets his axe fall and covers his face – hardly a fruitful response to adversity.
17 In De Paco's words, the whip symbolizes authoritative command and punishment (301), while the staff is "a magic weapon, an instrument used to mediate between the visible and invisible worlds, a symbol of the teacher's tutorship" (323). (My translation.)
18 Its name – Glamdring – is explicitly mentioned by the narrator twice during the battle. According to De Paco, in Christian iconography swords represent "the spirit and word of God, endowed with a will of their own, which is the reason why they were given names" (252). (My translation.)
19 Miller points out that the colour red is always dangerous, "reflecting the doubled potencies of blood and fire [...] the 'hot blood' of the furious warrior-hero [and] the destructively heated potentiality of the warrior" (285). De Paco relates white colour to indifferentiation, transcendental experience, innocence, and holiness (198). The analogue with the Biblical Archangel Michael, the messenger of the Last Judgment who usually appears as a warrior with a sword, also contributes to emphasize Gandalf's Christian connotations.
20 See also Noel 101.

blows his as he sets out to aid Gandalf – and the bridge collapses, as in the Norse myth.[21]

In the ensuing War of the Ring, we find more instances of the triple balance. When Gandalf returns after his fall in Moria, he urges Aragorn and the others on to Rohan in order to muster forces for the inevitable battles against Saruman and Sauron. Once they reach Meduseld, Gandalf speaks first with Gríma, King Théoden's counsellor, who works as a spy for Saruman, having deceived the King for a long time. Gandalf dismisses him and convinces Théoden of the need to actively fight Saruman and Sauron, saying "No counsel have I to give to those who despair" (*LotR* 537), appealing, simultaneously, both to Christian hope – underscored by his pointing to a patch of blue sky between the clouds – and the pagan mindset, bent on achieving glory on the battlefield by not yielding to despair when the going gets tough. Théoden is convinced, and even physically rejuvenated, both by the wizard's almost ritualistic magic and by his words, and determines to accept Gandalf's proposal. Gríma, for his part, is forgiven and offered a place in the cavalry next to the King. Even as he rejects the offer, they give him a horse so that he may leave Rohan unharmed.

Christian virtues are thus imposed on the more savage warrior ethics, that would have had Gríma executed for his treason, but at the same time it is worth noticing that the whole point of waking Théoden from his defeatist slumber is that he should engage his troops in the War of the Ring, which provides the King with an opportunity to redeem himself and clear his conscience on the battlefield. Théoden's words indicate that while he has no hope for an existence after death, the satisfaction of courageously doing his

---

21 The fact that Caradhras should deny the passage of the Fellowship over the mountains, close to the sky, is also significant for the transmission of this mélange of pagan and Christian traditions. The blizzard makes them descend to a subterranean space, with more immediate connections to the idea of the Christian Hell, something which prevents the Christian connotations of the duel from disappearing in the dialogue. A battle with spirits of the air would more easily have given rise to a different interpretation. Dufau persuasively explains that Moria can be interpreted as a place that eradicates the essence of the Self: "Moria shelters an anti-space that baffles all attempts at self-location […]. The traveller is bound to lose whatever bearings he used to have. How could he find a language of being in such a place since the concept of language refers to a system of signs? […] The self cannot evolve in collapse and breaking: it dies in such places" (115). The idea of chaos and the destruction of one's essence is, of course, compatible with the Christian idea of the soul's destruction in Hell. Obertino, for his part, highlights the parallels between Moria and pagan epic tradition in the *Aeneid*.

duty compensates for the possibly fatal outcome: "I myself will go to war, to fall in the front of the battle, if it must be. Thus I shall sleep better" (*LotR* 541). Théoden looks not to the sky for consolation, but to the mounds of the fallen kings of Rohan, hoping that he shall be worthy of the soil that keeps the bones of his predecessors – that his mound, too, will be looked upon with admiration by future generations. That grim prize is more than enough to motivate him.

Gríma, Saruman's spy, is here the main link to the twentieth-century conflicts, in which a new kind of diplomatic language emerged, which would express the most atrocious crimes in elegant wording.[22] Gríma's language anticipates Saruman's carefully phrased half-truths and plain lies that will acquire such importance when Gandalf later seeks out his former friend and colleague together with the Rohirrim. Both the physical space of Isengard and the character of Saruman[23] contribute to the creation of a symbolically charged negative vision of twentieth-century 'progress', much in the vein of the modern dystopias portrayed by T.S. Eliot (*The Waste Land*), George Orwell (*Nineteen Eighty-four*) or Ray Bradbury (*Fahrenheit 451*).

As they draw closer to Orthanc, Gandalf warns the others about the dangers of listening too closely to Saruman's voice, which will become prominent enough to lend itself to the title of the chapter. This prominence, together with the dystopian context of Isengard and Saruman's totalitarian projects, make it virtually impossible not to look for some symbolic interpretation of his melodious voice, that enchants the listeners with false promises of salvation. One fairly obvious reading is that the voice of Saruman can be seen to represent the enslaving power of the word – a symbol of the perversion that lies in attempting to rob

---

22 Fussell traces the use of euphemism for official accounts of the atrocities of modern warfare to the Great War (174-79).
23 Shippey (*Road* 170-72) believes that Saruman is the most modern character of *The Lord of the Rings* because of his strong ties to failed socialism, modern industry and technology. The descriptions of Isengard emphasize the destruction of the natural world that Saruman has brought to the valley, by means of tendencious similes and metaphors such as the substitution of trees for pillars joined by heavy chains, or the likeness of the valley to a cemetery inhabited by restless corpses – imagery with close ties to the literary dystopias of the first half of the twentieth century.

words of their original meaning, and use them merely for manipulative ends, as modern politicians[24] tend to do.

The duel of words and power between Saruman and Gandalf also hints at this symbolic interpretation. Saruman speaks of the comforts of modern life as the key to happiness in a system based on materialist values and imperialist exploitation – temptations that enchant the vast majority in spite of the obvious environmental and spiritual dangers they imply.[25] Gandalf, for his part, does not embellish reality in order to incite his audience to adopt a defeatist response to adversity – instead, he uses parables to make people aware of their moral duty. He is also similar to Christ in that he personifies material austerity, being the owner only of his clothes, sword and staff. The possibilities for Christian and pagan readings with parallels to twentieth-century concerns are enhanced by the many possible analogues between this episode and fictional works from both Christian and pagan traditions,[26] and by the fact that when Gandalf takes Saruman's colour (white) after the latter's fall, it coincides with the destruction of the industrial paraphernalia of Isengard.[27]

---

24 See Shippey, *Author* 75-6. The theory of the original unity between words and meaning was developed and explained by Owen Barfield, a friend of Tolkien and C S. Lewis, in his work *Poetic Diction: A Study in Meaning*. Flieger (*Light*) shows the influence of Barfield's theories on Tolkien. Wood explains how these theories apply to Saruman's speech (33-4).

25 This side of Saruman is further reinforced by the analogue between the wizard's voice and that of Kurtz, one of the protagonists of Joseph Conrad's *Heart of Darkness*. Kurtz's voice is also the voice of a man corrupted by his own savage instincts that inspire violent domination and exploitation, in the case of Kurtz as a result of the technological superiority of the Europeans in Africa at the end of the nineteenth century. The voice of Kurtz is in Conrad's narrative treated as if it were independent of its owner, symbolizing the imperialist spell and its potentially disastrous moral consequences – not in vain, Kurtz's last words are: "The horror!" Apart from the merely thematic similarities, Saruman's voice is likewise presented as something external to the wizard – it is not Saruman who does the talking, but the voice *itself*, which the narrator refers to as "the voice", or "it" several times (*LotR* 601-02). Though Conrad's novel refers to events prior to the Great War, the European intervention in Congo during the reign of King Leopold anticipated the attitude of several European totalitarian regimes during the first half of the twentieth century.

26 For instance, the way Théoden and his men react to Saruman's voice is similar to how Ulysses and his crew respond to the spoken or sung temptations they are exposed to during their return to Ithaca. Both kings suffer but are not shaken in their convictions, while their men, morally weaker, give in to the spells and temptations. This is particularly evident in the encounters with Circe and the Oxen of the Sun. Greene, for her part, underscores the likeness of Saruman with the figure of the villain in the prophetic works of Spenser, Milton and Blake, that usually was linked to temptation and hypocrisy, showing his indebtedness to Christian narrative tradition (49).

27 This symbolical interpretation is of course not the only possibility offered by the text. Saruman, for example, is a wizard, and so, of course, skilled in enchanting his audience with his voice. Apart from this, he is a character whose particular motivations are coherent both with his personal history and that of Middle-earth. In other words, Tolkien does not place this character in the story exclusively as a symbol of something else, like Orwell does with the pigs of *Animal Farm*, for instance – Saruman also has his place in the much larger mythological and (pseudo)historical context of Middle-earth.

At Minas Tirith, we find more examples of the triple balance. The scene in which Gandalf and Denethor debate over the body of Faramir, for instance, shows very clearly the tension between Christian and pagan points of view. The defeatist Denethor aims to surrender whole-heartedly, abandoning the responsibilities for his people, committing suicide and taking his son with him on the pyre. Gandalf disapproves of this most emphatically:

> 'Authority is not given you, Steward of Gondor, to order the hour of your death,' answered Gandalf. 'And only the heathen kings, under the domination of the Dark Power, did thus, slaying themselves in pride and despair, murdering their kin to ease their own death.' [...] '[...] The West has failed. It is time for all to depart who would not be slaves.' 'Such counsels will make the Enemy's victory certain indeed,' said Gandalf. (*LotR* 887)

The word 'heathen' is of course interesting here – heathen as opposed to what? Well, at least to something which would consider suicide, pride and despair immoral, a consequence of worshipping 'false' gods.[28]

At the same time, it is Denethor's lack of 'northern courage' that causes his fall, as St Clair's analysis of this character shows. St Clair links him to the pagan Njal of the eponymous Icelandic saga: Njal, who is intelligent, cunning, brave and perceptive, also loses his best-loved son and dies on the pyre – "[he is] what Denethor might have been without the palantír" (65). In another interpretation, Shippey underscores the lack of northern courage in Denethor, though he attributes this flaw to the effects of a civilized culture (*Road* 130).

It is precisely this civilized culture, represented by Denethor, which is threatened by Sauron and doomed to perish in order to be replaced by something else. In Tolkien's vision, at the end of the war it is not the primitive paganism of Théoden, nor the civilized paganism of Denethor, or, for that matter, a culture of self-denying Christian humility that triumphs, but the mixed outlook represented by Aragorn: a culture which reconciles northern courage and

---

28 Gandalf's words about 'heathen kings' probably refer to the Númenórean civilization of the Second Age, that captured Sauron but later came under his influence and began to worship Morgoth instead of Eru. In *The Lord of the Rings*, Denethor is under the influence of Sauron, having gazed too often into the palantír. As a result, Sauron acts through him to a certain extent. Whether the Steward's similarity to Satan, as he is portrayed in *Paradise Lost*, is a result of this or not may be debated, but it is true that he (and Saruman, too) shares certain features with this character – see, for example, Steadman's view, according to which the most salient features of Milton's Satan are "a leadership that misleads, a magnanimity that strives for unmerited honors, accomplishes acts of destruction instead of 'acts of benefit' and turns out to be vainglorious ambition and pride" (17).

Christian virtues[29] and is open to a multicultural union. In this, the first part of the process is somewhat similar to the cultural apocalypse brought about by the First World War, in which the civilized nineteenth-century English values disappeared,[30] but since Tolkien wished to propose a reversal of the modernist expressions and defeatist stance that dominated Western Europe after the war, the outcome is different. In Middle-earth, the apocalypse ends up bringing hope and vigour to those who did not lose faith while the darkness lasted – in fact, it is an opportunity to get rid of the last, feeble stage of the diluted Numenórean civilization, re-establish its past glory and create a stronger union which will ensure a good start for the Fourth Age.

That Gandalf sees the apocalypse not as inevitable doom but as an opportunity to prove that the best qualities of mankind, Christian as well as pagan, are stronger than Sauron's destructive machinery and oppressed warriors, is further stressed in the final phase of the war. In the last debate of the eponymous chapter, Gandalf's speech is marked by parables and sayings similar to those of the Bible, that exemplify his moral counsel regarding duty – "it is not our part to master all the tides of the world, but to do what is in us for the succour of those years wherein we are set, uprooting the evil in the fields that we know, so that those who live after may have clean earth to till"[31] (*LotR* 913) – with a strong emphasis on the need to make altruistic sacrifices:

> it may well prove that we ourselves shall perish utterly in a black battle far from the living lands; so that even if Barad-dûr be thrown down, we shall not live to see a new age. But this, I deem, is our duty. And better so than to perish nonetheless – as we surely shall, if we sit here – and know as we die that no new age shall be. (*LotR* 914)

---

29 For an outline of the combination of epic (pagan) and romance (Christian) motifs that shape the character of Aragorn, see Simonson ("Heroic Evolution").

30 See Fussell 18-29. Modris Eksteins claims that the fundamental difference in attitude between Britain and Germany was that the British fought to preserve a world of values (115-31) – "notions of justice, dignity, civility, restraint, and 'progress' governed by a respect for law" (118) – while the Germans strove to destroy the previous culture and create a new one from the ashes of the old. And this they achieved, to a great extent, in spite of the fact that they lost the war. The conflicting values of British and Germans would also seem to hold for the opposing forces that take part in the War of the Ring, though the German intentions with the First World War can of course not be equated to Sauron's. We should also notice that suicide is a general symbol of the destruction of the world (De Paco 356).

31 Cf. "the parable of the tares of the field" in Matt. 13.37-39, in which Jesus explains that the weeds of the evil one will be eliminated from the fields when the apocalypse comes: "He that soweth the good seed is the Son of man; The field is the world; the good seed are the children of the kingdom; but the tares are the children of the wicked one; the enemy that sowed them is the devil; the harvest is the end of the world; and the reapers are the angels."

Though it is easy to interpret the altruistic motivations in Christian terms, because of the insistent use of parables and Biblical phrasing, Gandalf obviously appeals to the qualities of northern courage, offering no salvation but just the grim satisfaction of knowing, in the moment when they "perish utterly" – that is, with no further hope of salvation – that they have done their duty.

The seven thousand men that Aragorn finally mobilizes for the war against Mordor are so obviously inferior in number to Sauron's forces that the attack seems almost ridiculous. Prince Imrahil compares it to a child that threatens an armoured knight "with a bow of string and green willow" (*LotR* 916). This simile obviously recalls the famous biblical story of David and Goliath, and the outcome is the same: against all odds, the smaller force wins. However, as in the scene at the bridge of Khazad-dûm, and that of the funeral pyre for Faramir, the mélange of northern courage and Christian virtues is also complemented by the possibility of expanding the applicability with a modern dimension: not only is the unexpected victory an obvious counter-attack on the twentieth-century defeatist attitude in general, given the analogues we have previously detected, it is also a rebuttal of Graves's poem "Goliath and David", which criticizes the innocence of the biblical story in the light of the poet's experiences in the Great War, expressing exactly the cynical spirit and somewhat helpless disillusionment that Tolkien so abhorred.[32]

Hence, while Tolkien's declared wish to avoid apathy in life and literature, and to make the reader perceive the world with new eyes, led him to use a 'secondary world' as the setting for his fiction, the resulting tale does in no way elude the most imperative concerns of the author's own age – something which reflects Tolkien's previously quoted words about escapism, that we should not "confound the escape of the prisoner with the flight of the deserter". By investing the text with multiple analogues and interpretative possibilities, the major historical backdrop of the story emerges as a scenario which coincides subtly but appreciably with some of the most dramatic events that took place in Europe in the first half of the twentieth century. At the same time, the ac-

---

32 The poem first appeared in Graves's collection *Goliath and David* (1917). Shippey also refers to Graves (though he does not mention this poem) when discussing the main differences between Tolkien and other writers of the era: "unlike many men of his age, [Tolkien] had not been alienated even by the Great War from the traditions in which he had been brought up. Unlike Robert Graves, his near-contemporary and fellow-Fusilier, he never said 'Goodbye to All That'" (*Road* 335).

count of the events of the invented world articulates a singular protest against the modernist attempts to portray modernity as a fragmented chaos in which elements from the past and the present mingle without any clear sense of direction. This disruptive interaction, based on ironical clashes between the old and the new, became in Tolkien's version a smooth and harmonious dialogue, which in turn enabled Christian and pagan attitudes to merge without much friction. Tolkien describes a world-scale aggression to which the most efficient response is based on a combination of both outlooks, which he may have seen as the key to avoid contemporary defeatism without resorting to blind violence and thereby losing touch with (Christian) ethical responsibility.

At the same time, the triple balance also provides us with a new approach to the curious blend of pagan and Christian elements in *The Lord of the Rings*, because the author may have used it to express a private inner tension, which he never fully admitted[33] but allowed to flourish in his tale, justified both by the tale's fictionality and the implicit applicability to twentieth-century predicaments. As he explained in the *Foreword* to the second edition, *The Lord of the Rings* "was primarily linguistic in inspiration and was begun in order to provide the necessary background of 'history' for Elvish tongues", partly the result of "the desire of a tale-teller to try his hand at a really long story that would hold the attention of readers, amuse them, delight them, and at times maybe excite them or deeply move them" (*LotR* 9-10). At a first glance, this would seem to be a hymn to fictional distance and a suitable ground for private thoughts to roam 'unseen'. However, the thoughts that articulate the tension between pagan and Christian elements in the fictional work become Tolkien's own as he continues: "As a guide I had only my own feelings for what is appealing or moving" (*LotR* 10). Being familiar with the author's thoughts about these personal preferences from his essays and letters, it does not seem unreasonable to conclude that the divided ideological

---

33 Tolkien remained ambiguous about this double stance all through his life. In an often quoted letter to Milton Waldman, he claims that "[m]yth and fairy-story must, as all art, reflect and contain in solution elements of moral and religious truth (or error), but not explicit, not in the known form of the primary 'real' world. (I am speaking, of course, of our present situation, not of ancient, pagan, pre-Christian days. [...])" (*L* 144). Significantly, he does not clarify which moral and religious standpoints he considers erroneous and which true, maybe because he believed that there was a measure of truth in both, as he explicitly claims further on in the same letter: "After all, I believe that legends and myths are largely made of 'truth', and indeed present aspects of it that can only be received in this mode; and long ago certain truths and modes of this kind were discovered and must always reappear" (*L* 147).

allegiance portrayed in the work probably reflects his "own feelings for what is appealing or moving". This, in turn, supports the idea that Tolkien's taste for old literature and admiration for the northern spirit, combined with his Christianity, his personal grudge against Hitler for having made the northern spirit "forever accursed", and his distaste for the defeatist and experimental modernist literature, add another, if not explicitly declared, intention to the author's list of purposes, namely to articulate a protest against what he perceived as a feeble twentieth-century response to adversity. I believe that the simultaneity of these three elements – the triple balance – is one of the main keys to understand both Tolkien as an author and the popular success of his most famous work.

Works cited

Arthur, Sara. *Walking With Frodo: A Devotional Journey Through The Lord of the Rings*. Wheaton, IL: Thirsty Books, 2003.

Birzer, Bradley J. *J. R. R. Tolkien's Sanctifying Myth: Understanding Middle-earth*. Wilmington, DE: ISI Books, 2002.

Brennan Croft, Janet. *War and the Works of J. R. R. Tolkien*. Westport, CT: Praeger, 2004.

Brooks, Cleanth. "The Waste Land: Critique of the Myth." *T. S. Eliot: The Waste Land*. Eds. C. B. Cox and Arnold B. Hinchcliffe. London: Macmillan, 1968. 128-161.

Bruner, Kurt, and Jim Ware. *Finding God in 'The Lord of the Rings'*. Wheaton, IL: Tyndale, 2001.

Burns, Marjorie. *Perilous Realms: Celtic and Norse in Tolkien's Middle-earth*. Toronto, Buffalo & London: Toronto University Press, 2006.

Carpenter, Humphrey. *J. R. R. Tolkien: A Biography*. 1977. Boston & New York: Houghton Mifflin, 2000.

Craig, David. "The Defeatism of *The Waste Land*." *T. S. Eliot: The Waste Land*. Eds. C. B. Cox and Arnold B. Hinchcliffe. London: Macmillan, 1968. 200-215.

Curry, Patrick. *Defending Middle-earth*. London: HarperCollins, 1997.

Day, David. *The World of Tolkien: Mythological Sources of 'The Lord of the Rings'*. London: Mitchell Beazley, 2003.

De Paco, Albert, ed. *Diccionario de Símbolos*. Barcelona: Editorial Optima, 2003.

Dickerson, Matthew. *Following Gandalf: Epic Battles and Moral Victory in 'The Lord of the Rings'*. Grand Rapids, MI: Brazos Press, 2003.

Dufau, Jean-Christophe. "Mythic Space in Tolkien's Work." *Reconsidering Tolkien*. Ed. Thomas Honegger. Zurich: Walking Tree Publishers, 2005. 107-128.

Eksteins, Modris. *Rites of Spring: The Great War and the Birth of the Modern Age*. 1989. Boston & New York: Houghton Mifflin, 2000.

Flieger, Verlyn. *A Question of Time: J. R. R. Tolkien's Road to Faërie*. Kent, OH: The Kent State University Press, 1997.

---. *Splintered Light: Logos and Language in Tolkien's World*. 1983. Revised ed. Kent, OH, and London: The Kent State University Press, 2002.

Fussell, Paul. *The Great War and Modern Memory*. 1975. New York: Oxford University Press, 2000.

Garth, John. *Tolkien and the Great War: The Threshold of Middle-earth*. Boston & New York: Houghton Mifflin, 2003.

Greene, Deirdre. "Higher Argument: Tolkien and the Tradition of Vision, Epic and Prophecy." *Proceedings of the J. R. R. Tolkien Centenary Conference, Keble College, Oxford, 1992*. Eds. Patricia Reynolds and Glen H. Goodknight. Milton Keynes: The Tolkien Society and the Mythopoeic Press, 1996. 45-52.

Hammond, Wayne. "The critical Response to Tolkien's Fiction". *Proceedings of the J. R. R. Tolkien Centenary Conference, Keble College, Oxford, 1992*. Eds. Patricia Reynolds and Glen H. Goodknight. Milton Keynes: The Tolkien Society and the Mythopoeic Press, 1996. 226-232.

Honegger, Thomas. "The Passing of the Elves and the Arrival of Modernity: Tolkien's 'Mythical Method'." *Tolkien and Modernity*. Vol. 2. Eds. Thomas Honegger and Frank Weinreich. Zurich & Berne: Walking Tree Publishers, 2006. 211-232.

--- and Frank Weinreich, eds. *Tolkien and Modernity*. 2 Vols. Zurich & Berne: Walking Tree Publishers, 2006.

Jackson, Rosemary. *Fantasy, the Literature of Subversion*. London: Routledge, 1981.

Lewis, Clive Staples. "The Dethronement of Power". 1955. *Understanding 'The Lord of the Rings': The Best of Tolkien Criticism*. Eds. Neil Isaacs and Rose Zimbardo. Boston & New York: Houghton Mifflin, 2004. 11-15.

Manlove, Colin. *Modern Fantasy: Five Studies*. 1975. Cambridge: Cambridge University Press, 1978.

Mardones, José María. *El Retorno del Mito: La Racionalidad Mito-Simbólica*. Madrid: Síntesis, 2000.

Miller, Dean A. *The Epic Hero*. Baltimore: John Hopkins University Press, 2000.

Noel, Ruth S. *The Mythology of Middle-earth*. Boston: Houghton Mifflin, 1977.

Obertino, James. "Moria and Hades: Underworld Journeys in Tolkien and Virgil." *Comparative Literature Studies* 30 (1993): 153-169.

Pearce, Joseph. *Tolkien: A Celebration*. San Francisco: Ignatius Press, 2001.

Segura, Eduardo. *El Viaje del Anillo*. Barcelona: Minotauro, 2004.

Shippey, Tom. *J.R.R. Tolkien. Author of the Century*. 2000. Boston & New York: Houghton Mifflin, 2002.

---. *The Road to Middle-earth*. 1982. Revised and extended ed. Boston: Houghton Mifflin, 2003.

---. *Roots and Branches: Selected Papers on Tolkien by Tom Shippey*. Zurich & Berne: Walking Tree Publishers, 2007.

Simonson, Martin. "Aragorn's Heroic Evolution: An Introduction to the Dynamics of the Intertraditional Dialogue in *The Lord of the Rings*." *Tolkien and Modernity*. Vol. 2. Eds. Thomas Honegger and Frank Weinreich. Zurich & Berne: Walking Tree Publishers, 2006. 75-114.

---. *'The Lord of the Rings' and the Western Narrative Tradition*. Zurich & Jena: Walking Tree Publishers, 2008.

Smith, Mark Eddy. *Tolkien's Ordinary Virtues: Exploring the Spiritual Themes of 'The Lord of the Rings'*. Dotener's Grove, IL: Intervarsity Press, 2002.

St Claire, Gloriana. "An Overview of the Northern Influences on Tolkien's Works." *Proceedings of the J. R. R. Tolkien Centenary Conference, Keble College, Oxford, 1992*. Eds. Patricia Reynolds and Glen H. Goodknight. Milton Keynes: The Tolkien Society and the Mythopoeic Press, 1996. 63-67.

Steadman, John M. *Milton and the Renaissance Hero*. 1967. London: Oxford University Press, 1969.

Tolkien, J. R. R. "On Fairy-Stories." *A Tolkien Reader*. New York: Random House, 1966. 33-99.

---. "The Homecoming of Beorhtnoth Beorhthelm's Son." *A Tolkien Reader*. New York: Random House, 1966. 3-27.

---. *The Lord of the Rings*. 1954/55. London: HarperCollins, 1993.

---. *The Letters of J. R. R. Tolkien*. Edited by Humphrey Carpenter with the assistance of Christopher Tolkien. 1981. Boston & New York: Houghton Mifflin, 2000.

Traversi, Derek. *T. S. Eliot: The Longer Poems*. 1976. London: The Bodley Head, 1978.

Wood, Ralph C. *The Gospel According to Tolkien: Visions of the Kingdom in Middle-earth*. Louisville & London: Westminster John Knox Press, 2003.

About the author

MARTIN SIMONSON holds a Ph.D. from the University of the Basque Country, and is the author of '*The Lord of the Rings' and the Western Narrative Tradition* (2008) as well as of several novels. He is currently teaching English language and literature at the University of the Basque Country, and has published translations into Spanish of several Swedish novelists and essayists, such as Jens Lapidus, Jonas Hassen Khemiri and Peter Englund.

Judith Klinger

Tolkien's 'Strange Powers of the Mind': Dreams, Visionary History and Authorship

Abstract

Although dreams frequently generate stories, their authors and origins are conceptualized differently within different cultures. While modernity posits the 'unconscious' as the dream's mysterious co-author, pre-modern cultures allow for the intervention of external forces within dreams. Thus dreams hover perpetually on the threshold between different states of awareness and reality. In Tolkien's works, (visionary) dreams and poetry are frequently intertwined as alternative modes of accessing a lost history and Other Time, thereby transcending linear historical narratives. Consequently, the related notions of authorship run counter to the modern concept of identifiable historical origins and point beyond the individual biographical author. My paper examines Tolkien's unique configuration of dream-visions, imagination/invention, and (re-)creative poetry across a range of texts, with a special focus on the correlation of visionary dreams and authorship in *The Notion Club Papers* and *The Lord of the Rings*: texts that reforge the tenuous connections between the historical, 'natural' and the mythical, 'supernatural' world. The resulting dialogue between modern and pre-modern epistemologies ultimately defines Tolkien's author-role as it is implied in his texts.

Dreams tell their own stories. Whether they seem to consist of modified fragments from daytime experience or to take the dreamer beyond the limits of his or her existence, once the dreamer has woken, they survive only in the telling. To achieve the transition into waking reality, dreams must be translated into another – usually verbal – medium. Since it is the dreamer who must make an effort to reconstruct and reassemble them into a proper narrative, the identity of their author seems to be certain. And yet, dreams may speak in ways that elude all attempts to transform them into a coherent account in accordance with the patterns that govern waking reality. Dream-theorists from antiquity to modernity have therefore developed concepts of a 'co-author' whose speech enters the dream in mystifying symbols or hidden messages. The dream's other voice may belong to supernatural agents, or it may belong to the unconscious: the involvement of an Other invariably guarantees that sense can be made of the dream's peculiar diction. Thus dreams are not as far removed from questions of authorship as it may seem at first glance. In the works of J.R.R. Tolkien, they are intrinsically connected to matters of literary creation and transmission. Narrated dreams may border on visionary journeys, providing insights that engender new tales; but when 'dreaming' is theorized as a specific mode of perception, it also overlaps and frequently interacts with 'imagination' and 'invention': categories that imply the process of literary creation.

I. Textual embedding:
Un-framed dreams and collective authorship

A particularly striking example from *The Lord of the Rings* may serve to illuminate the transition from dream to narrative and the questions of authorship raised by this process. Early in the Ring-quest, Frodo dreams of a 'far green country':

> either in his dreams or out of them, he could not tell which, Frodo heard a sweet singing running in his mind; a song that seemed to come like a pale light behind a grey rain-curtain, and growing stronger to turn the veil all to glass and silver, until at last it was rolled back, and a far green country opened before him under a swift sunrise. The vision melted into waking […]. (*LotR* 132)

This description returns as part of the narration at the very end of the book:

> And the ship went out into the High Sea and passed on into the West, until at last on a night of rain Frodo *smelled a sweet fragrance* on the air and heard the sound of singing that came over the water. And then it seemed to him that as in his dream in the house of Bombadil, the grey rain-curtain turned all to silver glass and was rolled back, and he beheld *white shores* and beyond them a far green country under a swift sunrise. (*LotR* 1007; emphasis added)[1]

This conclusion of Frodo's journey indicates that a visionary dream of his own future came to him in Tom Bombadil's house: he is about to reach Tol Eressëa, the Immortal Realm. But where did the dream originate and who is its author?

---

[1] Draft A of *The Grey Havens* did not contain the dream-vision, which was "roughed in marginally" (*SD* 109). But, as Christopher Tolkien points out, the connection had already been outlined in 1944, in a letter antedating the draft (*L* 104).

Why does the narration echo the dream-vision – instead of employing new descriptive means and imagery – when Frodo's final journey is described?

The book's framework establishes a multi-faceted perception of authorship. Tolkien adopts the role of author only in the *Foreword* to the second edition,[2] where he discusses his work on "the legend" (*LotR* xvi). With its *Notes on the Shire-Records*, the following *Prologue* then introduces the legend's source, the Red Book of Westmarch, a copy of the eyewitness record written by Frodo Baggins (based partially on notes by Bilbo Baggins and completed with additions from Samwise Gamgee). Unfolding a detailed manuscript tradition, the narrator of the *Prologue* presents himself as the translator-redactor of the tale.

The vision of approaching Eressëa implies a shared authorship along the same lines. Whether or not Frodo grasped the dream's meaning, he must have incorporated it into his records at some point. Since he hands his book over to Sam before they leave for the Grey Havens, Frodo's first glimpse of the Immortal Realm cannot be his own report; the reiteration of the dream-vision as actual reality must be part of Sam's text. Yet Sam remains behind on the shore, so that his authority on the matter may seem questionable.

The most plausible explanation would be that Sam, either remembering the dream that Frodo had described to him or discovering it in Frodo's written records, echoed Frodo's description. The remembered dream thus *becomes* reality in the book's narration and may reflect Sam's conviction that Frodo's vision precisely foretold a future event. Read this way, the realized dream contrasts starkly with Sam's mood as he watches the ship leave in shadowed isolation. The inclusion of a visionary future hence implies a double leap ahead: to Frodo's arrival at his destination and, simultaneously, to the point in time when Sam will fill the last pages of the book. As Tolkien's *Epilogue* discloses, Sam does not begin to work on his part of the book until fifteen years have passed (*SD* 122). While the temporal disjunction is not immediately obvious in *The Lord*

---

2 Only in the second edition by Ballantine Books in 1966 did *Foreword* and *Prologue* appear as separate texts with differently slanted author roles. By contrast, the *Foreword* to the first edition combined biographical comments with the reference to a translation from the Red Book (cf. *PME* 25f.): Tolkien "adopted the same pose that he had used in his prefatory note to the second edition of *The Hobbit* (1951) [...], that he was not the author of the work but merely its translator and redactor" (Hammond and Scull lxviii). See Flieger, *Music* 69-71.

of the Rings, it is nonetheless emphasized by the sharp narrative 'jump cut' from Frodo's perspective, concluding with the first sight of Eressëa at an undefined point in the future, back to Sam who remains, as if frozen for the entirety of Frodo's journey, on the darkening shore of Middle-earth. Short as this passage is, the temporal complexities touch upon the non-linear structure of dreams: a crucial aspect that emerges more fully in several other works.

A closer look also reveals minor changes to Frodo's description that nevertheless concern the underlying concept of authorship. Neither the "sweet fragrance" that precedes the sound of singing nor the "white shores" that lie before the "far green country" appear in Frodo's original dream.[3] If Sam is faithfully recreating Frodo's dream-vision as future reality, does he take liberties with the descriptive details? Did he in turn dream the journey from his own "point of vision"[4] in the years after Frodo's departure?[5]

The recreated dream-reality appears to be a fiction within the framework established in the *Prologue*, since its primary author, Sam, could not have witnessed Frodo's journey in the same manner that Frodo witnessed the historical events he recorded. Whether Frodo truly reached the Immortal Realm – and, if he did, whether he found it to be true to his dream – is a question which remains unanswerable. The details added to the dream-text therefore seem to highlight the fictional status of the passage and point back to the secondary author-translator, Tolkien, as the one authority who could well take liberties with the text of *The Lord of the Rings*. In this case, the apparent closure would reveal that Frodo's last journey ended in nothing but a hopeful fiction. The dilemma posed by the Red Book-framework, which does not permit any report of reaching Eressëa, would have been solved in rather postmodern fashion by pointing to the external author who invented not only the story but also the Red Book.

---

3 Another obvious addition is the reference to the earlier chapter ("as in his dream in the house of Bombadil"), a phrase that was "added only in proof" (Hammond and Scull 676), suggesting that Tolkien wished to emphasize a connection casual readers could easily overlook.
4 The term is used in *The Notion Club Papers* (*SD* 190).
5 The possibility that Sam may have had the same dream is suggested not only by his later journey to Eressëa (cf. *LotR* App. B 1072). In a draft for the *Fog on the Barrow-Downs* chapter, the dream of the 'far green country' came to all the hobbits (*RS* 127). Tolkien's early notes for the book's ending furthermore envision a joint journey: "Sam and Frodo go into a green land by the Sea?" (*TI* 212); "When old, Sam and Frodo set sail to island of West and [*sic*] Bilbo finishes the story. Out of gratitude the Elves adopt them and give them an island" (*TI* 287; cf. *SD* 53). This prospect may underlie the notion of a shared dream-vision.

The juxtaposition of dream-vision and vision-fiction raises questions about two issues: the matter of authorship and origin, with regard to both texts and dreams, and the status of dreams within texts presented as 'history'.[6] While it may be tempting to conclude that Tolkien decided to expose the fictionality of his own text at its very end, several letters as well as comments published in *The History of Middle-earth* point in another direction. In these texts, Tolkien insists that Frodo left the mortal world of Middle-earth to be healed in the Immortal Realm where Sam eventually joined him.[7] These statements rule out an interpretation of the final vision as a deliberate construct, designed to reflect the impossibility of reaching fictional closure. But these comments by no means resolve the larger questions, not least because Tolkien's authority on the matter is an intrinsic part of the puzzle.

By joining the role of author to that of a "recorder" (*L* 289), Tolkien extends authorship towards a collective and cedes authority to 'historical' eyewitnesses who, by sailing to Eressëa, have passed "out of time and history" altogether (*L* 198). The configuration emerging here, which connects authorship with visionary journeys beyond history and an entry into the Elven otherworld (or Faërie), is by no means a singular occurrence in Tolkien's works. *The Book of Lost Tales*, containing the earliest versions of what would later become *The Silmarillion*, opens with the arrival of a traveller from pre-Anglo-Saxon times in Eressëa where he gathers the tales that will eventually be recorded in the "Golden Book of Tavrobel" (*LT II* 290, 310), preserving the legends and histories of Elves for mortal men. The name of this first author-recorder, Eriol, is glossed as "One who dreams alone" (*LT I* 14), a name that gains added significance when the opening chapter introduces the "Path of Dreams" as another viable route to the realm of immortals (*LT I* 18).[8]

---

6 In Tolkien's *Foreword* to the second edition of *The Lord of the Rings*, the term "history" appears alongside the description of the work as a "legend" (*LotR* xvii, cf. 13). Tolkien correlates both terms where he describes the founding of the Shire: "About this time legend among the Hobbits first becomes history with a reckoning of years" (*LotR* 4). 'History' here refers to events that are firmly located in time and subjected to a calculable temporal progression.
7 *L* 198: "certain 'mortals', who have played some great part in Elvish affairs, may pass with the Elves to Elvenhome. Thus Frodo [...], and Bilbo, and eventually Sam (as adumbrated by Frodo); and as a unique exception Gimli the Dwarf, as friend of Legolas and 'servant' of Galadriel". Cf. *L* 411; *SD* 132; *MR* 341.
8 Indeed, Eriol's qualification as compiler of the Elvish 'legendarium' is implicitly linked to his abilities as a dreamer (cf. *LT I* 46, 129); his Eressëan informants in turn refer to insights gained on Olóre Mallë, the Path of Dreams (*LT II* 8, 70).

Authorship, combined with glimpses of Faërie and the mythical past, receives a pointed shift towards the visionary in Tolkien's unfinished time-travel stories, *The Lost Road* (1936) and *The Notion Club Papers* (1945). In these texts, dreams become the chief vehicle allowing the 20th-century protagonists to travel backwards in time and eventually to retrieve the lost history of Númenor as well as knowledge of the Immortal Realm. Time-travel in *The Notion Club Papers* is accompanied by intricate paths of transmission, "the nesting of text within text within text, each deriving from a successively earlier time" (Flieger, "Atlantis-Story" 55).[9] Ælfwine, who superseded Eriol as author-compiler in *The Book of Lost Tales* (*LT II* 300-05), now emerges as one of several author personae whose memories run through the generations. The process of rediscovery culminates in a visionary journey across the 'Straight Road' to Eressëa that Arundel Lowdham and Wilfrid Jeremy experience through the recollections of their Anglo-Saxon predecessors, Ælfwine and Tréowine (cf. *SD* 279).

The transmission device employed here points back to the *narrative framing strategies* already encountered in *The Lord of the Rings*. The text published under Tolkien's name is presented as the last link in a long chain of (oral and manuscript) traditions. While the "feigned manuscript topos" has numerous precedents, from the middle ages to 19th-century literature (cf. Hooker; Flieger, "Atlantis-Story" 55), the connection with dreams and the complexity of textual embedding achieved in *The Notion Club Papers* underline that its significance by far exceeds the function of lending "authenticity" or "credibility" to a work of fiction (Hooker 154, 177).

The implications of narrative framing are explicitly discussed in *The Notion Club Papers*, where Ramer, after presenting a new story to the Club, calls the frame "an awkward necessity of pictures". Guildford objects to the picture-frame parallel, however: "An author's way of getting to Mars (say) is part of *his* story of *his* Mars; and of *his* universe, as far as that particular tale goes. It's part of the picture, even if it's only in a marginal position; and it may seriously affect all that's inside" (*SD* 163). The frame is thus conceptualized

---

9 Cf. Flieger, "Atlantis-Story" 57: "Elendil's 'book' leads to Ælfwine's translation which leads to Edwin Lowdham's manuscript, of which the single leaf dropped by Lowdham and picked up by Ramer is embedded in the Notion Club 'papers,' the minutes found by Mr. Howard Green who then becomes both editor and publisher of *The Notion Club Papers*."

as intrinsic to the story. In *The Notion Club Papers* it becomes an essential part of the described events as well. The text explores previously undiscovered modes and channels of transmission as much as it discloses the downfall of Númenor and the existence of a Straight Road to the Undying Lands. Dreaming, in this context, functions as a vehicle of expanded perception – never as the frame for the "story inside".

Tolkien had already addressed this specific difference in *On Fairy-stories* (1939) where he distinguished dream as a literary framing device from dream as a mode of perception. In the essay, he rejects any employment of the 'machinery of Dream' as frame for a fairy-story:

> even if the reported dream was in other respects in itself a fairy-story, I would condemn the whole as gravely defective: like a good picture in a disfiguring frame. It is true that Dream is not unconnected with Faërie. In dreams strange powers of the mind may be unlocked. [...] But if a waking writer tells you that his tale is only a thing imagined in his sleep, he cheats deliberately the primal desire at the heart of Faërie: the realization, independent of the conceiving mind, of imagined wonder. [...] It is at any rate essential to a genuine fairy-story [...] that it should be presented as 'true'. [...] But since the fairy-story deals with 'marvels', it cannot tolerate any frame or machinery suggesting that the whole story in which they occur is a figment or illusion. (*OFS* 116f.)

With these remarks, Tolkien refers to a literary genre that became particularly popular during the (late) middle ages. Tales framed as dream-visions (such as the *Roman de la Rose*, *Piers Plowman*, or *Pearl*[10]) are defined by the "illusion that, prior to writing his poem, the author has made a transition into, and out of, a dream"; a literary mechanism that "functioned as a powerful device for signalling a state of altered consciousness" (Brown 24, 25). In his analysis of Middle English dream-visions, Peter Brown points out that tales of enchantment and a journey into Faërie function in a very similar manner, as the "altered state has been caused by the intervention of powers beyond the individual's immediate control" (38). When Tolkien argues that fairy-stories cannot tolerate a dream-frame, he underlines the distinction between enchantment and (ordi-

---

10 In his introduction to *Pearl*, Tolkien suggests that medieval vision-literature owed its popularity to the credibility the dream-frame lent to the reported events: "they [literary visions] allowed marvels to be placed within the real world" (*GPO* 9). Yet unlike a 'fairy-story' in a dream-frame, the medieval poem is not viewed as 'defective'. As Tolkien explains, contemporary beliefs allowed for the acceptance of such 'marvels': "we are dealing with a period when men, aware of the vagaries of dreams, still thought that amid their japes came visions of truth" (*GPO* 9).

nary) dreaming and reasons that the framing device determines the degree of reality – or truth – accorded to the story. The possibility of "imagined wonder" would be undermined by a frame exposing it as illusory. As in *The Notion Club Papers*, textual framing is not merely a matter of artistic consistency, rather it defines the prevalent mode of perception (and reception).

Tolkien's rejection of dream-frames and his obvious preference for elaborate textual genealogies furthermore demonstrate a historical awareness of appropriate gateways towards his tales of Arda. Dreams, according to common 20th-century convictions, are things 'imagined' in one's sleep, whereas a philologically sound descent of the tale ensures its credibility as "*vera historia*" (*L* 365). Within such a frame, however, dreams may unfold their "strange powers". While they are in themselves framed by waking perception, the course of events in *The Notion Club* Papers demonstrates how dreams can merge into waking reality, literally stepping out of their frame.

In *The Lord of the Rings*, Frodo's dream is equally unframed when it reappears as part of the narration. On the level of the story, it emerges as a dream-come-true. On the level of narrative strategies, the act of un-framing puts into practice what *On Fairy-stories* proposes theoretically: the "realization of imagined wonder". At the same time, the reconfigured dream at the very end of the book functions as a window on a different sphere of reality. The historical space of Middle-earth opens up towards the 'mythical' space of Eressëa and the Elven otherworld which otherwise remain outside the narrative range. The transition from a prophetic dream to narrated events effectively mirrors the transition into another reality. In the removal of the original frame, the poetological potential of dreams becomes momentarily tangible: as a bridge between different realities, dreams can function as the counterpart of textual embedding or of the genealogy of texts established in the *Prologue* to *The Lord of the Rings* and *The Notion Club Papers*. Such a genealogy distributes authorship among a succession of recorders, translators, compilers and redactors that may be traced back to an initial – though perhaps not original – text.[11] When the textual genealogy is

---

11 In *The Notion Club Papers*, the oldest text is ascribed to Elendil (*SD* 279); in *The Lord of the Rings*, Frodo's and Sam's book is partially based on Bilbo's 'diary'.

complemented by revelatory dreams, however, the ultimate source (or author) of these disclosures seems to recede into an unfathomable distance.

Consideration of dreams in relation to narrative framing devices has shown how dreams complement the concept of authorship as a collective process of compilation and transmission. As a specific mode of (non-linear) perception, dreaming may accompany and transcend the (linear) genealogy of texts. If unframed dreams can convey the truth of an entry into Faërie, as the ending of *The Lord of the Rings* suggests, the ability to dream may very well be conceived as a precondition for authorship – at least where the writing of 'fairy-stories' is concerned.

In order to pursue this line of inquiry further, it is necessary to examine the conceptualizations of dreaming in Tolkien's works and to identify points of connection with the storytelling/writing process. In the following, I will focus first on the theories and categories that surround and characterize dreams in some of Tolkien's texts. By outlining a theoretical model, I am not suggesting that the diversity of texts can be aligned to a single concept. While some basic commonalities may be traced, it is equally important to illuminate the different aspects of a complex connecting dream and vision to imagination, invention and authorship.

II. Intersections of dreams & literature: Visionary journeys

Even a cursory comparison of Tolkien's approach with the most influential dream-theories of European history discloses profound differences. These differences concern the role of *symbolism* on the one hand, and the *source* of dreams on the other. Sigmund Freud's theory relies on symbolic modes of representation (condensation and displacement in particular). The symbolic language of dreams bears witness to the activity of the unconscious that expresses unacknowledged fears and desires in often mystifying imagery. Freud therefore distinguishes manifest from latent content, which always aims at wish fulfilment. Dreams express a primary mental process that employs symbols and images according to its own logic, whereas the secondary – rational – processes employ linguistic signs and concepts.[12] In this context, it is important to note that Freud's theory salvaged dreams from a verdict largely imposed since the rise of Enlightenment. By light of reason, dreams could only be viewed as nonsensical ramblings of the sleeping mind, firmly located in the realm of irrationality and dangerously alike to pathological mental states (cf. Heise 23; Freud I.C: 55-76, I.H: 119-24). Freud's crucial theoretical move not only restored meaning to dreams, it also took up the ruptured threads of pre-modern traditions.

Prior to the Enlightenment era, certain types of dreams were considered meaningful and interpreted with recourse to complex theoretical models. For the purposes of this essay, it will suffice to outline the classifications developed by two influential authors: Artemidorus of Daldis (2nd cent.) and the late Roman writer Macrobius (4th-5th cent.) whose theories shaped the medieval understanding of dreams to a large extent.[13] Both authors distinguish visionary from meaningless somatic dreams caused by the affects of body and soul.[14] Divine agents are the ultimate co-authors of dream-visions[15] that may openly reveal important truths and future events. Artemidorus calls these theorematic dreams (I.2, 15), while Macrobius further distinguishes *visio* (prophetic vision of the future) and *oraculum* (in which an authority – divine or human – gives advice), both of which are owed to divine inspiration (I.iii, 87f., 90). However, visionary dreams may also arise in symbolic form. Artemidorus' class of 'allegorical dreams' is paralleled by Macrobius' description of the enigmatic dream (*somnium*) which "conceals with strange shapes and veils with ambiguity the true meaning of the information being offered, and requires an interpretation for its understanding" (I.iii, 90).[16] The pre-modern concepts share two basic convictions with Freudian theory: first, that meaningful dreams may signify in

---

12 See Freud, esp. chapter IV (manifest and latent content), 167-95; chapter VI.A-B (condensation and displacement), 312-44; and chapter VII.E (primary and secondary processes), 626-48.
13 On Macrobius' model and its influence on the development of medieval dream-theories, see Kruger 21ff., 58ff. and Peden.
14 Artemidorus distinguishes the visionary dream, *oneiros*, from the somatic variety, *enhypnion* (*Oneirocritica* I.1, 14). Macrobius' system contains two types of insignificant dreams (*insomnium* and *visum* or *phantasma*) that merely reflect the day's concerns or, when caused by indigestion, consist only of disconnected, fragmentary images (*Somnium Scipionis* I.iii, 88f.).
15 Artemidorus I.6, 20f. Artemidorus specifies that the 'encryption' of dreams occurs by "physical means" and images "that are natural products" (I.2, 15) when the soul is moved by a vision that originates beyond itself.
16 *Somnium* thus represents a truth in fictional or allegorical form (cf. Kruger 24). Peter Brown describes its position as "half-way between dreams caused by divine inspiration and those caused by physical and mental disorder" (23).

a symbolic mode that requires careful exegesis and, second, that their ultimate source is located outside the dreamer's rational mind. While Artemidorus, Macrobius and their successors identify supernatural powers as the authors of significant dreams, Freudian dream-analysis traces their symbolic language back to the individual unconscious.

By contrast, Tolkien's theories and literary descriptions of dreams are only marginally concerned with decipherable symbolism of any kind (cf. *SD* 183, 194). Dreams are hardly ever subjected to an exegetic process that decodes their bewildering images. While ancient and modern theories place much emphasis on the ultimate source or author of a dream, in order to determine its meaning, Tolkien seems to distinguish mainly between dreams reflecting activities of the dreamer's own mind and dreams originating elsewhere. What Tolkien examines and explores across various texts is the dreaming mind's *specific state of attention* (or mode of perception), which may include creative activities. 'Dream' is thus placed in the proximity of 'imagination' and 'invention' as well as 'vision'. *The Notion Club Papers* offers a convenient starting point for determining the connections between these categories, as this particular text provides Tolkien's most elaborate theory of dreams in relation to literature.

Discussion among the club members on 'Night 61' quickly focuses on Michael Ramer's experiments with dreams. While Ramer himself uses only descriptive approximations – such as 'deep', 'serious' or 'free' vs. 'marginal' dreams – to highlight distinctions, his explanations encompass the following types of dreams: ordinary or 'marginal' dreams made up of daytime experiences ("the mind, rootling about, as it does, in the day's leavings"; *SD* 181, cf. 186), those that continue the work of the dreamer's imagination in different form, occasionally challenging the dreamer to unravel the hidden significance of a dreamed scene or fragment (*SD* 189-93), and dreams in which the mind perceives locations and events beyond the time and space of waking reality. Within these "deep" or "free" dreams, the dreamer may be in contact with other minds, achieving a direct impression and an immediate understanding of events within Other Time or Other Space (*SD* 176) that can bypass even language (*SD* 200).

This brief overview indicates a certain affinity with the pre-modern understanding of dreams. 'Marginal' dreams are reminiscent of the somatic variety, whereas 'deep' dreams transcend the boundaries of the individual mind and allow contact with other beings; as a consequence, their revelations concern not only the individual dreamer. The Freudian approach, on the other hand, is explicitly discarded and ridiculed. Ramer asserts: "I can't, don't want to, and haven't tried to remember all the jumble of marginal stuff – the rubbish the analysts mostly muck about with, because it's practically all they've got" (*SD* 184f.).[17]

Yet despite the tangential connections with pre-modern theories, Tolkien's text focuses on an aspect as foreign to Artemidorus and Macrobius as it is to Freud. Central to Ramer's observations is the dream's specific mode of operation, rather than its content. Dreams are recognized as a vehicle for perceptions that transcend the ordinary continuum of time and space. His theory casts "free" dreams as a particular "movement" of the mind, which he describes as "transference of observation". Although this transference is not limited to dreams on principle, freedom from the "never-ending racket of sense-impressions" (*SD* 176) allows the mind to slip away from the conditioning of time and space (*SD* 178) that governs waking awareness. These "serious dreams, or visions" (*SD* 187) amount to "journeys" (*SD* 197), and therein lies their significance.

Where symbolism occurs, it proceeds from "a direct impression" received when the mind encounters the – utterly strange – presence of Others within dreams, as a "translation from meaning into symbol" (*SD* 202). A subsequent decoding of these specific symbols is neither desirable nor practicable, as they constitute the only language that the dreaming mind is capable of. Rather than attempting symbolic readings of any kind,[18] Ramer therefore derives explanations for the mystifying dream-fragments from their context. They are "like random pages torn out of a book" (*SD* 183), hence their meaning becomes apparent when the proper context of preceding or subsequent events can be established. This approach to comprehending the dream's significance also restores a linearity of cause and effect usually absent from the dream itself.

---

17 Subsequent anti-Freudian jibes are directed at the assumption that primal urges, controlled by a Censor, define the self (cf. *SD* 188).
18 'Symbols', in this context, operate like the conventional (linguistic) signs employed to translate a non-verbal or otherwise incomprehensible impression (cf. *SD* 203, 225). While symbolism in dreams isn't denied, it is generally not the focus of Ramer's attention (cf. *SD* 183, 194). He also suggests that the presence of symbols in dreams results from the same process as their literary employment (*SD* 193).

The parallels between dreams and stories that become tangible here are present from the very beginning of the Notion Club's discussion, initialized by Ramer's admission that he 'saw' what he described in his story and merely invented a frame.[19] This particular mode of seeing is generally distinct from imagining, so that the term 'free dream' becomes virtually interchangeable with 'vision'. Invention, the mind's creative faculty, enters at the other end of the spectrum of mental activities. Closely connected to it are 'construction' and 'fiction', though 'fiction' is surrounded by somewhat dubious connotations,[20] reminiscent of the sceptical medieval position that equated *historia* with truth and *fictio* with lie (cf. Leupin 18f.). The implied distinction between invention/construction on the one hand and fiction/fabrication on the other calls for a closer examination of 'invention'.

In his preface to Tolkien's *Etymologies* (late 1930s) Christopher Tolkien points out that the linguistic constructions are "in principle historically 'explicable'": "'Invention' was thus altogether distinct from 'artificiality'" (*LR* 341).[21] The history of the term itself points in a similar direction. In classical rhetoric, *inventio* meant the finding of a suitable theme or argument; in a medieval hagiographic context, *inventio* referred specifically to the discovery of a saint's relics.[22] It seems that related ideas shaped Tolkien's distinction of invention

---

19 The Club's other members immediately notice a peculiar quality in the framed story, too: "all of us, in some degree, had sensed something odd about that story, and now recognized that it differed from the norm *like seeing does from imagining*" (*SD* 172; emphasis added). At the Club's next gathering, Ramer begins to talk about dreams as vehicles of observing events beyond the ordinary constraints of time and space (*SD* 175f.).
20 *SD* 228: "you've got to make a distinction between lies, or casual fiction, or the mere verbal trick of projecting sentences back by putting the verbs into the past tense, between all that and *construction*. Especially of the major kind that has acquired a secondary life of its own and passes from mind to mind." When Stainer suggests that Lowdham has 'fabricated' mythical texts, Dolbear replies: "'Really you're unteachable [...]. Why do you always prefer a theory that cannot be true, unless somebody is lying?'" (*SD* 260). 'Invention' is therefore distinguished from 'fiction': "these ancient accounts, legends, myths, about the far Past, about the origins of kings, laws, and the fundamental crafts, are not all made of the same ingredients. They're not wholly inventions. And even what is invented is different from mere fiction; it has more roots" (*SD* 227). These roots, according to Jeremy, lie "in Being", i.e. "the pattern of our world as it uniquely is" and "the events in it as seen from a distance" (*SD* 227).
21 Cf. Shippey, *Road* 57: "This activity of re-creation – creation from philology – lies at the heart of Tolkien's 'invention' (though maybe not of his 'inspiration')." – Tolkien comments on the word 'hobbit' in similar fashion: "This, I confess, is my own invention; but not one devised at random. This is its origin. It is, for one thing, not wholly unlike the actual word in the Shire, which was *cûbuc* (plural *cûbugin*)" (*PME* 49).
22 See Cicero: *De inventione*. – Patristic and medieval legends that describe the recovery of a saint's mortal remains and other relics typically fall under the heading *De inventione et translatione...*, the most famous among them concerning the discovery of the Holy Cross (*Inventio Crucis*). See "Inventio et Translatio". *Analecta Bollandiana* 2 (1883): 341-354.

from fiction, with the implication that invention possesses a greater degree of relevance or truth because it draws on pre-existent materials and previously established patterns. In different contexts, the meaning of invention may thus oscillate between construction and reconstruction.

In *The Notion Club Papers*, discussion frequently returns to the inherent connections between dreams and (literary) invention. Dreams may continue where an author's waking mind leaves off, as Ramer states: "thought and 'invention' goes on in dreams, a lot of it; and of course you can [...] go on with the story-making, if that is what you were doing" (*SD* 187). Dreams of this type are also referred to as "working-dreams" (*SD* 201)[23] which draw on material already present in the mind (*SD* 189).[24] But "dream-storywriting" (*SD* 193) may be interspersed with "visions of real places" and "bits of long visions of things not invented" (*SD* 189). Indeed, the boundaries can be blurred in various ways.

Ramer speculates that "what one calls 'interests' are sometimes actually stimulated, or even implanted by contacts" (*SD* 197), and at another point in the discussion seems to amalgamate the previously separate categories when he states that composition within dreams "is not, of course, writing, but a sort of realized drama". This remark immediately reminds Jeremy of "Elvish drama" (*SD* 193), a concept first introduced in *On Fairy-stories*. In the essay, Tolkien states that

> Faërian Drama [...] can produce Fantasy with a realism and immediacy beyond the compass of any human mechanism. [...] If you are present at a Faërian drama you yourself are, or think that you are, bodily inside its Secondary World. The experience may be very similar to Dreaming and has (it would seem) sometimes (by men) been confounded with it. But in Faërian drama *you are in a dream that some other mind is weaving*, and the knowledge of that alarming fact may slip from your grasp. (*OFS* 142; emphasis added)

Elvish or Faërian drama is here conceptualized as entering the 'dream' or 'fantasy' of another – and indeed very strange – mind. But it also stems from a different mode of imagination whose power to conjure reality surpasses the ordinary (mortal) capacity: Tolkien likens it to 'dreaming' more than once.

---

[23] Ramer develops this distinction further in a fragment of Night 62: "it seems to me that the chief divisions are *Perceiving* (free dreams), *Composing and Working*, and *Reading*. Each has a distinctive quality, and confusion is not as a rule likely to occur, while it is going on; though the waking mind may make mistakes about disjointed memories" (*SD* 195f.).

[24] At this point, Tolkien's literary text directly contradicts *On Fairy-stories* where he maintains that in dreaming "there is no art" (*OFS* 139).

Elsewhere, in an etymological note glossing Gandalf's Valinorian name *Olórin*, he explains that Sindarin *olor*

> is a word often translated 'dream', but that does not refer to (most) human 'dreams', certainly not the dreams of sleep. To the Eldar, it included the vivid contents of their *memory*, as of their *imagination*: it referred in fact to *clear vision*, in the mind, of things not physically present at the body's situation. But not only to an idea but to a full clothing of this in particular form and detail. (*UT* 512f.)[25]

Despite the marked difference, vivid mortal dreams come closest to an otherwise unattainable (immortal) perfection of the imaginative faculty[26] that Tolkien also calls 'enchantment' (*OFS* 143). In *The Notion Club Papers*, Ramer describes dream-storywriting along very similar lines (*SD* 193). As Verlyn Flieger notes, dreaming is ultimately given "an immediacy, a presence and an impact that supersedes not just the 'dreamy' quality of the ordinary dream but the realistic clarity of the ordinary waking state as well" (*Time* 140).[27]

The passages quoted demonstrate that, depending on context, dream and imagination can be intrinsically connected with invention or creation. Imagination, the *ability to envision what is not present*,[28] holds the middle ground between (voluntary) invention and the observation of Other Time and Space that may

---

25 The note is part of *The Istari* (1954). Related to *olor* is *olo-s* ('phantasy'): "Common Elvish name for 'construction of the mind' not actually (pre)existing in Eä apart from the construction, but by the Eldar capable of being by Art (*Karmë*) made visible and sensible. *Olos* is usually applied to fair constructions having solely an artistic object (i.e. not having the object of deception, or of acquiring power)" (*UT* 513). An example of this vision-inducing power is given in *The Silmarillion*, when Finrod Felagund sings to mortal men of the Undying Lands (*S* 169).
26 This emphasis on imagination bears a certain likeness with the theory of Karl Albert Scherner who, in the later 19th century, explained dreams as the product of pure imagination or fantasy, operating unrestrained by conscious, rational thought (97-114). However, Scherner also asserted that these activities are caused solely by physiological stimuli.
27 That 'dream', in the supernatural realm, can merge with the creation of actual reality is suggested by the following passage from *The Music of the Ainur* that describes the making of Arda: "Know then that water was for the most part the *dream and invention* of Ulmo, an Ainu whom Ilúvatar had instructed deeper than all others in the depths of music" (*LT I* 56; emphasis added). Invention does not refer to an independent, original creation but to the realization of a previous (musical) vision.
28 Rather than 'fantasy', cf. *OFS* 138: "The human mind is capable of forming mental images of things not actually present. The faculty of conceiving the images is (or was) naturally called Imagination. But in recent times, in technical not normal language, Imagination has often been held to be something higher than the mere image-making, ascribed to the operations of Fancy (a reduced and depreciatory form of the older word Fantasy); an attempt is thus made to restrict, I should say misapply, Imagination to 'the power of giving to ideal creations the inner consistency of reality'." In the following, Tolkien specifies that imagination involves "perception of the image, the grasp of its implications, and the control", which is distinct from "the achievement of the expression", and introduces the term 'fantasy' "which shall embrace both the Sub-creative Art in itself and a quality of strangeness and wonder in the Expression, derived from the Image: a quality essential to fairy-story" (*OFS* 138f.).

occur within dreams. Intense dream-states approach Elvish imagination with its heightened capacity of conjuring the mind's contents as actual reality. Repeated references to the specifics of Elvish imagination furthermore suggest the possibility of a dialogue between entirely different modes of perception: one belonging to mortals, the other originating within Faërie, the domain of immortals (see below, section V).

On the whole, Tolkien's concept in *The Notion Club Papers* marks a clear division between insignificant and meaningful dreams, reminiscent of pre-modern theories. At the same time, rather than being caused by divine inspiration, significant dreams may be shaped by the dreamer's (creative) mind as well. Yet when Ramer speculates that personal preoccupations may have been 'implanted' by (unrecalled) experiences of contact, he also implies that the source of meaningful dreams is never entirely certain. To be sure, the origins of 'deep' dreams are never identified either. This unknown variable, alongside the possible blending of visionary elements with imaginative/inventive activities, points to an important feature: the significance of dreams cannot be established with recourse to an originator's authority. Instead, the Notion Club's dreamers have to rely on their own ability to discern and conceptualize different kinds of dreams.[29]

Subtle as their deliberations are, they never draw the boundaries between the diverse types of experience with absolute certainty – all the more so because dream-experiences and -theories continuously emerge from, and feed back into, the complex process of story-making. Even as he introduces his theory, Ramer describes the dreaming mind's "movement" beyond ordinary time and space (its "transference of observation") by drawing on a "literary parallel": "I don't think literary invention, or fancy, is mixed up in all this by accident" (*SD* 176). Hence dreams produce meaning when they contribute to the writing process or provide fragments of stories. And they become explosively meaningful when they reveal the presence of a lost past and establish new channels of transmission that may then transform waking reality and constitute a new tradition of texts.

---

29 This aspect points to a specific quality that Peter Brown discerns in late medieval dream-visions: The dream mechanism provides authors with "an instrument of radical analysis and evaluation" (44). Similarly Kruger 134: "The dream fiction, by representing in the dream an imaginative entity like fiction itself, often becomes self-reflexive. Dream vision is especially liable to become metafiction, thematizing issues of representation and interpretation."

The second part of *The Notion Club Papers* no longer focuses on theoretical considerations but moves from Arundel Lowdham's (chiefly linguistic) dreams to his and Jeremy's performance of experiences from a mythical past and their joint vision-quest. After their re-enactment of the flight from Númenor, Ramer muses that something has been "stirred up": "If not out of history, at any rate out of a very powerful world of imagination and memory. Jeremy would say 'perhaps out of both'" (*SD* 253). Once again, a critical boundary is questioned: historical events cannot be fully separated from their manifestations in the imagination. The past becomes tangible only through the transfer of stories (managed here by means of visionary experience), and 'imagination' once more displays the power to generate a reality that others may enter.

Two crucial factors shape both the understanding of dreams and the other major topics of *The Notion Club Papers*. Visionary experiences outside the order of time must be translated into the context of a historical process to make sense. These two facets, atemporal and historical, constantly complement each other and contribute to a *visionary history* converging with myth. Secondly, the proposed theory of dreams is eminently poetological.[30] As such it is inseparable from the conceptualization of literature and the textual genealogies that structure and accompany the plot. In the process, vital boundaries are crossed, not only between waking and sleeping, but also between present, past and future, between 'history' and 'myth'. Motivated and accompanied by an epistemological discourse that examines different modes of perception, this constant movement draws attention to the significance of the "dream threshold":

> Perhaps one of the most significant features of the boundary between waking and dreaming is its offer of a point of entry into new levels of perception otherwise inaccessible. [...] The dream threshold also transforms reality: the other world which the dreamer enters is both like and unlike the familiar one of waking experience (Brown 36).

This description of late medieval dream-visions is equally accurate when applied to the transformative potential of dreams in Tolkien's text. Here, as in

---

30 In his discussion of medieval dream-theories, Steven Kruger notes a "parallel complexity of oneiric and literary realms" (131) and points out the explicit parallels between Macrobius' categories and various literary genres: "Both dreams and fiction are 'double' experiences, and both are capable of bridging the opposed terms of falsehood and truth" (133). On the realization of this poetological potential in medieval texts see also Klinger, "Poetik der Träume".

the medieval genre, the series of surmounted boundaries signals an increasing receptiveness to, and intensification of, a state of altered consciousness (cf. Brown 40). Once they recognize the potential of their altered perceptions, the Notion Club's dreamers move within a changed reality. Peter Brown also notes that discontinuity in (literary) dreams can reflect a sense of fragmentation or alienation: "A dream is [...] well suited to the representation and analysis [...] of a searching for connections that have become hidden, tenuous, or problematic" (44). In *The Notion Club Papers* this search concerns the disjunction of 'myth' and 'history'. Complex textual embedding serves to question the linear, causal continuum of history that generates only certain types of stories (cf. Klinger, "More Poetical"). Dreams, however, provide an alternative when they range out of time and approach a mythical mode of imagination.

III. Leaps across time: The dreaming voices of history

An important pattern emerges from a text that is not connected to Tolkien's Middle-earth tales. In *The Homecoming of Beorhtnoth Beorhthelm's Son* (1953[31]), one of the two Anglo-Saxon protagonists, Torhthelm, falls into a trance-like state while resting on the cart beside his dead lord Beorhtnoth. With "the voice of one speaking in a dream", he "chants":

> Heart shall be bolder, harder be purpose,
> more proud the spirit as our power lessens!
> Mind shall not falter nor mood waver,
> though doom shall come and death conquer! (*HBBS* 141)

Torhthelm echoes words spoken by the men who appear before his mind's eye ("I hear them in the hall chanting, | stern words they sing with strong voices"; *HBBS* 141), but – apparent only to the reader – he is also repeating two lines from the Old English poem *The Battle of Maldon* (11th cent.), where they are spoken by Beorhtwold:

> Hige sceal þē heardra,   heorte þē cēnre,
> mōd sceal þē māre   þe ūre mægen lytlað. (l. 312f.)

---

[31] Although the text was published only in 1953, shortly before *The Fellowship of the Ring*, early drafts indicate that composition began in the early 1930s (*TI* 106f.)

Commenting on these verses that he describes as "a summing up of the heroic code", Tolkien specifies: "It is here [in *The Homecoming*] implied, as is indeed probable, that these words were not 'original', but an ancient and honoured expression of heroic will" (*HBBS* 124). Tolkien's appropriation of these verses does not end with incorporating them into his own text (itself set shortly after the historical battle of Maldon and composed in the metre of the older poem): while their message is expanded by two added lines that lack a counterpart in *Maldon*[32] and further illustrate the "heroic code", they are also reconfigured within a specific chain of transmission.

Rather than giving credit to the anonymous *Maldon* poet, Tolkien identifies the quoted verses as a traditional formula. This authorless text then moves on to Torhthelm who faces the apparition of several unnamed men – most probably the recently slain warriors – and echoes their voices during a visionary (or hallucinatory) moment. The origin of these lines loses itself in the twilight of unrecorded events. They belong to a collective, rather than any individual author, and travel quite freely from voice to voice, crossing even the border between different realities. While Beorhtwold may have been repeating words he had heard on other occasions, Torhthelm receives them as a message from another world.

'Dream', used figuratively in this case, seems to signify a receptive state of mind that permits such a transmission, but at the same time it is linked to a specific mode of speech ("the voice of one speaking in a dream"). Torhthelm's dreamlike speech furthermore approaches a 'speaking in tongues', an occurrence found more than once in Tolkien's works.[33] In this context, an implicit link with poetry must be noted. Torhthelm is introduced as the "son of a minstrel" and a "gleeman" (*HBBS* 123, 126) who quotes from poetic tradition occasionally (129, 131). The lines borrowed from *Maldon* in turn retain their poetic quality (tangible in the alliterative metre), and Tolkien does not suggest that

---

32 The Old English poem continues: *Hēr lið ūre ealdor eall forhēawen, | gōd on grēote: ā mæg gnornian | sē ðe nū fram þis wīgplegan wendan þenceð!* (ll. 313-316: "Here lies our lord, lethally wounded, | good man on the ground. May he grieve forever | who from his war-work would consider withdrawing"; translation by Bill Griffiths).

33 'Speaking in tongues' traditionally involves articulation in a completely unknown language (*glossolalia*) or in a foreign language (*xenolalia*); for a historical overview of the phenomenon see Christie-Murray. Tolkien's works feature only *xenolalia* in *The Notion Club Papers* and *The Lord of the Rings*.

their ultimate source might be found in a spontaneous utterance outside literary tradition. As a poetically condensed, "ancient and honoured expression of heroic will" these words may be actualized by different speakers. If the chain of oral transmission and memory is broken, the connection can be reforged in a 'dreaming' state: the lost history is recovered in visionary mode.[34]

The pattern established here is indeed visible in several other works, where its central elements recur in varied constellations. An authorless text emerges in a succession of voices that transcends oral/scriptural transmission when it involves a 'speaking in tongues', or a dream-state, or aspects of both. Such a text may refer to a historical event and thus convey a real experience, or it may be poetry, or both.

In *The Lord of the Rings*, a comparable incident occurs early in the Quest, when Frodo looks out across the eastern parts of the Shire and recites *The Road goes ever on and on* "aloud but as if to himself" (*LotR* 72). Only when Pippin asks if Bilbo was responsible for this "bit of rhyming" or whether it is one of Frodo's "imitations" does Frodo begin to wonder about the song's origin: "It came to me then, as if I was making it up; but I may have heard it long ago" (*LotR* 72). Without the larger context, this incident may seem ordinary enough, if not altogether banal. Frodo does not dream either, he merely echoes another's voice and words in a particularly fitting situation. However, one revealing element re-emerges here: the uncertainty of origins. Frodo cannot be sure whether he invented or echoed the (slightly modified) text,[35] and, as Tom Shippey has pointed out, the reference to Bilbo "does not mean that Bilbo made it up, or not that he made *all* of it up" (*Author* 189). This uncertainty is not entirely surprising within a predominantly oral culture, where traditional songs and poems may circulate freely without generating any particular interest in authorship or indeed any concern about 'originality'. Shared or collective authorship, 'imitation' and variation of already familiar texts can be expected to form the

---

34 Tolkien articulates a similar thought in a letter to W. H. Auden, in June 1955: "In any case if you want to write a tale of this sort you must consult your roots, and a man of the North-west of the Old World will set his heart and the action of his tale in an imaginary world of that air, and that situation: with the Shoreless Sea of his innumerable ancestors to the West, and the endless lands (out of which enemies mostly come) to the East. Though, in addition, *his heart may remember, even if he has been cut off from all oral tradition*, the rumour all along the coasts of the Men out of the Sea" (*L* 212f.; emphasis added).
35 In Frodo's version Bilbo's "eager feet" are replaced by "weary feet".

common standard of literature.³⁶ Yet this is neither the last nor the most striking instance of oral echoes in *The Lord of the Rings*.

Reminiscent of Torhthelm, Merry echoes the words of a nameless dead warrior when he wakes in the barrow, after the hobbits' nightmarish encounter with the Barrow-wight (*LotR* 140). On Weathertop, Frodo cries "*O Elbereth! Gilthoniel!*" in utter distress, repeating (apparently without conscious thought) the invocation first heard from Gildor's company of Elves in the Woody End. But to Sam "Frodo's voice [...] seemed to come from a great distance, or from under the earth, crying out strange words" (*LotR* 192). Later in the Quest, during the Cirith Ungol episode, both Frodo and Sam 'speak in tongues', which in Sam's case amounts to a variation of a Sindarin verse – the 'hymn to Elbereth' – heard at various points in the events (*LotR* 704, 712, 894; see section V).

However, the pattern emerges most strongly from the two time-travel stories, *The Lost Road* and *The Notion Club Papers*, where it provides the essential narrative drive. Two aspects that both works share must be of particular interest here: the discovery of a 'mythical' past through dreams and the materialization of these discoveries in literary or poetic form. Both are linked to the extent that non-linear temporal experience involves entering the (poetic, mythical) imagination that originates within Other Time.

In *The Lost Road* as well as *The Notion Club Papers* linguistic dreams, invention and discovery lay the groundwork for subsequent time-travel experiences. While Ramer provides the theoretical frame, the most prominent dream-traveller, Arry Lowdham, possesses a specifically linguistic talent. Practically throughout his life, he not only studied old languages and invented new ones but also heard – "both in dream or waking abstraction" – words and phrases from unknown languages "ringing in his ears" (*SD* 237). Similarly, in *The Lost Road* Alboin Errol, another scholar of ancient languages, picks up fragments of a language that he calls *Eressëan* or *Elf-latin* (*LR* 41). In both works, these "tantalizingly

---

36 Cf. Shippey, *Author* 188f., *Road* 185-88. In addition to "The Road Goes Ever On and On" another walking-song ("Upon the hearth the fire is red...") reappears transformed and with a different meaning later in the text. Cf. Shippey, *Author* 191: "Shire-poetry [...] can be new and old at the same time, highly personal and more-than-personal, subject to continuous change while retaining a recognizable frame." On the representation of oral traditions see also Flieger, *Music* 61-67.

linguistic" dreams (*LR* 45) eventually yield a poetic (albeit fragmentary) account of Númenor's downfall, a lament recorded in the Númenórean language(s).[37] This pivotal discovery provides the launching point for the ensuing visionary journeys. Alboin Errol encounters Elendil of Númenor the very next night, having "passed out of the waking world" (*LR* 48); Arry Lowdham and Wilfrid Jeremy begin to speak as Elendil/Nimruzīr and Voronwë/Abrazān after discussing the Númenórean text (*SD* 250-52).

In both works, the ultimate goal of a journey across time lies in the cataclysm of Númenor (the Middle-earth equivalent of Atlantis), already encapsulated in the *Lament*, as the origin of a twofold rupture. Númenor's downfall causes an irrevocable separation of the mortal world (Middle-earth) from the Immortal Realm (Valinor and Eressëa). After the cataclysm, the previously flat world is made round, so that the 'bent roads' of the mortal continuum are severed from the Straight Road to the Elven otherworld. The Straight Road thus supersedes the transhistorical *Olóre Mallë*, the Path of Dreams, as a more complex concept resulting from dramatic historical change. In *The Notion Club Papers*, the disjunction of Straight and bent roads is therefore identified with a "dividing line" between 'myth' and 'history'.[38] Yet revisiting this explosive disruption also means that an immediate connection between the world of men and Faërie is rediscovered, and that one enters a mode of perception in which "real history" can be experienced as "more mythical" and "more poetical" than linear history allows (*SD* 227; cf. Klinger, "More Poetical"). The concept of the Lost Straight Road embraces both aspects.

With regard to the implicit understanding of authorship and literature, two intertwined threads need to be traced further: the unravelling of linguistic history towards unknown origins and the process of poetic re-interpretation and re-production that accompanies it. Linguistic history becomes both a vehicle and an important goal of "the desire to go back":

---

37 *LR* 47; *SD* 246f. Virtually the same text appears in both works, but while *The Lost Road* features only a Quenya version, the 'lament' appears in Adûnaic and (an evolved version of) Quenya in *The Notion Club Papers*, thus combining the language of immortals with that of mortals.

38 *SD* 249: "Somebody once said, I forget who, that the distinction between history and myth might be meaningless outside the Earth. I think it might at least get a great deal less sharp on the Earth, further back. Perhaps the Atlantis catastrophe was the dividing line?" – Atlantis is cited as Númenor's equivalent within European mythology on various occasions: cf. *SD* 206, 232; *L* 197f., 206, 303.

> To walk in Time, perhaps, as men walk on long roads; or to survey it, as men may see the world from a mountain, or the earth as a living map beneath an airship. But in any case to see with eyes and to hear with ears: to see the lie of old and even forgotten lands, to behold ancient men walking, and *hear their languages as they spoke them, in the days before the days, when tongues of forgotten lineage were heard* in kingdoms long fallen by the shores of the Atlantic.
> (*LR* 45; emphasis added)

In *The Lost Road*, Alboin states: "language goes back by a continuous tradition into the past" (*LR* 40), and the text underlines the viability of this route when dreamed fragments from historical (Germanic) languages allude to the existence of a lost westward road. Alboin records the line *Westra lage wegas rehtas, nu isti sa wraithas* ("a straight road lay westward, now it is bent"; *LR* 43) as well as Anglo-Saxon verses in which Ælfwine invokes "West-regions unknown to men, marvels and strange beings, a land fair and lovely, the homeland of the Elves, and the bliss of the Gods" (*LR* 44). Nearly identical fragments emerge in *The Notion Club Papers*, where "echoes of very archaic English, even early Germanic" "came through" to Lowdham: *westra lage wegas rehtas, wraikwas nu isti* and *westweg wæs rihtweg, wóh is núpa* (*SD* 243). Ælfwine's verses also reappear, together with another Anglo-Saxon poem that describes the longing for "Elf-friends' island in the Outer-world" (*SD* 243f.). Eventually, the recurrent line that invokes the Straight Road is voiced in the Númenórean language: *adūn izindi batān tāidō ayadda | īdō kātha batīna lōkhī* – Once a straight road went into the West, now all roads are bent (*SD* 247; cf. *LR* 47).

But the lost road is not traced through newly found or 'invented' fragments in older languages alone; historical works of poetry, too, are drawn into the process of rediscovery. Parts of Lowdham's dream-verse about "Elf-friends' island" are easily identified as a variation of the Old English *Seafarer*, "that strange old poem of longing" (*SD* 243; cf. *LR* 84f.). Lowdham also quotes the lines *Éala Éarendel engla beorhtost | ofer middangeard monnum sended* from Cynewulf's *Crist* and speculates that "*Éarendel* [...] is not *only* Anglo-Saxon, but also something else much older" (*SD* 236). Later, in a chapter of which only a draft exists, the lines are repeated during Tréowine's vision of the Immortal Lands, upon sight of "a bright star" in the West.³⁹

As in *The Homecoming of Beorhtnoth*, fragments of older texts are embedded, complemented and re-interpreted. Transferred into the context of time-travel that aims at the rediscovery of the Straight Road these quotations yield a new meaning and point to a lingering awareness of Faërie beyond the western sea.⁴⁰ The same technique is applied to entire medieval texts and traditions as well. If it had been completed, *The Lost Road* would have included references to the *Navigatio Sancti Brendani* and the *Immram Maelduin* as well as a version of the *King Sheave* legend (*LR* 80, 83-91). In *The Notion Club Papers*, Frankley presents a poem titled *The Death of St. Brendan* that came to him in his sleep and which describes the Straight Road as an "unseen bridge" (*SD* 261-64). Subsequently, Lowdham and Jeremy relate their visionary experiences as Ælfwine and Tréowine in early medieval England: Ælfwine recites the already familiar verses that draw on *The Seafarer*, followed by the tale of *King Sheave* (*SD* 269-76).⁴¹

The legends quoted either relate voyages towards the 'Blessed Isles' of the West (*Brendan* and *Maelduin*) or speak of a stranger arriving from "the Unknown beyond the Great Sea" (*Sheave*; *LR* 95). Incorporated into *The Notion Club Papers*, they lend historical depth to the visionary journeys and extend the textual genealogy to include medieval traditions, just as the destruction of Númenor is identified as the true event behind the Atlantis legend. At the same time, these older texts are re-voiced and re-written by the protagonists of Tolkien's work, inspired not so much by philological erudition as by the Númenórean mystery that penetrates dreams and imagination. Textual archaeology thus transforms into poetic production. *The Notion Club Papers* thereby illustrates what, in *On Fairy-stories*, Tolkien wrote about literature (in contrast with all other arts): "Literature works from mind to mind and is

---

39 *SD* 278: "Tréowine sees the round world [?curve] below, and straight ahead a shining land, before the wind seizes them and drives them away. In the gathering dark [*or* dusk] he sees a bright star, shining in a rent in the cloud in the West. *Éalá Éarendel engla beorhtast*. Then he remembers no more." – See also Flieger, *Time* 144-49, on the inclusion of older texts.
40 Early notes from 1918 (assembled under the heading "Early Runic Documents") show that Tolkien collected quotations from medieval sources that can be re-interpreted along these lines (cf. *Parma Eldalamberon* XV, 96).
41 Maelduin, too, is mentioned in this context, alongside Brendan (*SD* 270). On the incorporation of *Navigatio* and *Immram*, see Flieger, *Music* 130-34.

thus more progenitive" (*OFS* 159). As a consequence, neither the dreams nor the poetry and legends that enter *The Notion Club Papers* can be traced back to a single author. Beyond the collective process of adaptation and variation, the original source remains unknown.

However, one major thread in *The Lost Road* and *The Notion Club Papers* suggests a linear history that might lead back to an ultimate origin. The time-travellers' philological and visionary inclinations extend back through the generations,[42] and a pair of travellers bearing names that translate as 'Elf-friend' and 'Bliss-friend'/'True-friend' respectively appear at each temporal stage in the journey to Númenor.[43] The dreams and visions of Arry *Alwin* Lowdham and Wilfrid *Trewyn* Jeremy open onto the experiences of Ælfwine and Tréowine in medieval England and merge with those of Elendil/Nimruzīr and Voronwë/Abrazān of Númenor. Verlyn Flieger has described this process as a "regression through serial identities and memories" ("Atlantis-Story" 58), based on "genetic recollections" (cf. *Time* 107, 113, 116-18). Tolkien's notes for *The Notion Club Papers* outline such a concept of ancestral memory (*SD* 278): "The theory is that the sight and memory goes on with *descendants* of Elendil and Voronwë (= Tréowine) but *not* reincarnation" (*SD* 279).

---

42 While Alboin's father Oswin Errol denies that one could ever "go back" in time (*LR* 44), his first name tells a different story: it translates as 'friend of the gods', corresponding exactly with the name of Elendil's father *Valandil* (cf. *LR* 53). Arundel Lowdham's father Edwin seems to have embarked on a very similar quest and eventually disappeared when he took his ship, *The Eárendel*, into a storm (*SD* 234). The name Arundel in turn is a worn-off version of Eärendil, Tolkien's most prominent mariner who managed to find a way to the Immortal Realm under extremely adverse circumstances. – In an earlier draft, the name of Lowdham's father was *Oswin Ellendel* (*SD* 284), plainly recalling not only Oswin Errol from *The Lost Road* but also the ultimate Elf-friend and Númenórean ancestor Elendil.
43 The name translating as 'Elf-friend' is the distinguishing mark for mortals who maintain an allegiance with the Eldar, as the Númenórean Elendil did, and who may be welcomed not only into their company but also to their protected realms in Middle-earth or even to Elvenhome in the West. Variations of the Elf-friend identity occur in the names Elendil/Nimruzīr/Ælfwine/Alboin/Alwin, paired with 'Bliss-friend/Friend of the Gods' (Herendil/Valandil/Eádwine/Oswine/Audoin) or 'True-friend' (Voronwë/Abrazān/Tréowine/Trewyn). The names are given in Anglo-Saxon, Lombardic, Adûnaic and Quenya, the oldest language, originating in the Immortal Realm.

At the same time, the paradigm of linear descent does not stand alone.[44] When ancestral memories erupt, they are more than "flashbacks":

> they might as well be called "flashforwards" or, better still, coincidents in the most literal sense. For they are neither backward nor forward but concurrent, both apparent directions simply choices in the static field of time over which the attending consciousness can move. (Flieger, *Time* 152)

Not only does transpersonal memory manifest unpredictably: the notion of a filial descent is also paralleled and underpinned by the far more prominent genealogy of (fragmentary) texts, reaching back to Elendil's book as the source of the Númenórean tale.[45] The recurring names that form a linguistic connection between the protagonists therefore stand out as the link between biological ancestry and textual genealogy. But if these names represent a linear succession, they also represent atemporal analogy and incalculable leaps across the linear continuum. More precisely, they represent the *collapse of linear succession* during moments of acute, simultaneous presence.

This collapse becomes visible at intervals, for instance when visionary experience dissolves historical linguistic difference: "He [Alboin] could not say whether he had conversed with Elendil in Eressëan or English" (*LR* 50). Similarly, Arry's father Edwin Lowdham records visionary insights in "Old English of a strongly Mercian (West-Midland) colour, ninth century" (*SD* 257), using Númenórean letters (cf. *SD* 255-59). Edwin's hybrid manuscript, reproduced in facsimile at the end of the Papers (*SD* 318-27), epitomizes the bewildering coincidence of the historically discrepant. But if these breakdowns in the historical continuum reflect the non-linear structure of dreams and time-travel, so does the process that turns historical texts like *The Seafarer* into 'inventions' of the Club's present – with allusions to discoveries in the future.

---

44 Alboin Errol's reasoning moves beyond linear (genetic) inheritance in *The Lost Road* as well when he argues that inherited (physical) traits may "leap" across many generations and describes the result of any historical process as a blend of "race", "culture" and "language" (*LR* 40: "Anyway, I like to go back – and not with race only, or culture only, or language; but with all three. I wish I could go back with the three that are mixed in us"). Although language plays a crucial role, it is nowhere stated whether the Germanic languages, so vividly present in both works, evolved from Númenórean Adûnaic. Equally, the text of *The Notion Club Papers* never explicitly identifies Lowdham and Jeremy as descendants of Elendil and Voronwë.

45 In his notes, Tolkien wrote that Elendil's "descendants get glimpses of it" (*SD* 279). Cf. Flieger, "Atlantis-Story" 57: "The journey into the past brings the protagonists closer with each successively older identity until they hold in their hands the book or books in which the earliest stories were brought forward."

These observations lead to an inevitable paradox. While the plots of *The Lost Road* and *The Notion Club Papers* are driven by the "desire to go back", and while linear historical threads can be isolated, time-travel itself moves beyond linear succession. Since authorship is an inherently historical concept that distinguishes source from product and origin from result, the concept itself must become obsolete where linear temporal progression no longer exists. This conclusion is indeed implied in the *Foreword* of *The Notion Club Papers*.

The *Foreword* not only introduces the complicated history of the Papers but also stages the disappearance of their author. While the Club's meetings supposedly took place in 1980-1990 and the Papers refer to events of the nineteen-seventies and eighties, the (invented) editor, Howard Green, cites evidence that places the Papers in the nineteen-forties (*SD* 155-57). Their unknown author, who seems to display a disturbing amount of "prevision" (*SD* 158), is thus temporally displaced between 1940 and 1990. Since Editor Green cannot assign a proper place in time to him or his text, he finally concludes:

> I am now convinced that the Papers are a work of fiction; and it may well be that the predictions (notably of the Storm), though genuine and not coincidences, were unconscious: giving one more glimpse of the strange processes of so-called literary "invention", with which the Papers are largely concerned (*SD* 158).

That "invention" more than deserves quotation marks is borne out by the Papers themselves, and the text in turn seeks to distinguish it from "mere fiction": invention "has more roots" (*SD* 227). Yet the author whom Howard Green suspects behind this devious literary construct remains an entirely unknown and unknowable entity,[46] and the 'roots' unearthed in the Notion Club's imagination ultimately belong to Other Time.

The archetypical moment of 'invention' – as well as recognition and reinterpretation – arrives, it would seem, with Tréowine's exclamation *Éalá Éarendel...* as he travels the Straight Road in a "dreamlike death" and sees "a shining land" before him (*SD* 277f.). But here not only the origin of poetic expression is uncertain, the dreamer's identity is equally unclear: "'Whether what follows is

---

46 Cf. *SD* 156: "The author appears in one or two passages, and in the occasional notes, to identify himself with the character called in the dialogues Nicholas Guildford. But Mr. J. R. Titmass, the well-known historian of twentieth-century Oxford, who has given all possible assistance to the present editor, has shown that this is certainly a fictitious name and derived from a mediaeval dialogue at one time read in the Schools of Oxford."

my direct dream,' said Jeremy, 'or the dreams of Tréowine and Ælfwine in the deeps of the sea I cannot say'" (*SD* 278). The nesting of dreams within dreams parallels the nesting of texts within texts in a potentially infinite succession which is – paradoxically – revealed in the mode of co-incidence. Consequently, the earliest 'source' hovers perpetually between presence and absence.[47]

As the difference between diachronic and synchronic structures dissolves, the boundary between actual history and imagination, too, may become questionable. When Lowdham describes his discovery of the Númenórean Lament as "a record, or a legend, of an Atlantis catastrophe", Jeremy asks: "Why or? [...] I mean, it might be a record and a legend" (*SD* 249). Indeed, dreams prove to be supreme vehicles for journeys beyond the dichotomy of fact and fantasy, history and myth: they open up a space that transcends the divisions of ordinary reality.[48]

IV. Enchantment: The space and time of imagination

Literature, Tolkien writes in *On Fairy-stories*, is richer and "more progenitive" than all other arts because it engages the reader's imagination: "If it speaks of *bread* or *wine* or *stone* or *tree*, it appeals to the whole of these things, to their ideas; yet each hearer will give to them a peculiar personal embodiment in his imagination" (*OFS* 159). Such an engagement can be heightened within dreams and becomes "enchantment" as an "elvish craft" (*OFS* 143), so that the power of stories can amount to a "spell".[49] In *The Notion Club Papers*, the dreamers not only observe the actual experiences or memories of other minds but may enter their imagination, their 'compositions' and dreams as well. The difference, however, may not be recognizable for the dreamer. It follows that the theory of dreaming also involves the more fundamental question of perception which

---

47 "The significant point in this welter of texts is the clear presence of an absence" (Flieger, *Music* 110). While Flieger refers to the Sindarin *Narn* as the (absent) original version of the Túrin Turambar story, the same is true of Elendil's book in *The Notion Club Papers*. See also Flieger's observation that the overtly linear sequence of books "seems to follow a kind of loop" from Ælfwine to Elendil and back to Ælfwine (*Music* 113f.).
48 This, too, is a structural trait that Tolkien's treatment of dreams shares with pre-modern approaches: "Because it leaves the dreamer in a position between clearly defined entities, the dream becomes an important way of exploring 'betweenness.' Poised between opposed categories of transcendent and immanent, divine and demonic, *the dream becomes an instrument for examining the gray areas that bridge the terms of polar oppositions*" (Kruger 65; emphasis added).
49 "Small wonder that *spell* means both a story told, and a formula of power over living men" (*OFS* 128).

shapes different spheres of imagination and invention. The previous section has shown that, in *The Notion Club Papers* (and, to a lesser extent, *The Lost Road*), the concepts of dreams and literature are intimately entwined. Authorship, then, must be defined by specific modes of perception as well.

That dreams give rise to epistemological questions is to be expected in the context of pre-modern concepts that distinguish meaningless dreams from true dream-visions inspired by external sources. Steven Kruger writes about the medieval dream-vision:

> In its self-reflexive movements, dream vision raises [...] questions about how literature grasps and represents real and true entities existing outside a strictly poetic realm. The dream poem's self-reflexivity, in other words, often leads into questions of epistemology. (137)

As a consequence, the literary work often "examines, as though in a mirror, its own imaginative [...] status" (Kruger 136). In Tolkien's texts, creative imagination may extend into and emerge out of dreams, while at the same time dreams can provide an entry into the (poetic) imagination of other individuals or cultures. The non-linear nature of dreams is reflected by a poetic process that transcends linear succession by re-inventing and re-locating literary traditions. As a result, the notion that the textual genealogy can be traced back to an identifiable author, too, is undermined.

The underlying epistemology – that is, the system of perception, imagination and knowledge – is necessarily complex. It involves not only a re-conceptualization of time but also historically distinct modes of perception. One of the possibilities discussed in *The Notion Club Papers* is that moving back in time could allow the traveller to experience a 'mythical reality': a precondition to grasping the reality of the Straight Road, which is at the heart of visionary travel in this most experimental of Tolkien's works. In the following, I will therefore analyze the connections between historically different modes of perception and poetic expression in *The Notion Club Papers*. Secondly, I will examine how an entry into a new imaginative – or 'enchanted' – space is realized in a text that provides no explicit theory of dreaming or (literary) imagination, *The Lord of the Rings*. Both aspects have bearings on the constitution of authorship within the texts (see also section V) and imply an understanding of authorship that shapes Tolkien's project of composing a 'mythology' (see section VI).

Verlyn Flieger has demonstrated that dream-travelling in *The Notion Club Papers* involves an understanding of time not as a process but as a field that one may survey depending on 'observer position' (*Time* 136f.). According to Ramer, the mind moves by transferring attention, so that it can range across a wider field of time. Another level of complexity is reached when the Club discusses whether dreaming could allow the time-traveller to enter a 'legendary' rather than an 'actual' past (*SD* 228f.). Ramer favours this idea but adds that it would depend "on what you yourself are like, and on what you are looking for" (*SD* 229). Just as the framing device determines the "story inside", the observer's mode of perception is inseparable from the vistas he may explore in Other Time.

More than individual differences are at issue here: the discussion ultimately concerns the discrepant epistemologies that constitute 'myth' and 'history'. Jeremy argues that, if one travelled back far enough, "one would find not myth dissolving into history, but rather the reverse: real history becoming more mythical – more shapely, simple, discernibly significant, even seen at close quarters. More poetical, and less prosaic" (*SD* 227). When he elaborates on this statement, he distinguishes "history in the sense of a story made up out of the intelligible surviving evidence (which is not necessarily truer to the facts than legend)" from "'the true story', the real Past": "much would be vividly real and at the same time ... er ... portentous; but there might be, would be, uncompleted passages, weak joints, gaps. You'd have to consolidate. You might need help" (*SD* 230). The necessity to "consolidate" the Past explains why Ramer feels that this sort of time-travel is "best done by one or two people in concert" (*SD* 230) and suggests a combination of observation and invention (as reconstruction), so that the 'recorders' of events become co-authors as well.

More complicated is the idea that one might visit a mythical reality and experience it as "more poetical" than history, "vividly real and at the same time portentous". First and foremost, Jeremy's distinctions imply that epistemologies are themselves subject to historical change. History, as he defines it, is a specific pattern of organizing reality by shaping it into a (causal and linear) narrative. The 'poetical' counterpart to this 'prosaic' narrative is myth. That Jeremy describes the mythical reality as "more discernibly significant" is best elucidated by drawing on Owen Barfield's theory of myth.[50]

Barfield situates myth in the context of a pre-historical perception defined by a comprehensive unity. Of the "relations between separate external objects, and between objects and feelings or ideas" he writes that the "language of primitive man reports them as direct perceptual experience. The speaker has observed a unity, and is not therefore himself conscious of a relation" (86). Since the primary meanings of words are immediately present, there can be no distinction between signifier and signified, just as words imply no distinction between literal and figurative sense either. Myth, in Barfield's theory, is the repository of this specific mode of thought and perception.[51] It preserves expressions of an immediate connection between 'natural' and 'supernatural' realms, between the presence of concrete appearances and their presence in the imagination.[52] In the context of this inquiry, it is particularly illuminating when Barfield writes about the "forgotten relationships" that "imagination can see them again" (87). Poetry, according to Barfield, may conceptually restore and recapture the primal perceptual unity (87, 207), which he also describes as poetry of an "instinctive kind" (111). Applying this concept to *The Notion Club Papers*, Jeremy's speculation that a mythical reality would appear "more poetical" can now be rephrased: when concrete appearance is joined to "feelings or ideas" in a single shape, it can be perceived as "discernibly significant" or "portentous" and at the same time "vividly real".

If the "mythical mode of imagination" (*BMC* 15) could be fully entered in visionary dreams, it might thus expose and inspire the dreamer to primary or 'instinctive' poetry. Under the conditions of history, however, the lost perceptual

---

50 See Flieger's summary of Barfield's theory and her analysis of Barfield's influence on Tolkien (*Light* 35-41, 67-72).
51 Even though by now their "living content has departed out of them" (Barfield 91). Cf. Barfield 92: "Mythology is the ghost of concrete meaning. Connections between discrete phenomena, connections which are now apprehended as metaphor, were once perceived as immediate realities."
52 Cf. Flieger, *Light* 37f.: "The word myth in this context must be taken to mean that which describes humankind's perception of its relationship to the natural and supernatural worlds. Words are expressed myth, the embodiments of mythic concepts and a mythic worldview. Language in its beginning made no distinction between the literal and the metaphoric meaning of the world, as it does today. [...] All diction was literal, giving direct voice to the perception of phenomena and humanity's intuitive mythic participation in them."

unity is ultimately unattainable. Primary meanings, as Barfield understands them, cannot be retrieved but must be remade, involving the activity of an author: "we shall find that, in the later kind of poetry, for which the individual poet is increasingly responsible [...] it is perfectly true to call the poet the creator, or re-creator of meaning itself" (Barfield 111f.). But *re-creator*, rather than independent creator, involves an understanding of authorship that relies on 'invention' in the sense of reconstruction and restores meanings that stem from collective imagination. In this sense, Torhthelm becomes the re-creator of a traditional and meaningful poetic expression of "heroic will" in *The Homecoming of Beorhtnoth*. 'Dream' is the vehicle that enables his act of re-creation, just as it enables Lowdham and Jeremy to re-invent Anglo-Saxon poetry – and to rediscover the presence and meaning of the Straight Road.

Instead of simulating an actual recovery of mythical imagination, Tolkien orchestrates a dialogue between the different modes of perception in *The Notion Club Papers*. The protagonists consider and experience myth from a historical "point of vision" and approach it most closely when they re-experience the original disruption: the "dividing line" or threshold between 'myth' and 'history' is "the Atlantis catastrophe", the downfall of Númenor (*SD* 249).

The importance of dream-vision precisely reflects this configuration of diverging epistemologies. Dream-vision represents "initiation *to*, not through, a threshold" (Brown 48; emphasis added); therefore "what seemed to be marginal, peripheral, a state of transition, both into and out of the dream, is on reflection central, essential" (Brown 48). While it remains impossible for modern historical subjects as the Notion Club members to enter fully into 'myth', the exploration of thresholds and divisions, and the successive crossing of boundaries in dreams within dreams, allows for a glimpse of the Straight Road into the mythical otherworld.

A similar constellation can be found in *The Lord of the Rings*, within a setting that is equally 'historical', if not as far removed from Númenor's fall as the world of the Notion Club. The most apparent connection between *The Lord of the Rings* and Tolkien's time-travel stories may be found in Faramir's dream of the Great Wave that drowns Númenor (*LotR* 941), incidentally the last dream reported in *The Lord of the Rings*.⁵³ Yet there is an early episode in *The Fellowship of the Ring* that combines Númenor, visionary experience and time-travel in a startling way. As Tom Bombadil hands ancient swords from the barrow to Frodo, Sam, Pippin and Merry, he talks about the "Men of Westernesse":

> The hobbits did not understand his words, but as he spoke *they had a vision as it were of a great expanse of years behind them, like a vast shadowy plain* over which there strode shapes of Men, tall and grim with bright swords, and last came one with a star on his brow. Then the vision faded [...].
> (*LotR* 142f.; emphasis added)

Time becomes visible as a field across which the Númenórean survivors enter Middle-earth. The unfolding tableau is strikingly reminiscent of Alboin Errol's desire "to walk in Time, perhaps, as men walk on long roads; or to survey it, as men may see the world from a mountain" (*LR* 45). Tom's words widen the hobbits' perceptions and conjure a past event that may have occurred in the very space they occupy in the present. Only shortly before, at the hobbits' escape from the barrow, Merry gave voice to a transpersonal memory, physically reliving history as he sensed the mortal anguish of a dead warrior.⁵⁴

This visionary episode must draw attention to the role Tom Bombadil plays for the emergence of dreams in *The Lord of the Rings*. Within the text's topography and structure, Bombadil's land occupies a significant site as a space of *transition*: it extends between the Shire and the outside world, the known and the (largely) unknown, and it confronts the four hobbit travellers with their first supernatural challenges, Old Man Willow and the Barrow-wight. That the hobbits' encounter with Bombadil involves a new mode of experience as well is signalled when Frodo and Sam stand "as if enchanted" at the sound of Tom's singing (*LotR* 117). Upon sight of Goldberry in Bombadil's house, Frodo feels an enchantment similar to that of "elven-voices", "but the spell that was

---

53 The Númenórean legacy forms an important theme throughout the text: It manifests in the role the *palantíri* play during the final stages of war, underpins the political significance of Gondor, shapes Faramir's character to a large extent and determines Aragorn's claim to the throne and the meaning of his re-established kingship, emblematized by the flowering of the new White Tree. In the realms of mortals, the fall of Númenor and the arrival of Elendil and Isildur are highly memorable founding events, and – due to their role in the war against Sauron – the story of Elendil and Isildur is interwoven with the One Ring's history as well.

54 *LotR* 140: "'Of course, I remember!' he said. 'The men of Carn Dûm came on us at night, and we were worsted. Ah! the spear in my heart!' He clutched at his breast. 'No! No!' he said, opening his eyes. 'What am I saying? I have been dreaming. [...]'" See Flieger, *Time* 177-79; *Music* 116.

now laid upon him was different [...]; marvellous and yet not strange" (*LotR* 121). The rhymes he then addresses to Goldberry seem like an extension of her earlier song, and Frodo is afterwards "overcome with surprise to hear himself saying such things" (*LotR* 122). Poetic speech arises as the spontaneous response to a sight that blends the 'marvellous' with the familiar and at the same time expresses a new understanding of poetry previously heard: "Now the joy that was hidden in the songs we heard is made plain to me", Frodo says (*LotR* 121).

But in Tom's house dreams of a visionary – or at least clairvoyant – nature abound as well, as Frodo's two dreams and the dreams of Pippin and Merry demonstrate. The blending of nocturnal dream with waking vision and re-embodied memory that pervades the episode is complemented by verbal enchantment. The stories Tom shares with the hobbits bring the past – perhaps visibly – alive for them,[55] so that his visitors finally sit "enchanted" before him, "under the spell of his words" (*LotR* 128). Tom's tales range beyond "waking thought", suggesting "that somehow, in this dreaming wakefulness that the hobbits are in, Tom has given them access to the whole field of time" (Flieger, *Time* 202).

Clearly, a significant boundary has been crossed. 'Enchantment', 'vision', 'dream' and 'spell' are key-words that cluster in this episode, embodied by Tom Bombadil who is able to command both the Willowman and the Barrow-wight. His spells are clothed in a poetic diction that seems to call all living things by their inborn names. In this context, his "nonsense" songs (*LotR* 116) that often consist of onomatopoeic syllables in infinite variations could well represent a kind of primary or 'instinctive' poetry as Owen Barfield's conceptualized it (103, 111).[56] Tom's power of imposing a spell or enchantment furthermore seems to emanate from his identity as "Eldest": "Tom was here before the river and the trees; Tom remembers the first raindrop and the first acorn. [...] When the Elves passed westward, Tom was here already, before the seas were bent" (*LotR*

---

55 "They lost the thread of his tale and shifted uneasily [...]. When they caught his words again they found that he had now wandered into strange regions beyond their memory and beyond their waking thought, into times when the world was wider, and *the seas flowed straight to the western Shore*; and still on and back Tom went singing out into ancient starlight, when only the Elf-sires were awake" (*LotR* 128; emphasis added).
56 In a letter, Tolkien indeed described Bombadil as the incarnation of "Poetry as opposed to Cattle-breeding and Agriculture and practicality" (*L* 179). See also *L* 192, where Tolkien speaks of Tom as an "exemplar [...] of pure (real) natural science: the spirit that desires knowledge of other things, their history and nature, *because they are 'other'* and wholly independent of the enquiring mind".

129). It is no coincidence either that this episode contains the first allusion to the Straight Road in *The Lord of the Rings*. Tom's awareness encompasses the time before the division that followed Númenor's fall. With dreams, visions and the specific kind of poetry that surrounds him, he initiates the hobbits to the threshold of Other Time.[57]

On the threshold towards the second stage of the Quest, in Rivendell, the blend of waking and dreaming vision coincides once again with an overlap of imaginative spaces and different modes of perception. In the Hall of Fire, Elvish poetry and music give rise to vision that blends into dream which again blends back into poetry:

> At first the beauty of the melodies and of the interwoven words in elven-tongues, even though he [Frodo] understood them little, held him in a *spell* [...]. Almost it seemed that the words took shape, and *visions* of far lands and bright things that he had never yet *imagined* opened out before him; and the firelit hall became like a golden mist above seas of foam that sighed upon the margins of the world. Then the *enchantment* became more and more *dreamlike*, until he felt that an endless river of swelling gold and silver was flowing over him, too multitudinous for its pattern to be comprehended; it became part of the throbbing air about him, and it drenched and drowned him. Swiftly he sank under its shining weight into a deep realm of sleep. *There he wandered long in a dream of music that turned into running water, and then suddenly into a voice.* (*LotR* 227; emphasis added)

Bilbo's song, which eventually draws Frodo back to waking attention, represents a more familiar kind of poetry, translating the legend of Eärendil into a new language and form. Elvish music and poetry, on the other hand, open up a new space of imagination that Frodo enters (a kind of Faërian drama), even if the images and impressions remain unreadable to him. Rather, the fluid interweaving of vision, enchantment and dream illustrates that Frodo is slipping back and forth across the boundaries between different kinds of perception.

This important difference is implied not only by Frodo's experience in Rivendell. While Elvish dreaming is rarely described in *The Lord of the Rings*, it is clearly distinguished by the ability to balance two different modes of perception

---

57 See also Flieger on the function of Frodo's dream-vision of Eressëa: "it begins the process of establishing for Frodo and thus for the reader a wider field of attention than the waking mind is alert to and so prepares the way for the dual time-scheme introduced through the different perceptions of Elves and Men that we are to meet in the episodes in Lórien" (*Time* 189).

within one awareness: "Legolas [...] could sleep, if sleep it could be called by Men, resting his mind in the strange paths of elvish dreams, even as he walked open-eyed in the light of this world" (*LotR* 418f., cf. 432). Characteristically, the dreams' contents are not revealed: what matters is the otherness of Elvish consciousness, cast into sharp relief by the external perspective adopted here.

While a number of significant dreams are related with a fair amount of detail in *The Lord of the Rings*, they contribute meaning to the unfolding story in a distinctly similar manner. Meaning arises not from any interpretation of the dreams and visions, however portentous or strange they may seem. Only in one case – Boromir's and Faramir's riddle-dream – do dreaming and the decoding of the dream's message motivate a course of action, so that it enters into the causal, linear progress of events. When visionary dreams foreshadow events elsewhere, however, they enrich textual meaning not by immediately adding to rational insight but rather by weaving cross-threads into the narrative tapestry of time. The images glimpsed in vivid, sometimes clairvoyant dreams certainly reveal something about the dreamer in relation to his (natural and supernatural) environment, for the sites of dreams appear to be at least as important as the dreamer's identity. But, above all, dreams highlight different states of awareness and imagination and portray the possibilities of widening vision. What remains to be examined, then, is to what an extent these possibilities are connected to the implicit understanding of authorship in *The Lord of the Rings*.

V. 'For eyes to see that can': Transformed vision and authorship

Frodo, who becomes the principal author of the source text for *The Lord of the Rings*, is also the most prominent dreamer of the tale. One of his dreams even springs directly from his duties as author: "He thought a fire was heating his toes, and out of the shadows on the other side of the hearth he heard Bilbo's voice speaking. *I don't think much of your diary,* he said. *Snowstorms on January the twelfth: there was no need to come back to report that!*" (*LotR* 282). While this is clearly a 'marginal' dream, expressing a latent concern about authorial responsibilities, Frodo's dreams are often clairvoyant or visionary. Yet it must be noted at once that the presence of actual nocturnal dreams dwindles in the course of the story. Of Frodo's nine dreams, five are described in detail, and all five occur in *The Fellowship of the Ring*. The un-framing of Frodo's dream-vision at the very end of the story suggests that a progress from dreams to other kinds of expanded perception may explain the gradual disappearance of the (framed) type of dream that occurs in sleep.

Changed vision is eventually articulated in poetic form. At the beginning of his journey, Frodo unthinkingly repeats Bilbo's verses about the unending road, adding only a minor variation. At the very end, on the way to the Grey Havens, Frodo modifies another hobbit walking-song in a highly significant manner: *A day will come at last when I | Shall take the hidden paths that run | West of the Moon, East of the Sun* (*LotR* 1005). As Tom Shippey notes, Frodo's "new road" that appears in this final variation of the traditional song is "the 'Lost Straight Road' of Tolkien's own mythology, the road to Elvenhome" (*Author* 191). At this point, poetic expression indicates a crucial shift in perception and a trajectory out of time, into Faërie. The progress from the initial vision of Eressëa to Frodo's song and Sam's dream-narrative at the end of the book furthermore suggests that authorship is inherently connected to a different mode of perception that transcends the mortal continuum of time and space.

Before I pursue this line of argument further, a brief introduction to dreams and the associated terminology in *The Lord of the Rings* is necessary. The vocabulary is certainly more diffuse than it is in *The Notion Club Papers*, and different types of dreams are nowhere classified. 'Dreaming' in the figurative sense can refer to states of waking abstraction (*LotR* 123, 613f., 631, 774) and to experiences that seem unreal or questionable to the waking mind (*LotR* 140, 233, 310, 373f., 582, 680, 859), but it may also describe the effect of spells and enchantments caused by supernatural powers (*LotR* 80, 81, 114f., 170, 505, 840). 'Dream' in *The Lord of the Rings* thus refers to a state of altered consciousness which may or may not originate somewhere beyond the dreamer's own mind: different meanings and implications are determined by the specific context. In the literal sense, the term encompasses every kind of nocturnal dreaming, regardless of its ordinary or revelatory nature. The only exception is Frodo's dream of Eressëa, which is specifically characterised as a "vision" (*LotR* 132).[58] Yet 'vision', in the general usage of the text, refers to (real and imagined) sights and visual impressions, so that context and content alone can make it clear whether a changed or heightened awareness is involved. Clearly, the terminology for revelatory dreams, dream-states and visionary experiences does not allow for absolute distinctions between different forms of experience. Compared to the differentiations in *The Notion Club Papers*, the fluidity of diction must be considered a conscious literary strategy, designed to reflect a specific operation of dreams.

Events in Rivendell disclose unequivocally that dreams in *The Lord of the Rings* can be prophetic or visionary. Frodo learns that his dream of Gandalf's escape from Orthanc reflected an actual event in the recent past (*LotR* 125, 254). The riddle-dreams that both Faramir and Boromir experience (*LotR* 239f., 655) closely approach the Macrobian *oraculum*, in which a superior authority offers advice, although the cryptic wording typically belongs to 'enigmatic dreams' (*somnium*). This dream clearly contains a message or a summons and although its source is never identified it is almost certainly supernatural.[59]

Frodo's vivid dreams during the early stages of the Ring-quest carry no messages, however. Instead they illustrate with increasing clarity that the dreaming consciousness may move freely across time and space. In the Shire, "strange visions of mountains that he had never seen" enter Frodo's dreams (*LotR* 42); in Crickhollow, he hears and smells the sea and climbs towards a tower on a ridge (*LotR* 106). His dream thus transports him to the Tower Hills, a real place in the topography of Middle-earth. In his first dream-vision at Bombadil's house, Frodo feels that he is lifted above the valley of Orthanc, whereas the second takes him within sight of Eressëa.

That this dream-series represents an initiation to the threshold of Other Time and Space is marked very clearly. Frodo's second dream-vision opens with: "either

---

58 In one other instance, 'vision' occurs in the context of Frodo's dreams: "Strangely enough, Frodo felt refreshed. He had been dreaming. The dark shadow had passed, and a fair vision had visited him in this land of disease" (*LotR* 620). But the context does not establish unequivocally whether this implies a visionary element as well.
59 Only within First Age mythology, in the *Silmarillion* texts, are dreams sometimes identified as divine messages (*S* 113, 135, 190).

in his dreams or out of them, he could not tell which" (*LotR* 132). Dreams not only become permeable for perceptions beyond the compass of waking awareness, dreaming also proves to be an intermediate stage in a process that eventually transcends the frame of sleep. When Frodo reaches another safe place of rest in Rivendell, the blending of dream, vision, enchantment and poetry once more illustrates this state of transition. After the sojourn in Rivendell, Frodo's dreams become rare and are no longer reported in detail,[60] but other forms of expanded perception and visionary experience occur more frequently.

It seems reasonable, then, to assume that the basic concept developed in *The Notion Club Papers* shapes the significance and the workings of dreams in *The Lord of the Rings* as well. The "transference of observation" or movement of the mind that defines altered vision is not limited to dreams; nocturnal dreaming merely facilitates the release from ordinary perceptual constraints. The primary difference between the two texts is that diverging realms of time and perception co-exist in the *waking reality* of Middle-earth, so that the boundaries between different states of awareness may be permeable.

Frodo's awareness is influenced by various sources in the course of the Ringquest. The presence and pursuit of the Ringwraiths and the injury Frodo suffers at Weathertop increasingly affect his waking and dreaming perceptions.[61] In Mordor, Frodo's "dreams of fire" (*LotR* 901) reflect the Ring's growing power which besets Frodo's mind as a "great wheel of fire" even in waking (*LotR* 898). But beside Tom Bombadil's land, other potent sites in Middle-earth introduce Frodo to a greater range of perception as well. On Amon Hen, the Hill of Sight, his vision roams freely over great distances. While the Ring turns the

---

60 Later in the Quest, Frodo wakes twice from refreshing, peaceful dreams that he cannot afterwards recall (*LotR* 620, 641). In the Tower of Cirith Ungol, Frodo says that he "fell into darkness and foul dreams" after Shelob's sting, but the context suggests that actual events took on the appearance of nightmares (*LotR* 889f.).
61 Frodo's dream at Crickhollow begins with a sense of pursuit and the "snuffling" that recalls previous encounters with the Black Riders (*LotR* 106). Similarly, the sound of "hoofs galloping from the East" ends his dream of Orthanc (125), and the same alarming noise enters Frodo's dreams again in Bree, on the night of the Ringwraiths' attack (173). While these dream-impressions may be due to memories and lingering fears, Frodo's dreams of his pursuers take on a visionary aspect after he has been injured at Weathertop. Dreaming and waking perception begin to merge for Frodo (197), and the more his injury affects him, the more his surroundings fade "to shadows of ghostly grey" (207) – exactly as they do in the previous dream of his garden. His awareness is beset by his pursuers: "Frodo lay half in a dream, imagining that endless dark wings were sweeping by above him, and that on the wings rode pursuers that sought him in all the hollows of the hills" (198f.). At this point, dream blends into an 'imagination' that foreshadows the Nazgûl's return on winged mounts.

surrounding world to "mist" and "shadows", the Seat of Seeing discloses "many visions" of far-off events (*LotR* 391f.).[62] At Cerin Amroth, in the Elven realm of Lothlórien, intimations of the future and past become tangible, enfolded in a "timeless land".[63] Similarly, Galadriel's Mirror offers glimpses of distant events in the past, present or future (*LotR* 354f.),[64] but – perhaps more importantly – Frodo's heightened vision is explicitly addressed as well: "your sight is grown keener", Galadriel tells him, referring both to Frodo's awareness of her thoughts and his ability to see her own ring of power which remains invisible to others (*LotR* 357). Lórien's complex relation to time forms the backdrop for perceptions that transcend linearity and encompass a wider field of observation (cf. Flieger, *Time* 99-115). The specific character of this space – akin to dreams in more than one respect[65] – delineates a potential for expanded vision that not everyone in the Fellowship can access.

However, Frodo does not experience these glimpses across time alone, for Sam is invited to join him by the Mirror. Although Sam cannot see Galadriel's ring, his visions present the greater challenge as they concern his choices and their impact on the linear continuum of cause and effect (*LotR* 353f.). Not only is Sam forced to decide between continuing his journey with Frodo and returning to the Shire in an attempt to prevent future disasters, the vision also foreshadows his most critical choice on the pass of Cirith Ungol, at Frodo's apparent death, which decides the success or failure of the entire Quest. Frodo's visions in the Mirror, on the other hand, traverse a wider field of time, containing "many

---

[62] The episode closes with an acute awareness of Sauron which seems to be owed to the Ring's presence. However, the emphasis placed on the connection between the location and sight ("He was sitting upon the Seat of Seeing, on Amon Hen, the Hill of the Eye of the Men of Númenor"; *LotR* 391) strongly suggests that the site, rather than the Ring, is the primary source of Frodo's expanded vision: There is no other instance in which wearing the Ring alone produces such an effect. See also Christopher Tolkien's comments: *TI* 374, 380f.

[63] *LotR* 342: "Frodo felt that he was in a timeless land that did not fade or change or fall into forgetfulness. When he had gone and passed again into the outer world, still Frodo the wanderer from the Shire would walk there." Soon afterwards, in the circle of white trees, he hears "far off great seas upon beaches that had long ago been washed away, and sea-birds crying whose race had perished from the earth."

[64] These visions resemble the visual fragments haunting Audoin Errol's dreams: "a sort of phantom story with no explanations. Just pictures, but not a sound, not a word. Ships coming to land. Towers on the shore. Battles, with swords glinting but silent. And there is that ominous picture: the great temple on the mountain, smoking like a volcano. And that awful vision of the chasm in the seas, a whole land slipping sideways, mountains rolling over; dark ships fleeing into the dark" (*LR* 52).

[65] Treebeard calls Lothlórien the *Dreamflower* (*LotR* 456). Cf. Flieger, *Time* 191: "There are hints suggesting that the whole of the Lórien episode, as well as taking place outside ordinary time, also takes place somehow outside ordinary consciousness."

swift scenes [...] that Frodo in some way knew to be parts of a great history in which he had become involved" (*LotR* 354; cf. Flieger, *Time* 194f.). The Lórien episode draws these shared visions together with shared poetic invention. In Galadriel's realm, Frodo composes a song to express his grief over the loss of Gandalf, to which Sam adds a verse of tribute to Gandalf's fireworks (*LotR* 350f.). This scene, prefiguring Frodo's and Sam's co-operation on the larger tale of their travels, immediately precedes Galadriel's invitation to look into her Mirror and see "things that were, and things that are, things that yet may be" (*LotR* 352). In her discussion of this complex scene, Amy Amendt-Raduege concludes that it "marks Sam's initiation into the realm of dreams and visions" (51). It is true that Sam, Frodo's eventual co-author, is not a very notable dreamer in *The Lord of the Rings*. If, as I have suggested, a connection between dreams and authorship exists in this text, one may therefore wonder if this applies only to Frodo.[66]

Sam's position in the field of dreams and visions is indeed less obvious. In Tom Bombadil's house, when his three companions are visited by intense dreams, Sam is singled out: "As far as he could remember, Sam slept through the night in deep content, *if logs are contented*" (*LotR* 126; emphasis added). The wording is laced with subtle ambiguity, as it hints that Sam may have dreamed but was unable to recall anything afterwards. More importantly, the final clause not only questions Sam's apparent contentment, it also alludes to the hobbits' earlier encounter with Old Man Willow: a thoroughly malcontent 'log'. This allusion must provoke the question why Sam alone remained unaffected by the Willow-man's spell. In this episode, too, Sam is singled out. Not only is he immune to the drowsiness and 'dreaming' inflicted on his companions (*LotR* 114f.), he also understands without effort what the Willow sings: "I don't like this great big tree. I don't trust it. Hark at it singing about sleep now!" (*LotR* 115). The source of this

---

66 The most notable effect of Bilbo's travels in *The Hobbit* is a new gift of poetry that emerges on his homeward journey (*H* 252f.). Bilbo's dreams are of a clairvoyant nature that may be compared to Frodo's dream of the Tower Hills or Merry's and Pippin's dreams in Bombadil's house. They disclose events and developments beyond the dreamer's ordinary range of perception, such as the opening of a secret entrance in the Misty Mountains cave (*H* 58) or the dance of bears near Beorn's house (*H* 115). Within enchanted dreams, both Bilbo and Bombur participate in the wood-elves' feast (*H* 131-33). However, none of these dreams display the visionary or prophetic traits seen in Frodo's dreams of Gandalf and of Eressëa.

surprising ability to understand Old Man Willow is never disclosed, but it places Sam within range of Tom Bombadil's mode of perception and suggests that Sam simply did not require the dream-initiation available at this site of transition.

Sam's initial appearance in *The Lord of the Rings* offers the first clues that support this inference. At home in the Shire, his imagination already comprises the existence of walking "Tree-men" and the Elves' passage towards the Havens (*LotR* 43f.). Sam's perspective thus foreshadows two crucial discoveries that define the mortal world's intersections with Faërie: the realm of Ents and the Straight Road. While Sam's companions in the *Green Dragon* consider his beliefs and preoccupations either illusory or irrelevant, he insists that "there's more truth" in old, half-forgotten tales than the others guess and asks: "Who invented the stories anyway?" (*LotR* 43) – suggesting that they are not 'made up'. While Sam's avowed belief in tales of Elves (*LotR* 62) draws on Bilbo's authority, he clearly inhabits a realm of imagination that ordinary hobbits cannot (or refuse to) access. Expectably, his first encounter with Elves in the Woody End has a profound effect on Sam's perception: "I seem to see ahead," he tells Frodo, "in a kind of way. I know we are going to take a very long road, into darkness; but I know I can't turn back. [...] I have something to do before the end, and it lies ahead, not in the Shire" (*LotR* 85). At this very early point in the Quest, Sam's sense of his purpose has changed irrevocably, and his perception encompasses inklings of the future. The quoted scenes illustrate that, even prior to leaving the Shire, Sam is on the boundary of a wider field of imagination. His love of old tales and his pronounced desire to see Elves eventually enable him to enter a larger world, beyond the limited vision of ordinary hobbits. If Frodo's entry is marked by dreams, Sam's mode of access is defined by wish and desire.[67]

The pattern of analogy and difference that shapes Sam's and Frodo's progressively widened awareness can be traced in relation to literature as well. While Bilbo

---

[67] Sam's ability to engage in (apparently unrealistic) wishing becomes particularly compelling during the most critical stages of the Quest: At Cirith Ungol, his "one wish" to find Frodo again preludes the unforeseeable joyous turn (*LotR* 716). In Mordor, his wishes for "a bit of light" and water appear to be miraculously granted (cf. Shippey, *Road* 231), and the sight of a star in the West reveals a timeless, untouchable beauty to him (*LotR* 897-99, 901). When Sam exclaims on the Field of Cormallen "All my wishes have come true!" (*LotR* 933), the fulfilled tale he imagined in the face of certain death has indeed become reality.

designates Frodo as the future author of the book, Frodo is "seldom moved to make song or rhyme" (*LotR* 350). Sam, on the other hand, steps into Bilbo's shoes as an exponent of poetry.[68] Significantly, Sam's engagement with tales and poetry also extends in every temporal dimension. The song of Gil-galad that he recites near Weathertop (one of Bilbo's translations) reaches far into the past and touches upon the ending age of Númenor. His song in the Tower of Cirith Ungol transcends the limitations of the present and invokes a timeless light (*LotR* 888). But Sam also imagines future songs and untold tales at the very moment when he faces an apparently inevitable end (*LotR* 718, 929). His association with poetry and tales thus mirrors the widening vision that Frodo attains by other means, culminating in their well-known dialogue on the Stairs of Cirith Ungol (*LotR* 696f.). Sam's discovery of the "great tale" that Frodo and he have "fallen into" encompasses an immense field of time and leaps ahead to a future moment when their story will be "read out of a great big book" (*LotR* 697). In this scene, the self-referential discussion of the book within the Book (cf. Flieger, *Music* 72f.) is complemented by trajectories that transcend the book's frame and extend into a mythical reality. The wider range of time and imagination that Sam delineates here contains Beren's quest for the Silmaril and Eärendil's voyage: mythical events that *The Lord of the Rings* repeatedly alludes to and represents in poetic fragments but does not disclose in full.

At this point, it seems that Frodo and Sam have reached complementary states of 'altered consciousness' that now manifest in accord. In the suffocating night of Shelob's Lair, memory of the Phial (Galadriel's gift to Frodo) comes to Sam with the full and vivid presence of Faërian drama (*LotR* 703f.), so that soon after "a minute heart of dazzling light" kindles in Frodo's hand, "as though Eärendil had himself come down from the high sunset paths with the last Silmaril upon his brow" (*LotR* 704). In the presence of this transcending light, Frodo and Sam 'speak in tongues': twice, as they fight Shelob and as they escape from the Tower of Cirith Ungol, they invoke Eärendil and Elbereth the Star-kindler in languages they do not know (*LotR* 704, 712, 894). The source of these inspired exclamations remains unknown, just as the origin of visionary

---

68 With one exception, where 'poetry' is used ironically by Pippin, the term itself occurs exclusively in connection with Bilbo and Sam and as part of their dialogue.

dreams is never identified, but they clearly articulate a non-linear correlation with mythical reality.[69]

Sam's heightened perceptions neither begin nor end with these vocal inflections of a transhistorical light. In Ithilien, he sees a light in Frodo that remains invisible to all other mortals, and this ability extends into the past as well. Only now does the text disclose that Sam had already noticed the light "shining faintly within" Frodo in Rivendell (*LotR* 638),[70] where Gandalf discerned a "hint of transparency" about the Ring-bearer: "He may become like a glass filled with a clear light for eyes to see that can" (*LotR* 217). During the later stages of the Quest, Sam sees Frodo twice with "other vision", once in the Emyn Muil and again on the slopes of Mount Doom.[71] Both visions contain manifestations of light (Frodo's hidden brightness and the Ring as a "wheel of fire"); both visions furthermore cast the fateful parts that Frodo and Gollum play for the Ring-quest and the history of Middle-earth in a mythical mode of imagination.[72] Sam's perceptions are at the same time "vividly real" and "more portentous" than ordinary sights. From the later stages of the Quest emerges a complex web of altered perceptions and invocations of a timeless light, giving rise to the notion that the wider field of attention to which Frodo and Sam have gained access is indeed illuminated by a light that belongs to mythical reality.

---

69 Frodo's exclamation *Aiya Eärendil Elenion Ancalima*! (*LotR* 704) recalls Tréowine's *Éala Éarendel* in an unfinished chapter for *The Notion Club Papers*. The difference between these analogous scenes is telling: while Tréowine responds to the sight of "a bright star [...] in the West", Frodo's connection with Eärendil (the star and the myth) is more closely knit, as his Phial renders Eärendil present in the darkness of Shelob's Lair. However, the underlying notion – imminent transition from history to myth and the discovery of the Straight Road – may be the same. If, as I have argued elsewhere, Frodo's perception of a 'door' or a 'parting gate' on the threshold of Cirith Ungol indicates an opening towards Other Time (cf. Klinger, "Hidden Paths" 168f., 190-96), his invocation of Eärendil arises from the same liminal experience that motivates Tréowine's cry.
70 Not least, this retrospective disclosure detaches Sam's perception of the light from linear temporality. The same narrative strategy occurs in the description of Frodo's dream in Crickhollow: Here the text discloses that the sound of the Sea, "a sound he had never heard in waking life, [...] had often troubled his dreams" (*LotR* 106).
71 *LotR* 604: "For a moment it appeared to Sam that his master had grown and Gollum had shrunk: a tall stern shadow, a mighty lord who hid his brightness in grey cloud, and at his feet a little whining dog. Yet the two were in some way akin and not alien: they could reach one another's minds." – *LotR* 922: "Then suddenly, as before under the eaves of the Emyn Muil, Sam saw these two rivals with other vision. A crouching shape, scarcely more than the shadow of a living thing, a creature now wholly ruined and defeated, yet filled with a hideous lust and rage; and before it stood stern, untouchable now by pity, a figure robed in white, but at its breast it held a wheel of fire. Out of the fire there spoke a commanding voice."
72 This form of altered vision fits a general tendency Lionel Basney describes when he observes that myth becomes increasingly tangible within history in *The Lord of the Rings*: "myth merges with experience, or into experience, its wonder intact, but having gained empirical solidity" (188).

When they walk through Mordor, Sam and Frodo have long crossed the boundaries of ordinary perception, and "the time lay behind them like an ever-darkening dream" (*LotR* 914). It seems like a logical consequence, then, that their transition back into historical reality is marked by a dream-flight: "Side by side they lay; and down swept Gwaihir, and down came Landroval and Meneldor the swift; and in a dream, not knowing what fate had befallen them, the wanderers were lifted up and borne far away out of the darkness and the fire" (*LotR* 930). The description implies that Frodo and Sam are now inside the same dream, one that is not (and perhaps cannot be) translated into linear narrative.

Although Frodo and Sam eventually return to the Shire, their previous home is no longer their ultimate destination: Sam, like Frodo, will set out on a journey across the Straight Road after he has completed his part of the book.[73] His temporary return to ordinary linear reality, too, is prefigured in visionary mode. In Galadriel's Mirror, Sam had already caught a glimpse of the Shire's (future) destruction. His only dream that *The Lord of the Ring* reports – which occurs relatively late, on the way to Cirith Ungol – seems to extend and transform this vision (cf. Amendt-Raduege 52): "He thought he was back in the Bag End garden looking for something; but he had a heavy pack on his back, which made him stoop. It all seemed very weedy and rank somehow, and thorns and bracken were invading the beds down near the bottom hedge" (*LotR* 684). While these sights anticipate the damage Sam will discover at his return, it is perhaps more significant that his only recorded dream takes him back to his 'starting point', the very borders of imagination, now left far behind and seen in a state of decay. Within the dream, Sam is stretched out between two different states. When his present weariness and the weight of his pack intrude on the dream-scenario, the wish to return to a familiar life is at odds with the heightened awareness and the burdens of the Quest. The tension that pervades the dream-experience – Sam's notion that he is "looking for something" – abruptly

---

73 The *Epilogue* links Sam's preparations to fill the final pages of the book with anticipation of this journey and a changed awareness of time: "Before he went Mr. Frodo said that my time maybe would come. I can wait. I think maybe we haven't said farewell for good. But I can wait. I have learned that much from the Elves at any rate. They are not so troubled about time" (*SD* 125). As Frodo predicts on the way to the Havens, Sam will remain in the Shire "as long as your part of the Story goes on" (*LotR* 1006).

focuses on his pipe, an attribute of ordinary comforts.[74] But, as Sam realizes in waking, it has been rendered useless. Sam's dream thus shows him in a state of 'betweenness' and prefigures what Frodo, too, eventually realizes: "There is no real going back. Though I may come to the Shire, it will not seem the same; for I shall not be the same" (*LotR* 967).[75]

The medieval dream-vision often reflects a state of 'betweenness', of being poised between natural and supernatural realms (Kruger 65; cf. Brown 45), and can therefore be employed to negotiate "the increasingly tenuous connections between mundane reality and the transcendent world" (Brown 23). In *The Lord of the Rings*, a similar process is memorably represented by the passing of the Elves from Middle-earth. During the 'Middle Days' (*LotR* 252) of the Third Age, the connections between mortal and immortal realms dwindle, and the living memory of the mythical 'Elder Days' is preserved only in guarded enclaves such as Lórien. Dreams are clearly symptomatic of this period of transition,[76] preceding the Fourth Age which is dominated by 'ordinary' mortal history (cf. *L* 186). Yet the vision of immortal Elves also represents a mode of perception in which different dimensions of time, the natural and the supernatural world are balanced.

By growing into such an awareness, Frodo and Sam reach a point of vision that reforges the connections between 'mundane' and 'transcendent' reality – to the point of allowing their conclusive entry into Faërie. The final step, however, is delayed by a troubled homecoming as well as indisputable duties to the Shire and to collective memory. The counterpart to Sam's dream-experience can be found in Frodo's exchange with Merry as they are about to re-enter the Shire:

> 'Well here we are, just the four of us that started out together,' said Merry. 'We have left all the rest behind, one after another. It seems almost like a dream that has slowly faded.' 'Not to me,' said Frodo. 'To me it feels more like falling asleep again.' (*LotR* 974)

---

74 Compare Bilbo's similar but less complex dream in *The Hobbit*: "But all night he dreamed of his own house and wandered in his sleep into all his different rooms looking for something that he could not find nor remember what it looked like" (*H* 99).
75 After their return, Sam himself feels "torn in two" between the wish to remain with Frodo (to continue their journey) and resuming an ordinary life in the Shire (*LotR* 1001, 1003, 1006).
76 Conversely, dreaming plays only a marginal role in texts concerning the First and Second Age: (waking) visions conjured and perceived by the Valar, Maiar and Elves dominate in *The Silmarillion*.

Merry's remark implicitly contrasts dream as a lesser reality with ordinary waking perception.[77] Instead of reversing the statement, Frodo's reply suggests a different opposition. If he is now "falling asleep again", he was awake throughout his journey – awake to, and aware of, a wider range of time and imagination.[78] The absence of 'dream' from the underlying logic of Frodo's answer once more reflects that his scope of perception has grown beyond dreaming. That evolved vision qualifies Frodo for the author-role cannot be doubted: the book he writes is a history as much as a 'fairy-story' that brings about the "realization of imagined wonder".

Crucial parallels connect *The Lord of the Rings* with *The Notion Club Papers*. Both texts feature a pair of travellers whose journey takes them beyond linear time until their perceptions eventually transcend dreaming, materializing in a joint 'speaking in tongues' and poetic expressions of transhistorical vision. In each pair, there is an *Ælfwine* or 'Elf-friend', as both Gildor and Elrond address Frodo (*LotR* 79, 264), while Sam certainly deserves to be called *Tréowine*, 'True-friend'. In both texts, the sounds of ancient languages, fragmented poetry and retrieved literary traditions establish a connection with Faërie.

But significant differences must be noted as well. For the modern time-travellers, linguistic and poetic rediscovery define their mode of access; only through the dreaming awareness of Ælfwine and Tréowine can they catch a glimpse of the Straight Road. The recession of historical frames in the time-travel context reflects specific epistemological conditions: history as the linear representation of cause and effect, "a story made up out of the intelligible surviving evidence" (*SD* 230), defines the overarching mode of perception. The non-linear, mythi-

---

77 Where expanding vision is concerned, the four hobbits part ways after their encounter with Bombadil: Pippin and Merry experience dreams with possibly clairvoyant elements only in Tom's house. Pippin's second dream, by contrast, is entirely ordinary and reflects recent experiences (*LotR* 434), and neither Merry nor Pippin respond to the visionary side of Lórien. Frodo's and Sam's Elvish invocations also contrast starkly with Merry's and Pippin's mirror experiences: While Merry's voice is taken over by a dead Man on the Barrow-downs, Pippin echoes Sauron's voice after taking a forbidden look into the *palantír* (*LotR* 579). These diverging paths come to their logical conclusion when Frodo and Sam end their journey in the Immortal Realm, whereas Merry and Pippin spend their final years among the Men of Gondor (*LotR* App. B 1072).

78 Flieger, *Time* 197f., concludes that Frodo's experience of the Quest can be described as a "waking dream", but 'dreaming' is not implied in Frodo's wording. Frodo returns to ultimate waking as he sails towards Eressëa: "Sam's day is ending, he is going back to the same Shire that has been night and dream for Frodo. Frodo's night is over, and his sunrise brings daylight and waking, a real awakening this time, in which what was dream is now the true reality" (Flieger, *Time* 205). It is all the more important then to note that this moment of awakening is Sam's contribution to the text.

cal counterpoint can be accessed only via dream-travelling and is recaptured conceptually in poetic 're-creation'.

Within the world that Frodo and Sam inhabit, the boundaries between different realms of perception are less strictly drawn, so that an actual journey across the Straight Road becomes possible. The vast tale that they have 'fallen into' reaches back into the past before the fall of Númenor which, in *The Notion Club Papers*, marks the division of myth and history. This larger story, transcending the frame of the Red Book and *The Lord of the Rings*, is imagined as an authorless tale, passed on, retold and continued by many voices.

Authorship, as it is represented by Sam and Frodo, ultimately recombines the two sides of reality, thereby providing a literary answer to Wilfrid Jeremy's speculation that real history might become more mythical and poetical if one travelled back far enough: both perspectives are contained in the book Frodo and Sam write. As eyewitnesses to major historical events, they become authors of their own chapters in the greater story.[79] The mythical mode of imagination breaks into this historical account at various points and manifests most potently where invocations to Elbereth and Eärendil ring through Sam's and Frodo's voices across the "deeps of time". How such an experience can inspire renewed poetry is illustrated by Sam's song in the Tower of Cirith Ungol: "And then suddenly new strength rose in him, and his voice rang out, while words of his own came unbidden to fit the simple tune" (*LotR* 888). What Sam expresses in his own words is borne by a sudden strength of unknown origin.

At the very end of the text, Frodo's un-framed dream-vision stands out as the ultimate "realization of imagined wonder", a capacity attributed to Sam from

---

79 Of course Frodo's book also contains events that he did not witness himself and therefore bears a much longer title than Tolkien's book: "The Downfall of the Lord of the Rings and the Return of the King (as seen by the Little People; being the memoirs of Bilbo and Frodo of the Shire, supplemented by the accounts of their friends and the learning of the Wise)" (*LotR* 1004). The compilation process begins with the Fellowship's reunion after the end of the war. That the narration does not adhere to Frodo's subjective perspective is furthermore to be expected within a pre-modern framework of storytelling: Frodo's book is not a personal "diary" (a term only Bilbo uses in *The Lord of the Rings*) but a history. There is no reason, then, to conclude that the concept of the Red Book "falls apart" if pursued too far: "Too many things will not fit comfortably into the concept – narrative voice, point of view, the amount of knowledge each of these 'authors' could have had at any one time" (Flieger, *Music* 79). In addition to the arguments already mentioned, the contribution of the external translator-redactor, too, must be taken into account. As Gergely Nagy writes about *The Silmarillion*: "Tolkien shows us how narratives are preserved [...]. The preservation of style together with matter is a wellknown phenomenon, as is the editor's and redactor's leveling of style" (36).

the very beginning of the book. The journey to Eressëa, as envisioned by Sam, exemplifies not only the convergence of history and myth but a state of altered consciousness;[80] it is at once real and imagined and blends visionary experience with an actual entry into Faërie. This conclusive moment of crossing the threshold into Other Time is Sam's contribution to the Tale and could not have been achieved by any other author or participant in the events. Within history and mortal time, Sam himself remains on the threshold, "hearing only the sigh and murmur of the waves on the shores of Middle-earth, and the sound of them sank deep into his heart" (*LotR* 1007) – yet by the same token the text foreshadows Sam's future journey.

Frodo's un-framed dream-vision marks both the end and the beginning of a 'fairy-*story*'. Its meaning relies on a conceptualization of imagination and literature that engages modern and pre-modern epistemologies in a dialogue. From a modern perspective equating history with factual reality and myth with symbolic representation,[81] however, the journey across the Straight Road can only be viewed as a fantastical 'fairy-*tale*' ending or, if it is to be taken seriously at all, an allegory of death. The external frame surrounding Tolkien's works must therefore come into view. The constituents of authorship so far discussed – from collective imagination and transmission to non-linear, transtemporal vision and 're-creative' poetry – clash, after all, with a context that identifies J. R. R. Tolkien as the historical author of a large body of fiction. A full investigation of this clash in the context of literary theory and history would by far exceed the limits of this essay, yet I will outline some of its textual traces within Tolkien's writings.

---

80 Another mark of this altered awareness and the resulting type of authorship is the 'sea-longing' of which Lowdham, speaking as Ælfwine, says in *The Notion Club Papers*: "And the sound of the winds and seas on the west beaches was ever a restless music to me, at once a pain and a desire; and the pain was keener in Spring, and the desire stronger in Autumn" (*SD* 271). This description recalls not only Frodo's crises in spring and autumn, after the Quest, but also Frodo's dream of the Tower and "the sound of the Sea far-off": a sound that "often troubled his dreams" (*LotR* 106). By the Grey Havens, Sam absorbs the sound of the Sea (*LotR* 1007), and the *Epilogue* discloses that, even back in the Shire, "he heard suddenly, deep and unstilled, the sigh and murmur of the Sea upon the shores of Middle-earth" (*SD* 128).
81 This dichotomy is of course questioned by postmodern theories, from Michel Foucault's contention that 'historical reality' is exclusively contained in the discourses shaped by different cultures to Hayden White's analysis of historiography as narrative, to name only two prominent proponents of this approach.

VI. An author's dreams:
In from the margins, out of the frame

> The Primary World, Reality, of elves and men is the
> same, if differently valued and perceived. (*OFS* 142)

So far, I have examined the implicit and explicit connections between visionary dreaming and authorship from within the texts. The divergent textual genres imply the author Tolkien in very different modes: in his academic essays as well as his letters his author-role is constituted not only as that of the speaking subject, authorized by professional expertise and personal insight, it is also at various points fleshed out with biographical commentary and information. In the literary works, on the other hand, the author Tolkien recedes behind narrative frameworks that establish textual genealogies and rely on collective authorship. If I turn now to Tolkien as the external author of all the works discussed, it is not my intention to transfer my interpretations and conclusions to the biographical realm. Tolkien's personal experience of authorship, though interwoven with his texts, must remain the subject of biography. What I intend to examine instead are the textual intersections of literary and biographical authorship. At certain points, references to the author Tolkien enter the literary works and become framed within them. At other points, literary events are un-framed and relocated within biographical reality. In both cases, a direct connection between the realms that Tolkien described as primary and secondary realities in *On Fairy-stories* is established.

Characteristically, such a connection may be couched in terms of dream-vision. The most prominent example is the dream of the Great Wave:

> I have what some might call an Atlantis complex. Possibly inherited, though my parents died too young for me to know such things about them, and too young to transfer such things by words. Inherited from me (I suppose) by one only of my children, though I did not know that about my son until recently, and he did not know it about me. I mean the terrible recurrent dream (beginning with memory) of the Great Wave, towering up, and coming in ineluctably over the trees and green fields. (I bequeathed it to Faramir.) I don't think I have had it since I wrote the 'Downfall of Númenor' as the last of the legends of the First and Second Age. (*L* 213)

The above letter to W. H. Auden was written in 1955, after the publication of *The Lord of the Rings*. Several other letters from the nineteen-fifties and -sixties mention the "vision and dream" which Tolkien also describes as a "legend or myth or dim memory of some ancient history" (*L* 347; cf. *L* 232, 361). The concept of ancestral memory, present in *The Lost Road* and *The Notion Club Papers*, is reflected here and supported by biographical evidence. Once again, dreaming serves as a vehicle of crossing boundaries: in this case, the boundary between secondary and primary world.[82]

This emphatic connection begs the question how Middle-earth as a whole is related to primary reality. "Middle-earth is not an imaginary world", Tolkien writes, drawing on the etymological and conceptual connections to "*midden-erd*" and "the *oikoumenē*": only "the historical period is imaginary" (*L* 239; cf. *L* 283, 186, 197). The disjunction of real place from imaginary time introduces a tension that grows where the parting of straight from bent roads moves into focus.[83] Tolkien reflects critically on the epistemological strain of imagining a mythical time with its corresponding flat world, of which the Straight Road is the final remnant:

> Actually in the imagination of this story we are now living on a physically round Earth. But the whole 'legendarium' contains a transition from a flat world [...] to a globe: an inevitable transition, I suppose, to a modern 'myth-maker' with a mind subjected to the same 'appearances' as ancient men, and partly fed on their myths, but taught that the Earth was round from the earliest years. So deep was the impression made by 'astronomy' on me that I do not think I could deal with or imaginatively conceive a flat world, though a world of static Earth with a Sun going round it seems easier (to fancy if not to reason). (*L* 197)

---

82 Modern industrial cultures still acknowledge that dreams induce a state of altered consciousness, even though external sources are generally excluded. It should be noted, however, that the unconscious as the only source of dreams was not the only commonly acceptable view in the earlier 20th century. Sigmund Freud himself wrote an article discussing possible connections between dreams and telepathy in 1922. Although his attitude is critical, he does not reject the possibility of telepathic interventions (neither does Scherner: 363-67, 370-74).

83 Of Middle-earth Tolkien wrote in another letter from 1954: "It lay then as it does. In fact just as it does, round and inescapable. [...] The new situation, established at the beginning of the Third Age, leads on eventually and inevitably to ordinary History [...]. If you or I or any of the mortal men (or hobbits) of Frodo's day had set out over sea, west, we should, as now, eventually have come back (as now) to our starting point. Gone was the 'mythological' time when Valinor (or Valimar), the Land of the Valar [...] existed physically in the Uttermost West [...]. After the Downfall of Númenor, and its destruction, all this was removed from the 'physical' world, and not reachable by material means. Only the Eldar (or High-Elves) could still sail thither, forsaking time and mortality, but never returning" (*L* 186). The fluid transition from an assumed continuity between the present world and Middle-earth to the discontinuity that ends "mythological time" leaves the reality of the Straight Road (even if it cannot be entered by "material means") unquestioned.

Two rhetorical moves can be identified in these comments connecting primary and secondary reality. On the one hand, Tolkien introduces himself as "historically minded" (*L* 239) and employs historical reasoning, both biographical and etymological, to anchor Middle-earth and certain critical events in the primary world. But on the other hand, the epistemology of history itself is undermined where the coherence of space and time, fundamental to the historical-empirical understanding of reality, is drawn into question. Such a question must arise when the spatial reality of Middle-earth is separated from its imaginary temporal status.

The point of view that can be construed from these comments is located on the very boundary of History as a constituent of modern epistemology. It points out the existence of such a boundary and the limits of historical imagination. What may lie beyond cannot be phrased in the historical mode, but it can be represented within the imagination or enchantment of Faërie as an external, though never fully accessible, point of vision.

This perspective is indeed represented in *On Fairy-stories*, where the reality of Elves is held in a state of ambiguity.[84] Of the "nature of *Faërie*", Tolkien writes: "I will not attempt to define that, nor to describe it directly. It cannot be done. Faërie cannot be caught in a net of words; for it is one of its qualities to be indescribable, though not imperceptible" (*OFS* 114). The description of Faërie as "the realm or state in which fairies have their being" (*OFS* 113) retains a characteristic 'betweenness', bridging the dichotomy of 'material' and 'spiritual', while the phrasing carefully avoids the suggestion of a definite origin. The 'being' that fairies have could originate within human imagination – or elsewhere. Consequently, the essay refuses to state unequivocally whether Faërie is located only within the secondary world of fairy-stories or whether it exists independently

---

84 Tom Shippey notes this as well but describes it as Tolkien's "trick of pretending that fairies are real": "This comes perilously close to whimsy, the pretence that something not true is true to create an air of comic innocence" (*Road* 49). However, *On Fairy-stories* gives no signs of intending a comical effect; the marked ambiguity must be taken seriously as a strategy of undermining certain suppositions about what can or cannot be true.

in the primary world.[85] Faërie is thus constantly framed and un-framed by the same technique applied to dream-visions in *The Notion Club Papers* and *The Lord of the Rings*.

The term 'imagination' is here employed to mediate between different epistemologies that constitute diverging realities. Where Tolkien discusses the "fantastic images" that imagination can embrace, the clear separation of primary from secondary reality is simultaneously upheld and questioned: "the images are of things not in the primary world (if that indeed is possible)" (*OFS* 139).[86] Within these complex negotiations, imagination can function as an experimental bridge reconnecting (apparently) separate realities: "It is not difficult to imagine", Tolkien writes in the essay's epilogue, "the peculiar excitement and joy that one would feel, if any specially beautiful fairy-story were found to be 'primarily' true, its narrative to be history, without thereby necessarily losing the mythical or allegorical significance that it had possessed" (*OFS* 156).[87] Finally, the joyous turn – for which Tolkien coins the term *eucatastrophe* – can "in a serious tale of Faërie" generate a joy "that for a moment passes outside the frame, rends indeed the very web of story, and lets a gleam come through" (*OFS* 154).[88]

The precarious position between epistemologies that *On Fairy-stories* negotiates – one belonging to history and modernity, the other to myth and Faërie – mir-

---

85 To quote only a few pertinent statements that suggest the reality of Faërie in the primary world: "For it is man who is, in contrast to fairies, supernatural (and often of diminutive stature); whereas they are natural, far more natural than he. Such is their doom" (*OFS* 110); "if elves are true, and really exist independently of our tales about them, then this also is certainly true: elves are not primarily concerned with us, nor we with them" (113); "It is often reported of fairies (truly or lyingly, I do not know) that they are workers of illusion" (116); "You are deluded – whether that is the intention of the elves (always or at any time) is another question" (142); "Art of the same sort, if more skilled and effortless, the elves can also use, or so the reports seem to show" (143); "Fairy-stories are made by men not by fairies. The human stories of the elves are doubtless full of the Escape from Deathlessness" (153).
86 Similarly, Tolkien immediately qualifies the statement that these "things are not only 'not actually present', but [...] indeed not to be found in our primary world at all", by adding: "or are *generally believed* not to be found there" (*OFS* 139; emphasis added).
87 The two perspectives are ultimately reconciled with recourse to divine authority and a religious perception of the world (which, within 20th-century industrialized cultures, amounts to the only generally acceptable assertion of a supernatural sphere): "God is the Lord, of angels, and of men – and of elves. Legend and History have met and fused" (*OFS* 156).
88 Frodo's first sight of Eressëa, at the end of *The Lord of the Rings*, "passes outside the frame" in a recognizably similar manner. Its juxtaposition with Frodo's previously portrayed loss and Sam's grief by the Havens furthermore reflects what Tolkien writes about *eucatastrophe*: "In its fairy-tale – or otherworld – setting, it is a sudden and miraculous grace: never to be counted on to recur. It does not deny the existence of *dyscatastrophe*, of sorrow and failure: the possibility of these is necessary to the joy of deliverance" (*OFS* 153).

rors the 'betweenness' of dreams in the literary works, albeit with a definite leaning towards a historical perspective. A similar tension can be found in the biographical representations of Tolkien's literary (re-)creation. His letters sometimes portray the writing process as an unfolding vision beyond the author's control and intention: "They [the stories] arose in my mind as 'given' things [...]: yet always I had the sense of recording what was already 'there', somewhere: not of 'inventing'" (*L* 149).[89] One letter that features a similar statement is quoted among Christopher Tolkien's commentary on the evolution of *The Lord of the Rings*: "I have long ceased to *invent* [...]: I wait till I seem to know what really happened. Or till it writes itself" (*TI* 411, cf. 390).[90] Christopher Tolkien frequently reiterates this and similar statements and thereby underpins a concept of authorship situated between conscious invention and inspired 're-creation'.[91]

Variations of the author as scribe (of a text that largely "writes itself") or as redactor-translator (of texts owed to fragmented traditions) occur throughout Tolkien's literary works, especially as part of framing devices like the *Prologue* to *The Lord of the Rings*. While such a frame adopts a modern historical (and philological) approach to the presented text, the idea of poetic 're-creation' implies a creative involvement beyond philology and editorial reconstruction. The succession of boundaries and frames in *The Notion Club Papers* illustrates most clearly how the recipients of visionary history and poetry become themselves re-creative poets. Consequently, another point of connection between the two perspectives has to be addressed: the trajectory from literary text to biographical frame is, after all, complemented by the reverse movement.

Poems that were first published under Tolkien's name, independent of any narrative framing within the 'legendarium', return as framed parts of larger

---

89 Cf. *L* 104: "the thing seems to write itself once I get going, as if the truth comes out then, only imperfectly glimpsed in the preliminary sketch." See also *L* 79, 212, 258.
90 The remark that precedes this statement is reminiscent of Ramer's theories in *The Notion Club Papers*: "I think a lot of this kind of work goes on at other (to say lower, deeper, or higher introduces a false gradation) levels, when one is saying how-do-you-do, or even 'sleeping'" (*L* 231). See also *L* 216f.: "I met a lot of things on the way that astonished me. [...] I knew nothing of the *Palantíri*, though the moment the Orthanc-stone was cast from the window, I recognized it, and knew the meaning of the 'rhyme of lore' that had been running in my mind: *seven stars and seven stones and one white tree*. These rhymes and names will crop up; but they do not always explain themselves." In the same letter, an interpretation of Shelob based on a traumatic biographical incident is firmly rejected.
91 Cf. *TI* 168; *WR* 18, 65, 104, 121, 147, 219; *SD* 37, 93.

works and are re-attributed to new authors.[92] Bilbo's *The Cat and the Fiddle*, sung by Frodo in *The Lord of the Rings*, was published in *Yorkshire Poetry*, 1923 (*LotR* 154-56; *RS* 144-47), Sam's Troll Song had a precedent in *The Root of the Boot*, first printed 1936 in *Songs for the Philologists* (*LotR* 201-03; *RS* 142-44; *TI* 59-61), and Bilbo's song of Eärendil at Rivendell emerges as a (largely revised and rewritten) version of the earlier poem *Errantry*, published in *The Oxford Magazine* in 1933 (*LotR* 227-30; *TI* 84-105).[93] Viewed from the surrounding framework of biographical authorship, the hobbits become re-creative authors of poetry first published as Tolkien's own.

These interactions across textual boundaries gain complexity as the poems are shifted to a different frame. Yet another version of *Errantry* eventually became part of *The Adventures of Tom Bombadil* (1961), a collection including, but not limited to, songs and poems from *The Lord of the Rings*. The framework for this compilation is established in the *Preface*: "The Red Book contains a large number of verses. A few are included in the narrative of the *Downfall of the Lord of the Rings*, or in the attached stories and chronicles; many more are found on loose leaves, while some are written carelessly in margins and blank spaces" (*ATB* 61). As the selection of 'marginal' poetry is moved to the centre of a new book, the editorial frame simultaneously gains importance. The *Preface* alone establishes the coherence of the corpus and its connections with the Red Book. Familiar characters – Bilbo and Sam – are identified as the authors (or adaptors) of songs and poems, and the evolution of *Errantry* into the later song of Eärendil is explained (*ATB* 61f.). While all other poems, except one, are attributed to anonymous hobbit authors of the late Third Age, it is the one exception that must be of particular interest here. No. 15, *The Sea-bell*, is singled out in the *Preface* and set apart from the rest of the collection:

> No. 15, certainly of hobbit origin, is an exception. It is the latest piece and belongs to the Fourth Age; but it is included here, because a hand has scrawled at its head *Frodos Dreme*. That is remarkable, and though the piece is most unlikely to have been written by Frodo himself, the title shows that it was

---

92 *The Lost Road* and *The Notion Club Papers* in particular also include biographical allusions: See Christopher Tolkien's comments (*SD* 150f.); Flieger, *Time* 73, 77, 126-29; *Music* 98f.
93 These are only the most obvious examples. Another prominent example is the reworking of *Light as Leaf on Lindentree* into Aragorn's song of Beren and Lúthien at Weathertop (*LotR* 187-89; *RS* 179-182).

associated with the dark and despairing dreams which visited him in March and October during his last three years. (*ATB* 64)

Tolkien's poem *Looney*, printed in *The Oxford Magazine* (1934), is the precursor of *The Sea-bell* in which a nameless traveller crosses the sea and seeks in vain to enter the Otherworld anticipated there. Aged and bent, the traveller finally returns to his own world where he finds himself equally isolated: the desired entry into Faërie has failed. While Tom Shippey proposes a largely biographical reading of this poem of "disenchantment", reflecting Tolkien's doubts and loss of inspiration in later years (*Road* 283-85), Verlyn Flieger follows the implications of the title '*Frodos Dreme*' by focussing on the connections with Frodo's journey and the recurring theme of perils or 'pitfalls' in Faërie (*Time* 207-18). As these readings indicate, *The Sea-bell* suggests two very different perspectives. While the diction and setting of the poem evoke Tolkien's poetic style and contemporary reality rather than Frodo's,[94] the *Preface* alone asserts a connection with the Shire of the Fourth Age and Frodo himself. However, uncertainties and displacements surrounding the given coordinates of *authorship*, *dream* and *time* complicate this connection and generate irresolvable ambiguities.

When the *Preface* qualifies the attribution of the poem to Frodo as "most unlikely", the coherence of author, dream and poem is implicitly dismantled. A later author may have imagined Frodo's dreaming[95] or expressed his own dream-experience in poetic form. Since the unknown writer of the title does not necessarily have to be the poem's author either, the misattributed *Dreme* could well be a mere fabrication. This conclusion receives support from *On Fairy-stories*, where the literary "machinery of Dream" is rejected as a "disfiguring frame" (*OFS* 116),

---

94 While this is not the place for a detailed analysis, the journey described in *The Sea-bell* begins and ends in a human environment that lacks all reference to hobbit culture: "harbours" and "buoys" clearly do not exist in the Shire, nor can one easily imagine Frodo walking "in blind alley and in long street" where the "men" he meets do not speak to him (cf. *ATB* 110, 113f.). As Verlyn Flieger also states: "his [Tom Shippey's] association of the voice with Tolkien's own is, in terms of the overall tone of the poem, both pertinent and persuasive" (*Time*, 210).

95 A further complication arises in connection with *The Lord of the Rings*: Frodo's 'dream-states' in March and October, if they can be called that, are waking disconnections from present reality, not actual (framed) dreaming. On the first 6th of October after the Quest, Frodo is "ill at ease" and "his eyes appeared not to see them or things about him"; on the next anniversary, "his eyes seemed to see things far away" (*LotR* 967, 1002). Secondly, the phrase "half in a dream" which occurs during the March 13th episode (*LotR* 1001) suggest an external influence reminiscent of supernatural spells: it occurs twice before in the text, once during the encounter with Old Man Willow (*LotR* 114) and again after Frodo's injury at Weathertop (*LotR* 198).

because it reduces the wonder of Faërie to mere illusion. That *Frodos Dreme* was added in a "scrawl" may suggest a disfigurement as well.[96]

The uncertainty of authorship, which is left hovering between a (falsely) identified individual and anonymous imitator(s), equally destabilizes the meaning of 'dream' and the references to Faërie. Tolkien's earlier assertion that the dream-frame would undermine a serious 'fairy-story' begs the question of whether *The Sea-bell* actually belongs in this genre. Familiar elements – such as the call of the sea, the voyage by ship, mysterious glimmering lights – do not yield a vision of the "strange land" as Faërie upon arrival. Only fleeting sounds of dancing, music, of "pipes, voices, horns on the hill" (*ATB* 111) suggest the unattainable presence of Elves.[97] The failed entry is complemented by a failure of poetic enchantment. In other words, Faërie is neither reached nor represented in the text,[98] so that the frame of illusory dreaming might, in fact, be justified.

Finally, the poem's position in time is rendered ambiguous. It "belongs to the Fourth Age", yet in *The Lord of the Rings* the Third Age ends with the Ring-bearers' journey across the Sea.[99] Since Frodo is not an author of the Fourth Age, the poem appears as a retrospective projection, a notion underlined by the use of *dreme* (recorded in Middle English since 1300) rather than 'dream' as in *The Lord of the Rings*.[100] The historicized title, a later addition, antedates the poem's more modern diction,[101] thereby reversing temporal progression.

---

[96] In *The Lord of the Rings*, "scrawl" always refers to defective writing, either caused by desperate haste (*LotR* 314), or because the writers are orcs and denizens of Mordor (*LotR* 687, 866).

[97] "I heard dancing there, music in the air, | feet going quick on the green floors. | But whenever I came it was ever the same: | the feet fled, and all was still; | never a greeting, only the fleeting | pipes, voices, horns on the hill." See also Tolkien's criticism of the Barrie play *Mary Rose* in *On Fairy-stories*: "No fairy is seen. The cruelly tormented human beings are there all the time" (*OFS* 160).

[98] By contrast, in the earlier poem *Looney* "the impression of paradise lasted for a couple of stanzas" (Shippey, *Road* 284).

[99] *LotR* 1006; App. B 1057, 1070f., App. A 1009. Additionally, the editorial comments refer back to Frodo's March and October crises during his "last three years", whereas the story of *The Lord of the Rings* as well as *The Tale of Years* show that Frodo spent less than two years in the Shire, after his return from the Quest.

[100] Or its Old English counterpart *swefn*, which Tolkien applied where he translated 'dream' in the *Quenta* and in the "Old English version of the Annals of Beleriand made by Ælfwine or Eriol" (*SME* 208, 339).

[101] Only one other archaism, "ruel-bone", appears in the poem itself and can be found in Tolkien's early *Lay of Leithian* (l. 2261) as well (*LB* 237, 371). On the other hand, the modern spelling "gladdon" in *The Sea-bell* contrasts with the adaptation of O.E. *glædene* as "gladden" (e.g. in names such as Gladden Fields) in *The Lord of the Rings* (cf. *L* 381).

If these ambiguities, too, define a state of 'betweenness', it concerns authorship in relation to visionary dreams of Faërie. Dreaming in *The Lord of the Rings* is bound up with the increasingly tenuous connections between Elvish realms of enchantment and the historical realms of mortals in Middle-earth at the end of the Third Age. The newly framed *Sea-bell*, on the other hand, reflects the underlying tension between a 'Fourth Age' perspective and the desire to reach (and poetically represent) Faërie. The boundary of the Fourth Age clearly marks the predominance of mortal history and at this angle intersects with the world of the modern 'editor' and the dominant epistemology of Tolkien's own time. The tone and setting of the poem itself and the historical-philological approach of the *Preface* point back to the realm of biographical authorship. The interplay of editorial frame and poem thus reflects the biographical conditions of writing and the limitations that a "historically minded" author confronts. From this point of view, the association with "dark and despairing" (rather than transcendent and revelatory) dreams seems inevitable. History has triumphed over Faërie in the Fourth Age as much as in the 20th century.

The added title *Frodos Dreme* may well signal that *The Sea-bell* can be read as "a commentary on Frodo" (Flieger, *Music* 82), but as commentary it is deeply self-reflexive.[102] More precisely, *The Sea-bell* in its editorial frame offers commentary on different modes of authorship. The 'visionary' authorship represented by Frodo eludes the grasp and recedes into a temporal vacuum that cannot be fathomed from an isolated historical perspective which defines the position of biographical authorship. Contemporary readers may in turn find the denied vision of *The Sea-bell* more credible and comprehensible than the visionary path into Faërie at the end of *The Lord of the Rings* which "passes outside the frame" of book and history. Counter to the un-framing of Frodo's vision, the editorial re-framing of *The Sea-bell* reflects the constraints of history that may

---

102 Flieger adds that Tolkien may have wished to underline "the tragedy of what had happened to his hero" (*Music* 83), but whether or not that was indeed Tolkien's motivation, the tragedy portrayed in the poem differs profoundly from the tragic aspects of Frodo's return to the Shire in *The Lord of the Rings*. There, Frodo cannot resume his previous life as he had hoped and wished: His transformation, combining growth in vision and wisdom with undeniable injuries, remains double-edged but also allows his entry into Faërie. In *The Sea-bell*, it is precisely that entry which tragically fails.

equally limit the reader's imagination.¹⁰³ But, by means of an exposed failure, it also demonstrates that an entry into the enchantment of Faërie relies on the dialogue of biographical with literary authorship, which speaks in many voices: only then will dreams and visions step out of their frame into primary, waking experience.

In the different textual genres discussed here, the concepts and articulations of authorship necessarily vary. Texts grounded in academic or biographical discourse, such as Tolkien's essays and letters, speak from a modern historical perspective dominated by the perception of the author as originator whose inspiration, if it cannot be rationally traced, is owed to the workings of the unconscious.¹⁰⁴ However, even within the framework of modern discourse, Tolkien emphasizes an understanding of authorship that retains an intrinsic connection to the metaphysical world. In *On Fairy-stories*, he develops the concept of 'sub-creation' to approach and explore – if not explain – the "mystery of literary creation" (*L* 231):

> Fantasy remains a human right: we make in our measure and in our derivative mode, because we are made: and not only made, but made in the image and likeness of a Maker. (*OFS* 145)¹⁰⁵

This insistence on transcending the realm of history seems mandatory for "the construction of elaborate and consistent mythology" (*L* 26). Of course "one cannot write a mythology, primarily because myths are not written" (Nagy 36), but also because myth "does not, cannot speak with one voice" (Flieger,

---

103 Related limitations are present in the portrayal of Sam's ultimate journey to Eressëa in *The Tale of Years*, written from a perspective that is limited to historical events in Middle-earth: Consequently, only Sam's journey to the boundary of that historical world, marked by the Tower Hills, can be recorded (*LotR* App. B 1072: "Master Samwise [...] comes to the Tower Hills, and is last seen by Elanor, to whom he gives the Red Book afterwards kept by the Fairbairns. Among them the tradition is handed down from Elanor that Samwise passed the Towers, and went to the Grey Havens, and passed over Sea, last of the Ring-bearers").
104 Only very rarely does Tolkien refer to 'unconscious' processes in the *Letters* (*L* 172, 375, 383, 418), but – considering his critical attitude towards psychoanalysis (*L* 60, 232, 288) – these references need not imply the Freudian concept.
105 Relating the literary concepts to 'sub-creation' would require a separate examination. Briefly put, Tolkien's theory of sub-creation derives an author's creative abilities from divine authority: The concept thus involves a linear genealogy and a hierarchy of transferred capacity and authority and in these respects differs from the non-linear emergence of poetry and the collective creative activities portrayed in the literary works. However, Tolkien's programmatic poem *Mythopoeia* addresses the "progenitive" (implicitly collective) aspect of literary sub-creation as well (*My* 87). The poem also invokes a perspective beyond history: "Blessed are the legend-makers with their rhyme | of things not found within recorded time" (*My* 88).

Music 54).[106] Although Tolkien never drew a clear distinction between 'myth' and 'legend', his term 'legendarium' – as a written and diversified body of texts relating the natural to the supernatural world – implies the transition from oral to scriptural traditions.[107] The large corpus of (often fragmentary) stories, embracing different styles, forms and genres, furthermore reflects central characteristics of historical mythologies: "Within the layers and complexities of an extended mythology, there will always be conflicting accounts and internal discrepancies" (Flieger, *Music* 54). But Tolkien's works not only speak with different voices, they also articulate diverging points of vision that relate the historical perspective to the mythical space and time of enchantment. The diverging conceptions of authorship are deeply involved in these relations and emerge primarily from the crossing of epistemological boundaries and the construction and dissolution of narrative frames. While it is certainly possible to relate the literary representations to biographical authorship, *reducing* them to biographical authorship as their ultimate source of meaning would also reduce the vivid concert to a single voice – unnecessarily privileged, if the programmatic statement in Tolkien's poem *Mythopoeia* is to be taken seriously: "I would that I might with the minstrels sing | and stir the unseen with a throbbing string" (*My* 89).

Tolkien's texts "stir the unseen" by envisioning a dialogue of epistemologies and a movement across the boundaries of historical perception. Dreams serve as primary vehicles for these transgressions. Of uncertain origin, they transcend linear time and initiate an altered consciousness situated between the historical and the mythical realms, between primary and secondary reality. They do tell their own stories in Tolkien's works – sometimes they even sing. But, most importantly, the stories and the poetry that arise out of dreams irrevocably transform the understanding of authorship.

---

106 For a more detailed discussion see the article by Allan Turner and Dirk Vanderbeke in this volume.
107 Gergely Nagy argues persuasively that Tolkien's sharp awareness of these processes allowed him "to write not only texts but traditions" and points out "how important textual transmission is to the interpretation of Tolkien – indeed, how very crucial textuality is in Tolkien's mythopoesis" (36).

Works cited

Amendt-Raduege, Amy M. "Dream Visions in J. R. R. Tolkien's *The Lord of the Rings*." *Tolkien Studies* 3 (2006): 45-55.

Artemidorus. *The Interpretation of Dreams. Oneirocritica* by Artemidorus. Translation and Commentary by Robert J. White. Park Ridge, NJ: Noyes Press, 1975.

Barfield, Owen. *Poetic Diction: A Study in Meaning.* 1928. London: Faber and Faber, 1952.

Basney, Lionel. "Myth, History, and Time in *The Lord of the Rings*." *Understanding 'The Lord of the Rings'. The Best of Tolkien Criticism.* Eds. Rose A. Zimbardo and Neil D. Isaacs. Boston & New York: Houghton Mifflin Company, 2004. 183-194.

The Battle of Maldon. Text and Translation. Edited and translated by Bill Griffiths. Frithgarth: Anglo-Saxon Books, 2003.

Brown, Peter. "On the Borders of Middle English Dreams Visions." *Reading Dreams: The Interpretation of Dreams from Chaucer to Shakespeare.* Ed. Peter Brown. Oxford: Oxford University Press, 1999. 22-50.

Christie-Murray, David. *Voices from the Gods. Speaking with Tongues.* London & Henley: Routledge & Kegan Paul, 1978.

Cicero, Tullius Marcus. *De Inventione, De Optimo, Genere Oratorum, Topica.* Translated by H. M. Hubbell. Cambridge: Harvard University Press, 1949.

Flieger, Verlyn. *A Question of Time. J. R. R. Tolkien's Road to Faërie.* London & Kent, Ohio: The Kent State University Press, 1997.

---. *Splintered Light. Logos and Language in Tolkien's World.* London & Kent, Ohio: The Kent State University Press, 2002.

---. "'Do the Atlantis-story and abandon Eriol-Saga'." *Tolkien Studies* 1 (2004): 43-68.

---. *Interrupted Music. The Making of Tolkien's Mythology.* London & Kent, Ohio: The Kent State University Press, 2005.

Foucault, Michel. *The Order of Things: An Archaeology of the Human Sciences.* New York: Vintage, 1970.

Freud, Sigmund. *The Interpretation of Dreams.* Translated from the German and edited by James Strachey. New York: Avon Books, 1965.

---. "Dreams and Telepathy" (1922). *The Standard Edition of the Complete Psychological Works of Sigmund Freud.* Vol. 18. Translated from the German under the General Editorship of James Strachey. London: Hogarth Press, 1955. 195-220.

Hammond, Wayne G. and Christina Scull. *The Lord of the Rings. A Reader's Companion*. London: Harper Collins, 2005.

Heise, Jens. *Traumdiskurse. Die Träume der Philosophie und die Psychologie des Traums*. Stuttgart: Fischer Taschenbuch Verlag, 1989.

Hooker, Mark T. "The Feigned-manuscript Topos: A Question of Authorship." *A Tolkienian Mathomium. A Collection of Articles about J. R. R. Tolkien and His Legendarium*. n.p.: Llyfrawr 2006. 153-177.

Klinger, Judith. "'More Poetical, Less Prosaic'. The Convergence of Myth and History in Tolkien's Works." *Hither Shore* 3 (2006): 53-68.

---. "Hidden Paths of Time. March 13th and the Riddles of Shelob's Lair." *Tolkien and Modernity*. 2 vols. Eds. Thomas Honegger and Frank Weinreich. Zurich and Berne: Walking Tree Publishers 2006. Vol. 2. 143-210.

---. "Die Poetik der Träume. Zum Erzählen von und mit Traum-Bildern im Prosa-Lancelot." *Lancelot. Der mittelhochdeutsche Roman im europäischen Kontext*. Eds. Christoph Huber and Klaus Ridder. Tübingen: Niemeyer, 2007. 211-234.

Kruger, Steven F. *Dreaming in the Middle Ages*. Cambridge: Cambridge University Press, 1992.

Leupin, Alexandre. *Fiction and Incarnation. Rhetoric, Theology, and Literature in the Middle Ages*. Minneapolis & London: University of Minnesota Press, 2003.

Macrobius. *Commentary on the Dream of Scipio*. Translated with an Introduction and Notes by William Harris Stahl. New York: Columbia University Press, 1990.

Nagy, Gergely. "The Adapted Text. The Lost Poetry of Beleriand." *Tolkien Studies* 1 (2004): 21-41.

Peden, A. M. "Macrobius and Medieval Dream Literature." *Medium Ævum* 54 (1985): 59-73.

Scherner, Karl Albert. *Das Leben des Traumes*. Berlin: Verlag Heinrich Schindler, 1861.

Shippey, Tom. *J. R. R. Tolkien. Author of the Century*. New York & Boston: Houghton Mifflin Company, 2002.

---. *The Road to Middle-earth. How J. R. R. Tolkien Created a New Mythology*. Revised and Expanded Edition. New York & Boston: Houghton Mifflin Company, 2003.

Tolkien, J. R. R. *The Hobbit*. 1937. London: Unwin Hyman Limited, 1990.

---. *The Lord of the Rings*. 1954/1955. London: Harper Collins, 1995.

---. "The Adventures of Tom Bombadil." 1962. *Tales from the Perilous Realm.* London: Harper Collins, 2002. 59-118.

---. "The Homecoming of Beorhtnoth Beorhthelm's Son." *Tree and Leaf. Including the Poem 'Mythopoeia'*. 1964. London: Harper Collins, 2001. 119-150.

---. "Mythopoeia." *Tree and Leaf. Including the Poem 'Mythopoeia'*. 1964. London: Harper Collins, 2001. 85-90.

---. *Sir Gawain and the Green Knight, Pearl, and Sir Orfeo.* Translated by J. R. R. Tolkien. Ed. Christopher Tolkien. 1975. London: Unwin Paperbacks, 1979.

---. *The Silmarillion.* Ed. Christopher Tolkien. 1977. London: George Allen & Unwin, 1979.

---. *Unfinished Tales of Númenor and Middle-earth.* Ed. Christopher Tolkien. 1980. London: Harper Collins, 1998.

---. *The Letters of J. R. R. Tolkien.* A Selection edited by Humphrey Carpenter with the assistance of Christopher Tolkien. 1981. London: Houghton Mifflin, 1995.

---. "Beowulf: The Monsters and the Critics." *The Monsters and the Critics and Other Essays.* Ed. Christopher Tolkien. 1983. London: HarperCollins, 1997. 5-48.

---. "On Fairy-Stories." *The Monsters and the Critics and Other Essays.* Ed. Christopher Tolkien. 1983. London: Harper Collins, 1997. 109-161.

---. *The Book of Lost Tales (Part One).* (*The History of Middle-earth* 1). Ed. Christopher Tolkien. 1983. London: Harper Collins, 2002.

---. *The Book of Lost Tales (Part Two).* (*The History of Middle-earth* 2). Ed. Christopher Tolkien. 1984. London: Harper Collins, 2002.

---. *The Lays of Beleriand.* (*The History of Middle-earth* 3). Ed. Christopher Tolkien. 1985. London: Harper Collins, 2002.

---. *The Shaping of Middle-earth.* (*The History of Middle-earth* 4). Ed. Christopher Tolkien. 1986. London: Harper Collins, 2002.

---. *The Lost Road and Other Writings.* (*The History of Middle-earth* 5). Ed. Christopher Tolkien. 1987. London: Harper Collins, 2002.

---. *The Return of the Shadow.* (*The History of Middle-earth* 6). Ed. Christopher Tolkien. 1988. London: Harper Collins, 1994.

---. *The Treason of Isengard.* (*The History of Middle-earth* 7). Ed. Christopher Tolkien. 1989. London: Harper Collins, 1994.

---. *The War of the Ring.* (*The History of Middle-earth* 8). Ed. Christopher Tolkien. 1990. London: Harper Collins, 1997.

---. *Sauron Defeated* (*The History of Middle-earth* 9). Ed. Christopher Tolkien. 1992. London: Harper Collins, 2002.

---. *Morgoth's Ring* (*The History of Middle-earth* 10). Ed. Christopher Tolkien. 1993. London: Harper Collins, 2002.

---. *The Peoples of Middle-earth* (*The History of Middle-earth* 12). Ed. Christopher Tolkien. 1996. London: Harper Collins, 1997.

---. "Early Runic Documents." *Parma Eldalamberon* XV (2004): 89-121.

White, Hayden. *The Content of Form. Narrative Discourse and Historical Representation.* Baltimore et al.: John Hopkins University Press, 1987.

About the author

JUDITH KLINGER, Dr. phil., studied German and English Philology and is currently employed at the chair of German Medieval Studies at Potsdam University. Her Ph.D. thesis explores concepts of identity in the medieval Prose-*Lancelot*; other publications focus on medieval poetics, negotiations of gender and desire, the interrelations of text and image within medieval manuscripts, and the transformations of medieval motives in modern literature and film. She has published various articles on Tolkien's works.

Margaret Hiley

(Re)Authoring History: Tolkien and Postcolonialism

Abstract

The present article begins with the following statement by Tolkien: "I cordially dislike allegory [...] I much prefer history, true or feigned, with its varied applicability to the thought and experience of readers." This quote becomes the point of departure for a discussion of in how far Tolkien's *Lord of the Rings* can be read as an example of such a 'feigned history', and to which ends concrete historical fragments are incorporated in the work itself. Focusing not just on *how* Anglo-Saxon fragments are used by Tolkien, but also on *why* they are used reveals a link to post-Empire resurgent English nationalism and places Tolkien's works within a postcolonial context. By using Old English texts and culture in his works, Tolkien is creating a version of Englishness that effectively writes the Norman Conquest and England's subsequent status as a Norman colony of sorts out of England's history. Running through this discussion of postcolonialism is the question of what model of authorship is necessary for this rewriting of history to become possible. Drawing on Nietzsche's statement that "history is the silent work of the dramatist", we can see that by the time Tolkien was writing, history was not simply the domain of historiographers, but also of authors of fiction; any type of history is, to a certain extent, 'feigned'. This is the position that many postcolonial writers take when dealing with their countries' fraught histories, and it is also the position that becomes evident in Tolkien's case in this postcolonial reading of his work.

> I cordially dislike allegory [...] I much prefer history, true or feigned, with its varied applicability to the thought and experience of readers.
> (*LotR* xv)

This statement of Tolkien's has inspired a number of studies on his treatment of history, and has led critics to read *The Lord of the Rings* as an example of this 'feigned history'.[1] Indeed, the issue of and problematics raised by history are central to Tolkien's entire *œuvre*, and the connections and discrepancies between history and myth, the 'question of time', and the

---

1 For example, Friedman.

importance of memory have been discussed by several scholars.[2] The present essay aims to examine this 'feigned history' and the concept of the author behind it, as the question of authorship becomes an especially interesting – not to say fraught – one in this regard, and opens up Tolkien's works to a postcolonial reading. The focus will rest, in accordance with the opening quote, upon *The Lord of the Rings*.

Writing history

Traditionally, the aim of history was to provide an objective portrayal of past events, and its claim was absolute. History had no 'author', its events were simply recorded; if someone 'wrote history', it was on account of their deeds, not of their pen.[3] Friedrich Nietzsche criticised this idea of history and historiography in his *Vom Nutzen und Nachteil der Historie für das Leben* (first published 1874), and his ideas had become widely influential by the beginning of the twentieth century. He stated, "die Geschichte [...] ist die stille Arbeit des Dramatikers" – "history is the silent work of the dramatist" (Nietzsche, *Historie* 57). Far from being impersonal and impartial, history represents a certain point of view and is the work of a particular author rooted in a particular time and place – in fact, it is a fiction like any other. Thus, it can be 'feigned' – perhaps it is, of necessity, feigned. It is perhaps all the more insidious (at least according to Nietzsche) as it aspires to hide this – the author's work is 'silent'. However, the consequence of this re-evaluation of history is that the artist, who creates fictions, becomes a historian as legitimate as the historiographer.

Thus it is not surprising that writers especially during the first half of the twentieth century (when Nietzsche's works were perhaps at their most influential) engage with the increasingly problematic concept of history, questioning its traditional narratives and substituting their own. In literature, both past and present are constructed imaginatively, rather than objectively as in linear positivistic historiography. "End fact. Try fiction" Ezra Pound writes in his poem "Near Perigord", which deals with the Provençal troubadours of the twelfth

---

2 A few examples are Verlyn Flieger's *A Question of Time*, or more recently Judith Klinger's "Hidden Paths of Time".
3 In some cases, historical agents and recorders were the same, such as Julius Caesar for example.

century (*Selected Poems* 60). This substituting of 'fiction' for 'fact' was felt to be particularly necessary in light of the cataclysmic events of the early twentieth century – the World Wars, the Irish Civil War, and the gradual breakdown of the British Empire. All these events made it abundantly clear that the Victorian idea of history as a tale of unstoppable progress could no longer be held valid.[4] Intellectuals and writers found themselves searching for new historical models, returning to ancient concepts such as history as eternal decline, or a cyclical view of history. Both of these models can be found in Tolkien's works. His legendarium constructs history as a series of cycles, ages of the world demarcated by repeated violent conflict, often between the same sides (the War of Wrath, the Fall of Númenor, the Last Alliance, the War of the Ring); at the same time, Middle-earth's inhabitants are subject to constant decline – the Elves and Men of the First Age are greater in power and strength than those of the Third, who have become "lesser" and "diminished" (*LotR* 1018, 1023).

In espousing these historical models, it might be argued that Tolkien and his contemporaries were simply seeking to substitute one 'grand narrative' of history (that of progress) with another (that of decline). However, when the texts themselves are examined closely, they reveal a more ambiguous position towards history, which appears in a variety of ways, and is often both affirmed and negated. For example, in T. S. Eliot's *Four Quartets* – one of the key works of the twentieth century dealing with time and history – Eliot talks of "The backward look behind the assurance / Of recorded history, the backward half-look / Over the shoulder, towards the primitive terror" ("The Dry Salvages", *Collected Poems* 209). History is necessary for making sense of the past; indeed it is a condition of existence, without which we would be the victims of "primitive terror". However, this existence comes at a price – that of knowingly living a falsehood: "The knowledge imposes a pattern, and falsifies, / For the pattern is new in every moment / And every moment is a new and shocking / Valuation of all we have been" ("East Coker", *Collected Poems* 199). History is simultaneously necessary

---

4 This had again already been expressed by Nietzsche: "Die Menschheit stellt nicht eine Entwicklung zum Besseren oder Stärkeren oder Höheren dar, in der Weise, wie dies heute geglaubt wird. Der 'Fortschritt' ist bloss eine moderne Idee, das heisst eine falsche Idee" (*Der Antichrist* 193). (Humanity does not represent progression towards something better or stronger or higher, the way it is believed today. 'Progress' is only a modern idea, that is a wrong idea.)

and impossible, or only possible as 'falsifying', as 'feigned'. As we shall see, it appears in a similarly ambiguous way in Tolkien's works.

A 'feigned history' for England

"End fact. Try fiction." A case might be made for taking this line of Pound's as a mission statement, not just for his circle of fellow modernists, but also for Tolkien and his tales of Middle-earth. In the Prologue to *The Lord of the Rings*, Tolkien hints at a connection between Middle-earth and our world;[5] indeed, Middle-earth is constructed as a kind of pre-history to our world, and more specifically, as a pre-history to modern England.

The fact that Tolkien's work is remarkable for its consistent Englishness has already been the focus of much critical attention.[6] This national bias is something that stands in contrast to, for example, his friend C. S. Lewis's fantasy, which is purposely more international or 'classical' in its references.[7] As is well known, with his legendarium of Middle-earth Tolkien wished to write a 'mythology for England', and in a long (and again well-known) letter he describes this in detail:

> I was from early days grieved by the poverty of my own beloved country: it had no stories of its own (bound up with its tongue and soil), not of the quality which I sought, and found (as an ingredient) in legends of other lands. [...] Do not laugh! But once upon a time (my crest has long since fallen) I had a mind to make a body of more or less connected legend, ranging from the large and cosmogonic, to the level of romantic fairy-story – the larger founded on the lesser in contact with the earth, the lesser drawing splendour from the vast backcloths – which I could dedicate simply to: to England; to my country. [...] I would draw some of the great tales in fullness, and leave many only placed in the scheme, and sketched. The cycles should be linked to a majestic whole, and yet leave scope for other minds and hands, wielding paint and music and drama. Absurd. (*L* 144-45)

---

5 "Even in ancient days, [the hobbits] were, as a rule, shy of 'the Big Folk', as they call *us*, and *now* they avoid us with dismay and are becoming hard to find" (*LotR* 1; emphasis added). Elsewhere Tolkien states, "Middle-earth is our world" (cit. Carpenter 98), and "Middle-earth is not an imaginary world" (*L* 239).
6 For example, Tom Shippey's *The Road to Middle-earth* or Jane Chance's *A Mythology for England*.
7 Lewis' work would of course not necessarily be 'English' as he is Irish, not English; the fact that his works seem to refuse a nationalist ideal could be seen as due to his displaced identity as an Ulsterman living in England.

Tolkien notes a dearth or lack of continuity in English legend and myth, and it is indeed the case that the English (in marked contrast to, for example, the Irish they occupied for centuries) have no distinct mythology of their own, the closest being the Arthurian 'Matter of Britain', which is however a mix of Celtic and Romance influence, besides being distinctly Christian in character.[8] This dearth is what Tolkien set out to correct, and can probably be ascribed to the repeated invasions of the island of Britain in early times, when one wave of invaders after another drove the previous inhabitants out, largely destroying their culture in the process. Thus, while the Celtic fringe of Britain persists in seeing the English as a Saxon race (still seen for example in the contemporary Gaelic term of 'Sassenach', Saxon, for an English person), the English even before the Norman Conquest were not a homogenous Germanic race in possession of their own mythology, but a mixture of Saxon, Celt, Norseman, and Roman.

Tolkien himself however appears to subscribe to the (not entirely accurate) view of Englishness as essentially Saxon, placing himself in a tradition of 'Saxonism' that begins in the 17th century with Milton's *History of Britain*.[9] Perhaps his Saxon ideal and insistence on Englishness, rather than Britishness, is also what makes the Arthurian myth problematic for Tolkien, as in it the Saxons are portrayed as enemy barbarians.[10] 1066 saw the complete destruction of the 'Saxon' culture and the imposition of a French Norman system of society and the French language. Tolkien himself saw the Battle of Hastings as one of the most tragic events in his country's history, the worst result of which in the eyes of Tolkien the philologist was the virtual extinction of Old English, which lost all status, becoming the language of the serfs, then gradually merging with French to become what we know today as Early Modern English. Tolkien's passion for Anglo-Saxon made

---

8 Tolkien was not the only one to think so. Forster writes in *Howards End*: "Why has England not a great mythology? Our folklore has never advanced beyond daintiness, and the greater melodies about our countryside have all been issued through the pipes of Greece. Deep and true as the native imagination can be, it seems to have failed here" (262).
9 The rise of Anglo-Saxon studies significantly also begins around this time. Thus it is also an academic tradition of 'Saxonism' that Tolkien places himself in. How indebted Tolkien's creation of Middle-earth is to his academic background in Old English philology in particular is described in detail in Shippey's *Road to Middle-earth*.
10 Conversely, this is the very fact that makes Arthurian legend ideal for appropriation by other writers such as the Welshman David Jones in his long work *In Parenthesis*.

him ever suspicious of French, the language that had displaced and (as he felt) deformed the tongue he felt to be inherently his own.[11]

When Tolkien went about creating his mythology, he consciously made use of those fragments of Anglo-Saxon that had survived the Norman Conquest and into his own day, building them into his subcreation and weaving them into his own ideas. For example, the very first inspiration of what was to become *The Silmarillion* was an Old English poem from the *Exeter Book*, which runs

> Eala earendel,   engla beorhtast,
> ofer middangeard   monnum sended

This means "Oh, Earendel, brightest of angels, sent to men above Middle-earth [...]" (both poem and translation are taken from Shippey, *Road* 218). And thus the germ of the myth of Eärendil the Mariner, whose star (the Silmaril) rose over Middle-earth as a sign of hope to Men and Elves at the end of the First Age, was sown. The Rohirrim, the race of men in *The Lord of the Rings* who are basically Anglo-Saxons on horses,[12] are inspired both by the Anglo-Saxon language (they speak a lost form of Old English, Mercian) and by the pre-Norman images of horses cut into southwest England's chalky soil, one of which is close to Oxford and which Tolkien doubtlessly saw often. The Old English epic *Beowulf* also plays a significant role in imagining the Riddermark (as the Rohirrim call their land in their own language); at one point it is even quoted directly (although in translation) when Legolas describes the Golden Hall of Meduseld: "The light of it shines far over the land" (*LotR* 496).[13] It is also of note how the expressly English or Anglo-Saxon nature of Tolkien's sub-creation is reflected in his choice of language; for example, the simple name 'Bag End', the dwelling-place of the Baggins family, is at the dead end of a road that would in conventional English be called a 'cul-de-sac' – a French term (although not used in France!) of which 'Bag End' is a literal translation – and in Tom Shippey's eyes is "a defiantly English reaction" (*Road* 66). The Baggins's nasty relatives, the Sackville-Bagginses, have by contrast "severed their connection with Bag End by calling it cul-de-sac(k)

---

11 Humphrey Carpenter describes the passionate personal feelings Tolkien had for Anglo-Saxon in his *J.R.R. Tolkien. A Biography*, esp. in the chapter "He had been inside language", 136-46.
12 See Honegger, who provides the most recent discussion of the Rohirrim's Anglo-Saxon roots.
13 These examples are all taken from Shippey, *Road* 111-13.

and tagging on the French suffix -ville!" (Shippey, *Road* 66). Amusing as this particular instance of insistent Englishness may seem, Tolkien was serious about keeping French influence to a minimum in his works.[14]

Through its use of actual historic sources, Tolkien's Middle-earth is clearly related to the England it wishes to provide a mythology for. But the deliberate avoidance of any post-Conquest material and language reveals that Tolkien's endeavour to create a specially 'English' mythology represents an attempt to write foreign (i.e. Norman) invasion out of his country's history. It attempts to establish a specifically 'English' identity that equates Englishness with the Anglo-Saxon culture and language, dismissing any Norman and French influence.

At this point we must return briefly to the question of the relationship between history and mythology in Tolkien's work. Myth usually is conceived of as ahistorical (cf. Emig 90); thus it is interesting that Tolkien, in trying to create a mythology, uses concrete historical fragments that can be linked to a specific period of England's history. The rags of time, one might say, are being used to overcome time. Perhaps it is this fact that lies behind his statement from *On Fairy-Stories*: "History often resembles 'Myth', because they are both ultimately of the same stuff" (*OFS* 127). In this essay, Tolkien seems to see history as the precondition for myth;[15] this would then tie into the fact that (parts of) England's history become (parts of) Tolkien's mythology.

However, if Tolkien's *œuvre* as a whole is taken to constitute his mythology for England (which the present essay assumes), it must be pointed out that this mythology is itself inherently historical, forming a history of Middle-earth, and not an ahistorical cycle of related tales in the way, for example, of the

---

14 The question of Celtic influence is another one. The Elves seem to evince many traits characteristically (if not necessarily correctly) ascribed to the Celts, and Tolkien's Sindarin is modelled on Welsh. For more on this and Tolkien's own contradictory position on Celticism, cf. Marjorie Burns, *Perilous Realms: Celtic and Norse in Tolkien's Middle-earth* and and Dimitra Fimi, *Tolkien, Race and Cultural History*. However, Tolkien did not use actual Celtic fragments or quotations to create his world the way he does with Anglo-Saxon.

15 He states that "If indeed Ingeld and Freawaru never lived, or at least never loved, then it is ultimately from nameless man and woman that they get their tale" (*OFS* 127) – before again complicating matters by adding "or rather into whose tale they have entered".

Norse *Edda*.[16] This, I believe, is again due to the fact that he is using historical fragments and bears out the hypothesis that he is, in effect, rewriting history as well as (or perhaps rather than) providing a mythology.

History and postcolonialism

In their attempt to write the Norman Conquest out of their version of Englishness, Tolkien's works perhaps can be seen, strangely enough, as a postcolonial literature written 900 years after colonisation. Now 'postcolonialism' is a hotly contested term, and perhaps a short explanation of what is meant by it here is in order. In its most common usage, the term 'postcolonial' applies to former colonies of European countries and is taken to refer historically to the time following their independence upon the collapse of European imperialism, and ideologically to a stance that is anti-colonial and questions the dominance of Western thought and its imposition upon other cultures. It is thus controversial to refer to imperial states such as Great Britain as postcolonial, and it should be stated that the present study uses the term in a broader sense as suggested by Peter Hulme, who writes: "If 'postcolonial' is a useful word, then it refers to a process of disengagement from the whole colonial syndrome, which takes many forms and is probably inescapable for all those whose worlds have been marked by that set of phenomena." Hulme also points out that "a country can be postcolonial and colonizing at the same time" (120-22). In this sense, the term becomes meaningful for the present study and can be used to describe features of Tolkien's works, which have hitherto more often than not been seen as evincing typically imperialist values.[17]

Tolkien's insistent Englishness and also his work's connection to (post)colonialism can be seen within historical context of the preliminary dissolution of the British Empire following the World Wars. Far from this being universally perceived as

---

16 One can naturally also distinguish between 'ahistorical' or mythic locations and characters and historical, temporal ones *within* Middle-earth and Tolkien's narrative; examples of timeless mythic places might be Lórien the "timeless land" (*LotR* 342) or Valinor, and characters of such great antiquity they appear mythical (such as Elrond and Galadriel); even the Fellowship appear like figures out of legend to the Rohirrim (cf. *LotR* 423). However, this has already been analysed by many critics (e.g. Flieger) and is not the focus of the present essay.
17 Elizabeth Massa Hoiem discusses this with reference to other studies in her article "World Creation as Colonization".

a dramatic decline, Jed Esty notes that "English intellectuals translated the end of empire into a resurgent concept of national culture," and that some "canonical English writers [...] measured the passing of British hegemony not solely in terms of vitiated imperial humanism but also in terms of a recovered cultural particularity, that is, at least potentially, the basis for both social and aesthetic renewal" (2, 3). Among the writers cited by Esty are T. S. Eliot, Virginia Woolf, and E. M. Forster, but also Tolkien himself. The insistence that can be traced in their works on a specifically English culture, as opposed to the diversity of imperial Britishness, becomes increasingly important as that diversity breaks up. This insistence on Englishness does not necessarily mean that their writings become provincial and narrowed down; their aim is to "implicitly reinscribe universalism into the language of English particularism [...] so that Englishness represents not just a type, but the very archetype" (Esty 14).

T. S. Eliot for example cites Yeats as his model, noting that "in becoming more Irish [...] he became more universal" ("Yeats", *Selected Prose* 252). Esty points out that in doing this, "Eliot and his London contemporaries were beginning to borrow the logic of cultural nationalism back from the colonies" (14).[18] In this way, English nationalism can be interpreted as a postcolonial syndrome. Postcolonial cultural nationalism, as in for example the case of Yeats, searches for a unified and integrated national culture and identity; accordingly, the "metaphor of lost totality" (Esty 7) that characterises imperial literature might be overcome in a postimperial England, and "the end of empire might be taken to augur a basic repair or reintegration of English culture itself" (7). Interesting for us is the fact that it was seen as the responsibility of the writers to (re)create this 'Englishness'; it is they who want to author a new English identity.

Tolkien fits perfectly into Esty's reading of late modernism and resurgent nationalism in postimperial England. As seen above, his work can in a way be seen as postcolonial, if postcolonial in a peculiar form. His letters reveal a dislike and indeed condemnation of imperialism, a fear of cosmopolitan-

---

18 This universality of the particular is also taken up by Patrick Kavanagh, who writes: "The parochial mentality [...] is never in any doubt about social and artistic validity of his parish. All great civilizations are based on parochialism – Greek, Israelite, English. Parochialism is universal; it deals with fundamentals" (cit. in *The Contemporary Book of Irish Poetry* xviii). It is interesting that Kavanagh lists English parochialism here as a model for the Irish to follow, and not the other way round, as Eliot does.

ism (particularly in the guise of Americanization), and a self-declared love of England, rather than (modern) Britain.[19] His insistent 'Englishness' is perhaps all the more emphatic because he was himself at least partly a colonial subject, born in South Africa, and carrying a name of German origin.[20] Patrick Curry cites Tolkien as calling his move to England "a double coming home [...] with the memory of something different – hot, dry and barren – and it intensified my love of my own countryside. [...] I loved it with an intensity of love that was a kind of nostalgia reversed" (cit. Curry 60). (It speaks for the strength of Tolkien's conviction that England was his home that Curry states that Tolkien *returned* to England, when he had never been there before.)

Tolkien's works, particularly *The Hobbit* and *The Lord of the Rings*, can be seen as partaking in "a national pastoral fantasy" (Curry 37) that takes the Shire as its starting and its end point – the Shire that is, in Tolkien's own words, "based on rural England" (*L* 250). Interestingly, it was only when he conceived of the Shire and used the hobbits as protagonists that Tolkien found himself able to write a coherent narrative about Middle-earth. One might say that this specifically English and thus nationally coherent space of the Shire is the necessary precondition for narrative coherence. Tolkien's masterpiece, *The Lord of the Rings*, which forms the greater part of his mythology for England, also puts Englishness at the heart of its created world. Indeed, as Esty notes, with the Shire Tolkien manages to simultaneously "reenchant England and recover its ordinariness" (122). Virginia Luling claims that Tolkien's focus on England as "not a conquering but a conquered nation" (53) places Middle-earth, England's fantastic twin, close to the "'fourth world' of indigenous minorities" (53); however, one could develop this argument further by observing that this focus on a pre-industrial, pre-imperial England is also a way of effectively whitewashing it of the guilt of British colonial exploitation.

Thus Tolkien's work can indeed be read as partaking in "a process of disengagement from the whole colonial syndrome" (Hulme 120), as it rejects a past both

---

19 For example, "I do find this Americo-cosmopolitanism very terrifying. [...] For I love England (not Great Britain and certainly not the British Commonwealth (grr!)" (*L* 65); or, "I know nothing about British or American imperialism in the Far East that does not fill me with regret and disgust" (*L* 115).
20 Marjorie Burns writes: "His father's family was not purely English, and Tolkien would have preferred to be English irrefutably, to be English to the core" (8). She also states that because of Tolkien's Catholicism he might have been made to feel un-English (8).

of colonisation (the Norman Conquest) and of imperialism (the British Empire). He both attempts to construct an alternate history for England, one in which foreign invasion and the ensuing fragmentation of culture and language never took place, and contributes to a typically 'English' identity, providing a desirable alternative to the 'Britishness' that increasingly lost credibility after the collapse of the British Empire. Similar endeavours can be observed in the writings of for example Yeats, who wished to construct a nationalist Irish identity, free of British oppression, and does so in his works by seeking to return to a time in Irish history that pre-dates British/English occupation. It becomes the task of the postcolonial poet and writer to re-imagine and re-write their country's history: "End fact. Try fiction."

Cycles of ruin

For all this, it must remain doubtful whether this vision of a unified English culture and mythology is actually achieved in Tolkien's works. The vision of the past given in *The Lord of the Rings* is not one of a continuous history, but one where noble lines are broken, heirlooms are lost, and ancient citadels and fortresses are destroyed or fall into ruin. Thus the Elves have dwindled until only four of their dwelling-places remain: Rivendell, Lórien, Mirkwood and the Grey Havens; and this last is only really a place of departure. While these places and indeed the Elves encountered in the narrative have their importance as points where the action is slowed down and the motivations behind it are made clear (as in the Council of Elrond and the Mirror-gazing in Lórien), it is actually Elvish *relics* that take on a vital role in the narrative, such as the Elvish swords from the lost kingdom of Gondolin, Gandalf's Glamdring and Bilbo and later Frodo's Sting.

Similarly, the line of the Kings of Gondor, the South Kingdom of the Númenóreans, is broken when their King Eärnur falls in Minas Morgul (cf. *LotR* 1062), while although in the North Kingdom of Arnor the line is kept intact, the kingdom itself is lost and the heirs of Númenor become Rangers of the wild. It is of course significant that the heirloom of these Kings is a broken sword. The great realm of the Dwarves, Moria, is destroyed by the Balrog and the lesser one in Erebor by the dragon Smaug (in a similar fashion, too: both evil powers are fire-monsters). While the latter realm is eventually re-established, an attempt to recolonise Moria ends in a repetition of its first downfall.

While travelling across Middle-earth, the Fellowship of the Ring repeatedly encounters the remains and ruins of these past kingdoms: first of all, the hobbits traverse the Barrow-downs, the graves of the old Kings and Queens of Arnor, then encounter what used to be the "great watch-tower [called] Amon Sûl" upon Weathertop (*LotR* 181); after an interlude in Rivendell, the Fellowship passes through Hollin, where Elves used to dwell. Now, however, the only trace of the Elves is the stones they carved; as Legolas says, "the trees and the grass do not remember them. Only I hear the stones lament them: deep they delved us, fair they wrought us, high they builded us; but they are gone" (*LotR* 276). The companions then pass through the ruined Dwarf kingdom of Moria, and finally cross into Gondor, the border marked by two ancient statues of Isildur and Anárion and the hills of Amon Hen and Amon Lhaw, upon which there used to be "high seats [...] and watch was kept" (*LotR* 384). The journeys of the Fellowship are thus almost like an archaeological trip, cataloguing the ancient ruins of Middle-earth's history.

Significantly, each of these sites of ruin becomes a place of threat or danger: the hobbits are trapped in the Downs by the Barrow-wight, the Nazgûl attack Aragorn and the hobbits on Amon Sûl, in Hollin flocks of black crows and a mysterious flying shadow "moving fast [...] and not with the wind" (*LotR* 279) disturb the travellers, in Moria they re-encounter "Durin's Bane" the Balrog and lose their leader Gandalf, and finally the Fellowship is attacked and breaks up on Amon Hen. History is not only ruinous; it seems to possess a malevolent power that dooms those passing through its ruins to re-enact the destruction that laid them waste in the first place. In some cases this is almost a literal repetition of the initial disaster: for example, Amon Sûl was destroyed by the Witch-King of Angmar (cf. *LotR* 1060), who becomes the Lord of the Nazgûl and leads the attack upon Weathertop in which Frodo is wounded. Even more striking is the episode in Moria. In Moria's Chamber of Records the Fellowship discover a book that, although partly slashed and stained and thus rendered illegible, tells them the fate of the Dwarves that lived there:

> 'It is grim reading,' [Gandalf] said. 'I fear their end was cruel. Listen! *We cannot get out. We cannot get out. They have taken the Bridge and second hall. Frár and Lóni and Náli fell there.* Then there are four lines smeared so that I can only read *went 5 days ago.* The last lines run *the pool is up to the wall at Westgate. The Watcher in the Water took Óin. We cannot get out. The end comes, and then drums, drums in the deep.* I wonder what that means. The last thing written is in a trailing scrawl of elf-letters: they are coming. There is nothing more.' (*LotR* 314)

It may seem strange that a Dwarf should have made a record of his colony and kept it, very practically for the Fellowship, up till the moment he died (though maybe not so strange if one gives credit to Tolkien's statement that he wrote parts of his mythology "down in dugouts under shell fire"; *L* 78). However, it is important for the novel not just because it fills in information; it sets the scene for a repetition of that very tragedy:

> Gandalf had hardly spoken these words, when there came a great noise: a rolling *Boom* that seemed to come from the depths far below, and to tremble in the stone at their feet. They sprang towards the door in alarm. *Doom, doom* it rolled again, as if huge hands were turning the very caverns of Moria into a vast drum. [...] 'They are coming!' cried Legolas. 'We cannot get out,' said Gimli. 'Trapped!' cried Gandalf. 'Why did I delay? Here we are, caught, just as they were before.' (*LotR* 315)

It is not just by chance that Legolas and Gimli repeat the sentences they have just heard Gandalf read out. Thus we can see that in Middle-earth history becomes the perpetuation of violence.

Of course, one can argue that with the reestablishment of Gondor and Arnor and the return of the King (and the symbolic reforging of the sword), this pessimistic view of history is proved wrong and a new order is set up. Similarly, the Shire, threatened with industrialisation and modernisation, is saved and its rural order preserved. This seeming restoration is however undermined by the fact that it can no longer satisfy the very ones who laboured to bring it about – Frodo departs from Middle- earth, and as we hear in the Appendices, so does Sam (cf. *LotR* 1072). "The Tale of Aragorn and Arwen", also found in the Appendices, casts a note of gloom even upon Aragorn's success, for he, as all mortals, must die, and Arwen ends her days alone in abandoned Lórien, to be "utterly forgotten" after her death (*LotR* 1038). The hope that with the end of the Third Age, wholeness and unity is established, is actually belied by the very form of *The Lord of the Rings*, which, although it contains a long coherent narrative, is actually in its entirety made up of (supposedly historical) fragments. Of all Middle-earth's rich and varied history, all that remains are these fragments, embodying in their incomplete state the "loss and the silence" (*LotR* 1037) that is thematised repeatedly in Tolkien's tales.

Thus we can see that Middle-earth, the mythological England, actually repeats England's loss of a unified cultural heritage instead of reestablishing it. It is founded on the fragments that survived the Norman Conquest, but instead of truly erasing that part of English history as it sets out to do, Tolkien's sub-creation repeats the history of destruction and fragmentation. Within the narrative of *The Lord of the Rings*, the weight of history unavoidably results in destruction, and this is paralleled in the novel's structure, which, instead of creating a coherent new whole, reproduces the fragmentary form of the culture that inspired it. The forces of history cannot be denied.

Tolkien's attempt to rewrite his nation's history to produce a unified English national culture based on a newly created mythology thus ultimately ends by acknowledging the impossibility of doing so. The attempt to contain the forces of history within a constructed mythology results in failure when that construct is harnessed to a nationalist agenda. Tolkien's 'mythology for England', based upon an Anglo-Saxon concept of Englishness, wishes to contribute to a nationalist English culture, but repeats the inherent fragmentation that makes a unified Englishness of the kind he desires impossible, and the picture given of history is thus one of discontinuity and rupture.

The 'silent work of the dramatist'

The ambiguous relationship to history that manifests itself in Tolkien's works is reflected in their ambiguous positioning of the author. On the one hand, the grand claim that the writer is able to create a new mythology and thus, a new history for his country places the author in a position of absolute power; on the other hand, we have seen that the forces of history are not so easily purged from the work of art that tries to deny them, undermining this claim of authority.

Thus the author's position is uneasy, hanging in between (re)creating history and (re)recording it.

In his study *Secondary Worlds*, W. H. Auden distinguishes between the two fundamental desires of the historian and the poet respectively: the historian "desire[s] to know the truth about the primary world", whereas the poet "desire[s] to make new secondary worlds or share in secondary worlds created by others" (48). Tolkien would appear to be torn between these two positions; his works create a new secondary world, yet this creation is inspired by the primary world and its history. If the postcolonial project is about challenging established history and offering alternative readings of it, then Tolkien's works offer us such an alternative through which we can discern an alternate 'truth' about the primary world. And if, as Auden claims, "the primary world is untidy, only capable, as James said, of splendid waste" (57), then perhaps Tolkien's literary efforts can be seen as trying to tidy up the primary world, almost (to stay within the semantic field) as trying to recycle its 'splendid waste'. He thus is both a historian *and* a poet.[21]

Accordingly, within *The Lord of the Rings* the figures of author (or poet, in Auden's terminology) and historian are frequently fused, and their importance is subtly highlighted by the very form of the text, which appears to be both a new creation and a recorded account of the events of the War of the Ring. This would appear to lend itself to the claim that the artist is an authentic historiographer, perhaps the most authentic. Although this has hitherto not been recognised in criticism, perhaps the most significant role the hobbits take on is that of recorders of history and song. As historians, they write down their own versions of the end of the Third Age, and they note down Elvish songs and translate them besides writing down songs of their own creation. Despite the wealth of beautifully crafted manuscripts on display in Rivendell in Peter Jackson's film version of Tolkien's novel, it is never mentioned anywhere in the actual text that the Elves write down their tales and songs – they require the

---

21 Auden does concede that – as Nietzsche had made eminently clear – even "the most rigorous Historian cannot entirely dispense with the poet. In the first place, any history is already a secondary world in that it can only be written or told in words, and the only elements in the primary world which language can reproduce are the words that people speak there" (50). He also points out the criterion of selection that determines history.

hobbits to do this for them.²² And if we hear of some manuscripts of Men (such as Isildur's parchment where he writes of the finding of the Ring), it is also made clear that Aragorn has his own copies made of the hobbits' Red Book, their account of the War of the Ring, showing the high value placed upon the hobbits' historical accounts.

The Red Book takes on particular significance: Bilbo leaves it to Frodo, and he in turn leaves it to Sam to complete: "I have quite finished, Sam. [...] The last pages are for you" (*LotR* 1004). While the Baggins family disappears from Middle-earth at the end of the novel, they leave behind their Book which makes sure that their legacy endures even though they themselves have gone, acting as a kind of *Ersatz* child. As Frodo says to Sam: "But you are my heir: all that I had and might have had I leave to you. [...] you will read from the Red Book, and keep alive the memory of the age that is gone" (*LotR* 1006). This the Red Book does: it endures into our own time, eventually becoming *The Lord of the Rings* itself – for that is what the novel represents, a modern-day edition of the Red Book, and all that remains of (pre)historical Middle-earth in our day and age. Within the book, the position of the poet-historian seems secure, and the fact that their works endure appears as their ultimate validation.

However, as we have seen, these works do not survive in their entirety, enduring merely as fragments that testify to the ruins of history rather than to a continuous, smooth transmission. And when we regard the text(s) from the outside, it becomes clear that Middle-earth's history never appears overtly as 'authored': instead, it seeks to derive its authority from impersonality, thus referring to the traditional ideal that history should be objective and unbiased. Looking at the form of *The Lord of the Rings*, we can see that it appears as a collection of fragments surrounding a longer, coherent narrative. Both narrative and fragments are presented as a kind of critical edition of 'historical' documents by an 'editor', thus creating a polyvocal text supposedly written by several different people, some known (Bilbo, Frodo, Sam) and some unknown, and commented upon by an unidentified editor. The picture is thus that history is not authored by

---

22 This can be seen as relating to the point made earlier about how coherence is given through 'Englishness' in the Shire and that this can be seen as contributing to the overall coherence of the narrative. One might see the hobbits, through their self-appointed task of historical documentation, as providing a frame that gives historical coherence to the mythological subject-matter (many thanks to Judith Klinger for pointing this out to me).

any one person; authorship itself becomes something multilayered rather than monadic, reflecting perhaps a mediaeval concept of the author more suited to the text's pseudo-mediaeval material. This would appear to undermine the claim to authority posited by the fact that an author can indeed write history. However, it also means that the material presented in *The Lord of the Rings* gains authenticity, as it appears to be 'history' in the traditional sense of being impersonal and unbiased, gaining the sanction of an academic treatment, and thus subtly strengthening the position of its author. In this way the text's true author is concealed; he becomes invisible behind the masks of the many other authors and the editor, and his work truly becomes 'silent' as Nietzsche claims, his voice concealed behind the many other supposedly historical and academic voices in the text.

Thus the whole notion of authoring history as it appears in *The Lord of the Rings* becomes fraught and full of tension: the text hangs somewhere between asserting its authority as a history for England, and evincing the failure of that endeavour. *The Lord of the Rings* both pretends to record history and, by virtue of its detachment from the primary world, stand outside it. However, if the book were to stand fully outside time it could have no subject-matter: there is no history in undying Valinor, and no need for historians. Its position thus truly is that of 'feigned history'.

Conclusion

We have seen how ambiguous the picture of authorship given in the *The Lord of the Rings* is in regard to its 'feigned history', and how that feigned history can be interpreted as a postcolonial endeavour that ultimately fails. Perhaps one cannot rewrite that which has come to pass, write that which the passage of time has made impossible: a return to a time before colonial conquest. In contemporary postcolonial literature and criticism, it is generally accepted that the colonial experience must be acknowledged in order for its trauma to be dealt with; as Chinua Achebe writes, "The storyteller creates the memory that the survivors must have – otherwise their surviving would have no meaning" (cit. Gikandi 10). A literature that tries to wipe the mind blank, destroy memory rather than create it – even with the best of intentions – must be seen as escapist in a truly negative sense. In this particular regard, despite claims to the contrary by his defenders, the aim of Tolkien's work *is* escapist: it tries to negate part of England's history (essentially from 1066 till the end of the British Empire),[23] but thus falls into the trap of repeating history and reproducing its structures instead of moving on. For ultimately, there can be no Escape: "A people without history / Is not redeemed from time" (Eliot "Little Gidding", *Collected Poems* 222).

Works cited

Auden, W. H. *Secondary Worlds*. New York: Random House, 1968.

Burns, Marjorie. *Perilous Realms: Celtic and Norse in Tolkien's Middle-earth*. Toronto: University of Toronto Press, 2005.

Carpenter, Humphrey. *J. R. R. Tolkien: A Biography*. London: HarperCollins, 1977.

Chance, Jane. *Tolkien's Art: A Mythology for England*. London: Macmillan, 1979.

Curry, Patrick. *Defending Middle-earth*. London: HarperCollins, 1997.

Eliot, T. S. *Collected Poems* 1909–1962. London: Faber, 1963.

---. *Selected Prose of T. S. Eliot*. Ed. Frank Kermode. London: Faber, 1975.

Emig, Rainer. *Modernism in Poetry*. London: Longman, 1995.

Esty, Jed. *A Shrinking Island: Modernism and National Culture in England*. Princeton: Princeton University Press, 2005.

Fallon, Peter and Derek Mahon, eds. *The Penguin Book of Contemporary Irish Poetry*. London: Penguin, 1990.

Fimi, Dimitra. *Tolkien, Race and Cultural History: From Fairies to Hobbits*. Basingstoke: Palgrave Macmillan, 2008.

Flieger, Verlyn. *A Question of Time: J. R. R. Tolkien's Road to Faërie*. Kent, OH: Kent State University Press, 1997.

Friedman, Barton. "Fabricating History: Narrative Strategy in *The Lord of the Rings*." *Clio* 2 (1973): 123-144.

Forster, E. M. *Howards End*. London: Penguin, 1989.

---

23 By this I do not mean that he wanted to get rid of history altogether (although there are certain parts of his writing that do betray a desire to escape from time), and this essay has shown that many of his works can be seen as entering into dialogue with history. But he definitely wishes to erase the historical phenomena of the Norman Conquest and British imperialism from his version of Englishness.

Gikandi, Simon. *Reading Chinua Achebe: Language and Ideology in Fiction.* Portsmouth, NH: Heinemann, 1991.

Hoiem, Elizabeth Massa. "World Creation as Colonization: British Imperialism in 'Aldarion and Erendis'." *Tolkien Studies* 2 (2005): 75-92.

Honegger, Thomas. "The Rohirrim: 'Anglo-Saxons on Horseback?' An Inquiry into Tolkien's Use of Sources." *Tolkien and the Study of His Sources. Critical Essays.* Ed. Jason Fisher. Jefferson NC and London: McFarland, 2011. 116-132.

Hulme, Peter. "Including America." *ARIEL* 26.1 (January 1995): 117-123.

Jones, David. *In Parenthesis.* London: Faber, 1963.

Joyce, James. *Ulysses.* London: Penguin, 1939.

Klinger, Judith. "Hidden Paths of Time: March 13th and the Riddles of Shelob's Lair." *Tolkien and Modernity.* Vol. 2. Ed. Thomas Honegger and Frank Weinreich. Zollikofen: Walking Tree, 2006. 143-210.

Luling, Virginia. "An Anthropologist in Middle-earth." *Proceedings of the J. R. R. Tolkien Centenary Conference.* Ed. Patricia Reynolds and Glen H. Goodknight. Milton Keynes: Tolkien Society, 1995. 53-57.

Nietzsche, Friedrich. *Vom Nutzen und Nachteil der Historie für das Leben.* 1874. Basel: Diogenes, 1984.

---. *Götzendämmerung. Der Antichrist.* Stuttgart: Kröner, 1964.

Pound, Ezra. *Selected Poems.* London: Faber, 1975.

Shippey, Tom. *The Road to Middle-earth.* London: HarperCollins, 1992.

---. *J. R. R. Tolkien: Author of the Century.* London: HarperCollins, 2000.

Tolkien, J. R. R. "On Fairy-Stories." *The Monsters and the Critics and Other Essays.* London: HarperCollins, 1990. 109-161.

---. *The Letters of J. R. R. Tolkien.* Ed. Humphrey Carpenter. London: George Allen & Unwin, 1981.

---. *The Lord of the Rings.* (3 volume edition). London: HarperCollins, 1997.

About the author

MARGARET HILEY studied at the Universities of Regensburg and Glasgow, specialising in fantasy, science fiction and literary modernism. She has taught, lectured and published on these topics both in the UK and abroad. Since 2007 she has taught at the University Centre Peterborough, where she also coordinated the degree programmes in the Arts and Sciences before establishing a new career as an academic and literary translator. Please visit her website at www.margarethiley.com for more information!.

Patrick A. Brückner

One Author to Rule Them All

Abstract

Contemporary writing on Tolkien – especially in the aftermath of Tom Shippey's *J.R.R. Tolkien: Author of the Century* – often focuses on the perceived 'modernity' of his texts. Yet before the 'author' Tolkien can be employed to access his œuvre, the author has to be constructed by drawing on Tolkien's biography. This author figure then functions to explain (or explain away) apparent anachronisms and incoherencies that scholars routinely encounter in Tolkien's writings. The key words 'Catholicism', 'post-war-writer', 'trauma' and 'coming-of-age-novel' figure prominently in biographically oriented readings of his works (especially of the *The Lord of the Rings*). The essay shows that constructing Tolkien as a modern author – and, consequently, reading *The Lord of the Rings* as a modern text – generates additional problems with anachronisms instead of solving them. I therefore aim to counter the most common critical strategy in current Tolkien research. Instead of harmonising textual incoherencies, by focusing exclusively on the 'author' Tolkien, my argument hinges on the alterity of Tolkien's œuvre and discusses *The Lord of the Rings* as an exemplary work. Based on Tolkien's own reasoning in *On Fairy-Stories*, it can be demonstrated that the frequently cited medieval sources should not be read as underwriting a notion of original authorship but as an instance of the writer's commitment to epic traditions.

> But the true secret of being a hero
> lies in knowing the order of things.
> (Peter S. Beagle, *The Last Unicorn*)

1. Tolkien – An author of the twentieth century?

J. R. R. Tolkien spent most of his life in the 20th century – that is a fact. One cannot deny that he was also British, a soldier in the First World War, an Oxford don, a husband, a father, and a Catholic (cf. Carpenter). Even less disputable is the fact that Tolkien authored *The Hobbit*, *The Lord of the Rings*, *The Silmarillion*,[1] and a host of other fictional and non-fictional texts.

It is only the last statement that lends relevance outside the private realm to the facts mentioned above. J. R. R. Tolkien was an author – therefore any information about his personal life may be used as an interpretive tool to better understand his work (or rather his works). Consequently, the readings that hark back to Tolkien's biography (and let us not forget the attempts to construct a coherent 'œuvre') are legion. Let me mention but a few: "Tolkien was also a deeply moral and a devoutly religious man" (Burns 163). "It [*The Lord of the Rings*] is, nevertheless, to some extent a product not of World War II, but of the six months during which Tolkien fought with the 11th Lancashire Fusiliers during World War I" (Hooker 125). "The story of Beren and Lúthien remained deeply personal to Tolkien till he died: he had the names 'Beren' and 'Lúthien' carved on his and his wife's shared tombstone, a striking identification" (Shippey, *Author* 247). All of these readings take their cue from known facts about Tolkien's life. Thus far, so good.

It is a truism that a text without an author is not thinkable – at least for a modern audience (cf. Lauer 164).[2] In addition, it also seems a given that whatever is known about the author delineates the scope of what can be gleaned from interpreting the text: a sensible approach, if one subscribes to Foucault's observation that "the author explains the presence of certain events within a text, as well as their transformations, distortions, and their various modifications (and this through an author's biography or by reference to his particular point of view, in the analysis of his social preferences and his position within a class or by delineating his fundamental objectives)" (Foucault, "Author" 128).

At first glance, these remarks seem to provide the ultimate vindication for biography-based readings. Foucault, however, also points out that this approach

---

1 It must be pointed out, however, that Tolkien's authorship of *The Silmarillion* is – to say the least – a lot less clear-cut as it is a posthumous work. The textual corpus was produced and edited by Christopher Tolkien to a significant degree, so that questions about the texts' origin are difficult to answer. I will leave it at that for the moment (even though this problem is of sufficient relevance to justify an essay of its own), since literary criticism seems to be in agreement that it is indeed Tolkien who authored these texts.
2 Original quote: "Wir können nicht anders, als uns zu einem Text auch einen Autor hinzuzudenken." All quotes in languages other than English were translated by Siobhán Groitl.

depends on an author constructed by the reader or another interpreting entity (cf. Foucault, "Author" 127). Because Tolkien, the author, and his readers lived in the 20th century, the discourses that play out in his texts have thus often been located in the 20th century as well.[3]

It is indeed conspicuous that the biography-based readings mentioned above all rest on discourses that became normative only with Modernity. In times of war, men strike up friendships that must differ fundamentally from the relationship of a man and a woman, defined as love. The fact that Tolkien fought in a war is invoked again and again to explain the relationship between Frodo and Sam: they are 'friends' (and 'friends' only). Tolkien was a Catholic: therefore even a text invoking a world without gods or religious practice (*The Lord of the Rings*) must yield elements that support a Catholic or, at the very least, a Christian reading. Such an approach is most strikingly illustrated by Martin Meyer's reading that describes Sam (and, of course, Frodo) in Christian terms as meek, humble, and *sündenfrei* ('free of sin'; cf. 275, 281) without providing evidence or further argument. In Meyer's view, Tolkien's Catholic faith apparently lends sufficient plausibility to this observation. That Tolkien was a married man is furthermore fundamental to constructing a strictly heteronormative world view within his texts. The male/female relationship alone qualifies as 'love' – the privileged, sole locus where sexuality may be experienced – and is thereby distinguished from the friendship between males, even though the text (*The Lord of the Rings*) does not touch on the issue of sexuality at all.[4] As a consequence, Arwen and Aragorn have to be perceived as romantic lovers. These are but a few examples of readings based solely on Tolkien's life.

Which discourses are advanced by these readings? The discourses that may be identified within the text? The discourses proffered by Tolkien the author?

---

3 This statement should not be read as a dismissal of discourse analyses. If they are to be useful, however, the mechanisms underlying the construction of the author function must be questioned, and the discourses on which readings are based must be sufficiently and rigorously historicized.

4 It is hardly a coincidence that all three examples of biographism mentioned above add up to one coherent argument concerning the main pair of protagonists: Sam and Frodo are a product of Tolkien's war-experiences, representing a variation of an assumed (itself already constructed) friendship bond between an officer and his batman. A relationship other than friendship is inconceivable, for this would constitute a sin and – as we all know – Tolkien was a Catholic and a happily married one on top of that. (While individual readings of this kind may be more elaborate, that is their reasoning in a nutshell.) At the centre of this argument, one of the major pervasive discourses of Modernity can be located: the discourse of heteronormative sexuality (cf. Foucault, *History*).

Or an author's discourses constructed by readers (hence originating from their discourses and world view)? Tom Shippey states: "I believe that it is our ability to read metaphorically which has made Tolkien's stories directly relevant to the twentieth century. We do not expect to meet Ringwraiths, but 'wraithing' is a genuine danger; we do not expect to meet dragons, but the 'dragonsickness' is perfectly common" (*Author* 328).

One could argue that the ability to read 'metaphors' is directly related to the Foucaultian concept of an author constructed by a reader.[5] 'Metaphorical reading', in this context, designates an approach that draws on discourses outside the text in order to interpret it. More specifically, the reader's knowledge of personal and socio-cultural circumstances that define the 'writer' (who seems entirely real, once the reader has assembled the information into a coherent construction) becomes the primary instrument of interpretation. In the case of a modern author like Tolkien, such an approach is facilitated by the assumption that reader and author share an identical experience of the world. Against this backdrop of a common world view, all occurrences within the text become explicable with recourse to events within the 'real' life of the 'writer'. As keys that unlock textual meanings, the discourses found within the text are replaced by the reader's knowledge about the author. Yet it is generally overlooked that this perception of the author is generated by the reader. Any facts within the text that lack an equivalent within the reader's reality will therefore – as Shippey demonstrates – be construed as 'metaphors' for entities in the reader's world. However, the question remains how close such a 'metaphorical reading' can get to the discourses within the text and their historical specificity.

It is a platitude to state that in the Middle High German epic *arbeit* does not connote the same as the modern German *Arbeit* (work), the meaning of *êre* differs from *Ehre* (honour), and an *âventiure* is not an *Abenteuer* (adventure). Paradoxically, though, if one were to 'read'[6] the texts with a modern understand-

---

5 Everything we know about the 'real' Tolkien – say, the fact that he fought in a war or has left us letters with 'interpretations' of his texts – can be viewed as the source of a discursive field. Instead of drawing on the literary work itself to access and make sense of the text, the reader constructs the author Tolkien as the interpretive fulcrum. The assumption that the reading of 'metaphors' is a method of understanding the text is again based on the idea that another entity – the author in the Foucaultian sense – can be found behind the text.
6 In this context, 'reading' is not to be taken as an interpretive process but as an act of emphatic understanding.

ing of these terms, one could attain an interpretation that makes sense, even if it is incorrect. Alternatively, one could safeguard "against such a subjective reading by actively seeking out and grappling with its [the text's] historic differences. The author in his historical specificity is thus not to be employed as the basis of making sense of the text but as a regulatory function" (Haug 332).[7]

Are we to assume that Tolkien is a modern author after all? That his main work, *The Lord of the Rings*, is a modern novel? Is Shippey correct in his statement "the concept [...] and the hints [...] are responses to something found in his own [Tolkien's], and our, life experiences" (*Author* 128)? Shippey's argument assumes that the modern reader's ability to interpret the 'metaphors' in Tolkien's texts points to the modernity of Tolkien the author. This, he argues, leads to the modern author Tolkien, who composed modern texts, especially the modern novel known to us as *The Lord of the Rings*. This construction in turn justifies inquiries into post-war writing related to traumata (cf. Shippey, *Author* xxix), modern conceptions of marriage, love and reproduction, the problem of what constitutes a sin, etc. (cf. Shippey, *Author* 196). The same construction also allows for the discovery of (more or less clear) answers to these questions in the text itself, answers provided by the discursive fields where the reader (and, consequently, the author) resides.

If one were to follow Walter Haug's suggestion – that is, to position the author as a regulative force against all too subjective readings – one would have to examine the *congruence* of social realities experienced by an author of the first half of the 20th century on the one hand and by a reader of the early 21st century on the other. Finding answers might prove difficult. Additional difficulties arise if one inquires what Tolkien's remarks in *On Fairy-Stories* refer to: "The dragon had the trade-mark *Of Faërie* written plain upon him. In whatever world he had his being it was an Other-world. Fantasy, the making or glimpsing of Other-worlds, was the heart of the desire of Faërie" (*OFS* 135).

Shippey, aware that there is no place for dragons in the waning 20th century (and even less in the early 21st century), explains: "we [the readers] do not ex-

---

7 Original quote: "gegenüber [solch einer] subjektiven Lektüre [ist es notwendig] den Text historisch zurückzubinden [und] sich an dessen historischer Differenz abzuarbeiten. [Dazu] gehört [...] der Autor in seiner Zeitgebundenheit [nicht] als Basis des Verständnisses, sondern [eben] Regulativ."

pect to meet dragons, but the 'dragonsickness' is perfectly common" (*Author* 328). Yet another statement by Tolkien casts some doubt on this generalisation, giving reason to suspect that this particular 'reading of the metaphor' might work only within limits: "It is not difficult to imagine the peculiar excitement and joy that one would feel if any specially beautiful fairy-story were found to be 'primarily' true, its narrative to be history, without thereby necessarily losing the mythical or allegorical significance that it had possessed" (*OFS* 156).

Consequently, all results generated by a metaphorical reading remain deficient: they will neglect anything that might be 'primarily true' and thus also the necessary (conceivably true) historical background of the story related in *The Lord of the Rings*. If one were to take the latter seriously, the simple transformation of the story into a metaphor that can be 'read' without difficulty would clash with the historical positioning of texts, discourses and motives on which an academically responsible approach would have to insist. According to Tolkien, the ideal fairy-story is 'primarily true in history' and therefore does not lend itself quite so easily to the ahistorical applications Shippey tends to discern.

Umberto Eco once remarked that it is indispensable for a romance[8] – and he explicitly includes Tolkien's works in that genre – *not* to take place in the Here and Now, nor to refer to the Here and Now, not even allegorically (547). Leaving aside for the moment the problems of genre (discussed in detail below), it needs to be noted that Eco's position is diametrically opposed to Shippey's while closely approaching Tolkien's remarks on fairy-stories. The Old English, Old Norse and other medieval sources (and genres) Tolkien drew on suggest that his texts – and I will argue my case by discussing *The Lord of the Rings* specifically – call for a different reading than modern novels, as they have little or nothing to do with the Here and Now. How this basic condition affects the text's author requires further examination as well.

---

8 Eco uses 'romance' as a modern genre category, in which "any danger functions as a means of challenging and then cementing the love relationship. [...] The moral fantasy of the romance is that of love triumphant and permanent, overcoming all obstacles and difficulties" (Lacey 221). I would like to add that applying this notion to the relationship of Sam and Frodo might yield interesting results.

2. Novel? Fairy-Story? Epic? – The question of genre

Shippey notes that "more subtly [...] *The Lord of the Rings* is evidently [a] work of the twentieth century, not [...] readily describable as [a] novel" (*Author* 311). But what should we call it? Shippey seems to avoid an answer, but declares: "he [Tolkien] took the ideals of modernism seriously instead of playing around with them" (*Author* 315f.) – a rather surprising conclusion, given the fact that the chapter of his book dedicated to the literary characteristics of Modernity points out contrasts rather than similarities in Tolkien's œuvre (cf. *Author* 312-15). If Shippey, as one might assume, is intent on proving the modernity of Tolkien's writing by employing the construction: author of the 20th century = modern author = modern text (although not a novel), the question of genre must become crucial. What kind of text is *The Lord of the Rings*?

Commenting on *The Hobbit* (yet his observations apply even more to *The Lord of the Rings*), Papajewski states: "On reading Tolkien's *The Hobbit*, one is disinclined to speak of a 'fairy-story' not only, but also because of its sheer length. One might, however, be justified in likening its compositional elements to that of a 'fairy-story'" (47).[9] Hans Peter Bauer elaborates on this thesis by referring to the lay (or 'heroic song', defined as an orally transmitted literary form) as the "basis on which the epic is built by extension" (10).[10] Following Bauer, lay, epic, and fairy-story are comparable with regard to the manner of storytelling,[11] whereas the manner by which "the communicative context is textualised [...] differentiates [the genres]" (10).[12]

Bauer's mention of the lay is especially relevant in the context of Sam's and Frodo's conversation on the Stairs of Cirith Ungol: "Why, to think of it, we're in the same tale [i.e., that of Beren and Lúthien] still" (*LotR* 697). This tale came down to them (and hence to us) not in prose but as a 'chant' (*LotR* 187). If one were to trust the text, it would make sense to follow Bauer's lead and

---

9 Original quote: "Bei der Bewertung von Tolkiens *The Hobbit* [...] kann man schon wegen des großen Umfangs [...] nicht ohne weiteres von einer 'fairy story' sprechen, aber man kann ihre kompositorischen Elemente [...] mit denen einer 'fairy story' vergleichen."
10 Original quote: "grundsätzlich die Basis darstellt, auf welcher durch Erweiterung das Epos entsteht."
11 Concerning both the paradigmatic and the syntagmatic axis, that is: the selection and composition of motives.
12 Original quote: "die Vertextung der Kommunikationssituation [...] ein differenzierendes Kriterium [der Gattungen]."

view *The Lord of the Ring* as a fairy-story that has been "epically broadened using compositional elements" (10).[13] Yet this insight cannot solve the question of genre as long as Tolkien's formal requirements for a fairy-story – beyond his exclusion of drama (*OFS* 140) – remain unclear.

There are reasons, however, to assume that his text is a fairy-story after all. The least compelling argument can be gleaned from Tolkien's own statement:[14] "It [*The Lord of the Rings*] is a 'fairy-story'" (*L* 232). Since every genre can apparently generate fairy-stories, this remark alone cannot decide the question of genre we are pursuing. Bauer suggests the following definition: "a fairy [story] is an adventure story which focuses on a hero operating in a very specific sort of world. [...] This world operates like ours, but is has different relationships" (14). This description basically mirrors Tolkien's observation that it is not desirable in any world (like ours) to marry frogs, but that worlds do exist (i.e., the world of Faërie) where such relationships are indispensable (*OFS* 152). To decide the matter of genre, we therefore need to answer the following question: what is it that *The Frog King*, *Beowulf*,[15] and *The Lord of the Rings* (all of them fairy-stories) have in common? At first glance, the temporal placement seems to be of importance. *The Frog King* begins with "In olden times, when wishing still helped one..." (Grimm 17) and *Beowulf* opens with:

> Hwæt! Wé Gárdena   in géardagum
> þéodcyninga   þrym gefrúnon
> hú ða æþelingas   ellen fremedon.
> (*Beowulf* ll. 1-3)[16]

The Lord of the Rings commences: "This book is largely concerned with Hobbits" (*LotR* 1), and after a few more few lines we read:

> The beginning of Hobbits lies far back in the Elder Days that are now lost and forgotten. [...] But in the days of Bilbo, and of Frodo his heir, they [the hobbits] suddenly became, [...] both important and renowned, and troubled

---

13 Original quote: "mit seinen kompositorischen Elementen als 'episch verbreiterte'."
14 The relevance of this quote does not depend on the author as a privileged source for the interpretation of his work; rather it illustrates how Tolkien, the literary critic, set forth his concept of the fairy-story as a genre.
15 Tolkien identifies *Beowulf* as a fairy-story (cf. *OFS* 127), even though he is aware of its traditional classification as an epic (cf. *BMC* 9). I am interested not in *Beowulf* as such but in Tolkien's perspective on the text.
16 "Listen! The fame of Danish kings in days gone by, the daring feats worked by those heroes are well known to us" (*Beowulf*, verse transl. 2).

the counsels of the Wise and the Great. Those days, the Third Age of Middle-earth, are now long past. (*LotR* 2)[17]

All three texts begin by invoking an age long past. With regard to the German *Märchen* (but equally applicable to the English fairy-story), Jolles states that, in addition to the complete absence of real historical characters, the distance between the narrated historical time and the time in the fairy-tale serves to annihilate a "contemporary time that is experienced as immoral" (243).[18] This insurmountable gap precludes any immediate connection with the world of the reader (which is bound up in an ethics of action). A world is thus produced where an "ethics of action"[19], characteristic of novels, is suspended by an "ethics of events"[20] (cf. Jolles 244).

Consequently, the princess must marry the Frog King: not because she wants to, but because her golden ball fell into his well. It is this very ethics of events that – taking a cue from Tolkien – one could identify as a prominent theme of *Beowulf*, centred on "men caught in the chains of circumstance [...] dying with their backs to the wall" (*BMC* 17). (The major difference between the fairy-tale and *Beowulf* is that events in *The Frog King* appear coincidental, whereas in *Beowulf* an ethics of events structures the textual world and all conceivable decisions within it.)

Tolkien is aware that this world view can hardly be called modern. Modernity would require "a judgement that the heroic or tragic story on a strictly human plane is by nature superior. Doom is held less literary than ἁμαρτία [guilt]" (*BMC* 15). Doom, however, seems to be a more appealing subject for Tolkien. It is noteworthy that the focus of interest is not on the hero's inner landscape, his inner division, his lack of perfection and guilty ensnarement (resulting from a discrepancy between the interior and the external world), but his way of behaving in a world predestined by doom.

It is not at all difficult to demonstrate that this concept is equally valid for *The Lord of the Rings*. Shippey proposes that the Council of Elrond serves to organ-

---

17 It is striking that two temporal planes are alluded to: the 'far back' of the Third Age in relation to the Elder Days and the 'long past' that describes the relationship between the text and the Third Age.
18 Original quote: "der als unmoralisch empfundenen Welt der Wirklichkeit."
19 Original quote: "Ethik des Handelns."
20 Original quote: "Ethik des Geschehens."

ize the plot (cf. *Author* 77f.), and Bilbo seems to agree: "And who are they [the messengers sent with the Ring] to be? That seems to me what this Council has to decide" (*LotR* 263). A decision is indeed reached:

> A great dread fell on him [Frodo], as if he was awaiting the pronouncement of some doom that he had long foreseen and vainly hoped might after all never be spoken. An overwhelming longing to rest and remain at peace by Bilbo's side in Rivendell filled all his heart. At last with an effort he spoke, and wondered to hear his own words, as if some other will was using his small voice. 'I will take the Ring,' he said. (*LotR* 263f.)

It is neither the Council that eventually decides who the Ring-bearer should be, nor is it Frodo. In fact, no 'organizing' but rather the unveiling of a plot occurs. The response to Bilbo's offer to take the Ring may serve to elucidate the point: "'Of course, my dear Bilbo,' said Gandalf. 'If you had really started this affair, you might be expected to finish it. But you know well enough now that starting is too great a claim for any, and that only a small part is played in great deeds by any hero'" (*LotR* 263). Nothing that Frodo (or any other member of the Council) does decides who the Ring-bearer should be. The whole scene is characterised by a complete lack of self-determination. Frodo was and always has been "appointed" (*LotR* 264) for this choice; it is his doom to carry the Ring to Mount Doom.

Beowulf dies battling the dragon because "the wages of heroism is death" (*BMC* 26), and only because of the dragon does Tolkien remark that *Beowulf* "stands amid but above the petty wars of princes, and surpasses the dates and limits of historical periods, however important" (*BMC* 33). In the fairy-tale, the Princess is finally granted subject status only because the Frog King wants to make her his wife. Bakhtin's comments on the epic hero are particularly illuminating in this context:

> In the epic, characters are bounded, preformed, individualized by their various situations and destinies, but not by varying 'truths.' [...] Outside his destiny, the epic and tragic hero is nothing; he is, therefore, a function of the plot fate assigns him; he cannot become the hero of another destiny or another plot. (35f.)

By contrast, "the epic wholeness of an individual disintegrates in a novel in other ways" (Bakhtin 37). The hero of a fairy-story and the hero of an epic are, in their totality, predefined by their fate and their function: such a totality cannot be found in a novel. At this point, a characteristic that fairy-story and epic storytelling have in common, and which distinguishes the two genres from the novel, becomes apparent. In both genres, the ethics of events seems to occupy the centre stage. (The disavowal of any reference to the present constitutes another similarity.) This is a convenient point to leave *Beowulf* and the princess with her Frog King and to turn our attention to the protagonists of *The Lord of the Rings*.

We have already demonstrated that Frodo's fate is fully determined and circumscribed by the Ring and his task as a Ring-bearer. This, however, holds true for almost all the protagonists of *The Lord of the Rings*. Sam's role, especially, is not one of arbitrary decisions made by a self-determined individual, as he himself puts it so eloquently on the Stairs of Cirith Ungol, faithfully reflecting the overall logic of the text:

> The brave things in the old tales and songs [...]: adventures, as I used to call them. I used to think that they were things the wonderful folk of the stories went out and looked for, because they wanted them, because they were exciting and life was a bit dull, a kind of a sport, as you might say. But that's not the way of it with the tales that really mattered, or the ones that stay in the mind. Folk seem to have been just landed in them, usually – their paths were laid that way [...]. But I expect they had lots of chances, like us [Sam and Frodo], of turning back, only they didn't. And if they had, we shouldn't know, because they'd have been forgotten. We hear about those as just went on. (*LotR* 696)

This definition of subject matters that may become a 'tale' in *The Lord of the Rings* exactly mirrors the mechanisms Bakhtin postulates for the epic:

> One may, and in fact one must, memorialize with [...] language only that which is worthy of being remembered, that which should be preserved in the memory of descendents; [...]. The interrelationship of times is important here. The valorized emphasis is not on the future and does not serve the future, no favors are being done it (such favors face an eternity outside time); what is served here is the future memory of a past, a broadening of the world of the absolute past, an enriching of it with new images (at the expense of contemporaneity) – a world that is always opposed in principle to any merely transitory past. (18f.)

If one accepts this principle (as Sam's musings suggest), one must assume that Frodo and Sam inhabit a story structured not by contact with the present with its "potential for re-thinking and re-evaluating" (Bakhtin 18), but by a relationship with an 'absolute past'. The presence of this absolute past is indeed palpable throughout the story. Knowledge about the One Ring is old, even ancient: "*One Ring to rule them all* [...] is [...] a verse long known in Elven-lore" (*LotR* 49). When Elrond relates the story of the Ring and the first Ring-war to the Council, Frodo is amazed: "You remember? [...] I thought that the fall of Gil-galad was a long age ago" (*LotR* 237). Frodo takes it for granted that "both the singer and the listener [...] are located in the same time and on the same evaluative (hierarchical) plane, but the represented world of the heroes stands on an utterly different and inaccessible time-and-value plane, separated by epic distance" (Bakhtin 14). In the character of Elrond, the temporal planes of the present and the absolute past collide with particular clarity: he[21] points out that the mortal members of the Council are completely detached from the epic past while tracing his own presence and fate back to this same past.[22]

According to Georg Lukács, the epic may be understood as the construction of a contained totality of life, opposed to the novel as the representation of a private fragment of the world, "whose extensive totality of life one cannot presume any longer" (47).[23] In Bakhtin's writings, epic totality results from absolute epic distance: "memory, and not knowledge" (15) define the epic.

One could therefore speculate that, where epic distance and the protagonists' contemporary reality meet, a shift from the How to the Why of events might occur. Because epic distance becomes manifest in the present of the tale itself, the characters might gain a new freedom of action: instead of drawing on past events in order to make sense of the world, they would base their insights on individualised interactions. (For example, the question might be raised which specific reasons, weaknesses, and motives prompted Isildur to keep the Ring, and what Elrond made of it.) The world would then only exist as a 'private fragment'; an ethics of actions might burst forth.

However, no one at Elrond's Council is interested in Isildur's motives for keeping the Ring. No one present doubts the inevitability of what came to pass. Everyone knows that the Ring is Isildur's Bane. Mirroring Frodo's surprise at Elrond's presence in both temporal planes, Boromir responds with disbelief

---

21 In this context, Elrond can be viewed as a representative of all elves.
22 The peculiar passage of time in Lórien exemplifies the manner in which the elves are fused with the epic past: "In that land, maybe, we [the Fellowship] were in a time that has elsewhere long gone by" (*LotR* 379).
23 Original quote: "extensive Totalität des Lebens nicht mehr sinnfällig gegeben ist."

to Aragorn's announcement: "The Sword of Elendil would be a help beyond our hope – if such a thing could indeed return out of the shadows of the past" (*LotR* 241). Boromir came to Rivendell, or so he apparently believes, to attend to current political affairs. Yet the prophecy –

> *All that is gold does not glitter,*
> *Not all those who wander are lost;*
> *The old that is strong does not wither,*
> *Deep roots are not reached by the frost.*
> *From ashes a fire shall be woken,*
> *A light from the shadows shall spring;*
> *Renewed shall be blade that was broken:*
> *The crownless again shall be king* (*LotR* 241)

– clearly correlates the topics under discussion with the epic past.

Bilbo's recital of this prophecy[24] illustrates that the matters discussed in Elrond's house pertain to the present and future only insofar as they reveal their meaning in relation to the past. In Bree, Aragorn confirms: "I am Aragorn, and those verses go with that name" (*LotR* 168). Bakhtin points out that "the novel might wish to prophesize facts, to predict and influence the real future, the future of the author and his readers [...]. Characteristic for it [the novel] is an eternal re-thinking and re-evaluating. That centre of activity that ponders and justifies the past is transferred to the future" (31). Applying this logic, Boromir's disbelief is all too understandable,[25] for the future, in this view, is incomplete and determined by the question how Aragorn will approach his 'task' (once again the question is what he will do). The plot, however, describes a configuration which Tolkien has already identified for *Beowulf*: "men caught in the chains of circumstance [...] dying with their backs to the wall" (*BMC* 17). It is more than obvious what Aragorn will do: the focus lies on how he will do it.

> In the epic world view, 'beginning,' 'first,' 'founder,' 'ancestor,' 'that which occurred earlier' and so forth are not merely temporal categories but valorized temporal categories, and valorized to an extreme degree. This is as true for relationships among people as for relations among all other items and phenomena of the epic world. [...] All the really good things (i.e., the 'first' things) occur

---

24 That Bilbo presents himself as the 'author' of the text (cf. *LotR* 241) will be discussed below.
25 One might even ask whether the ties to an incomplete future account for Boromir's failure (and, even more so, for that of Denethor, his father). This might also explain why it is Boromir who feels unsafe in Lothlórien (cf. *LotR* 349), the site of a "time that has elsewhere long go by" (*LotR* 379).

only in this past. The epic absolute past is the single source and beginning of everything good for all later times as well. (Bakhtin 15)

The prophecy connected to Aragorn refers to the epic past when the high kings of Gondor ruled. This rule will be re-established in a new form (for Men), but re-established, nevertheless, when Aragorn eventually ascends the throne. All available signs point to this conclusion: the "ancient crown" placed on Aragorn's head corresponds to the ritual formula "Out of the Great Sea to Middle-earth I am come. In this place will I abide, and my heirs, unto the ending of the world" (*LotR* 946), invoking Elendil and thereby the absolute epic past of Middle-earth. The construction of historical continuities and facts in *The Lord of the Rings* diverges from what Modernity has taught us to expect: "National tradition (not personal experience and the free thought that grows out of it) serves as the source for the epic" (Bakhtin 13).[26]

This observation delineates a fundamental difference between epic and fairy-tale. Aragorn's ascension to the throne dissolves the temporal gap between tradition and the present: the act defines the future as predestined by the epic past. Aragorn's 'ideal kingship', therefore, will not be made apparent through his future achievements as a ruler; the quality of his rule and kingship has already been revealed within the epic past. Ultimately, Aragorn's deeds can all be traced back to the prophecy which – in contrast to a prediction – "is characteristic for the epic [and] is realized wholly within the limits of the absolute past [...]; it does not touch the reader and his real time" (Bakhtin 31). When Aragorn is crowned, it is not his individual fate that is fulfilled: he merely meets his epic destiny. (His individual fate, in fact, only comes into existence because of this predetermination.) The scion of the White Tree, the "sapling of the line of Nimloth the fair; and that was a seedling of Galathilion, and that a fruit Telperion of many names, Eldest of Trees" (*LotR* 950), found by Aragorn, newly planted in Gondor, is the most obvious example of this connection to the absolute epic past. This past precedes even the era of the first kings – "Yet the line of Nimloth is older far than your line, King Elessar" (*LotR* 950) – and

---

26 'National' should not be understood as referring to the modern construction of a state but in the sense that Tolkien employs: "Yet it is written in a language that after many centuries has still essential kinship with our own, it was made in this land [...], and for those who are native to that tongue and land, it must ever call with profound appeal" (*BMC* 34).

correlates the kingdom of Men with a past outside 'history' (as defined by modern historiography).

Is this principle in operation as well where the hobbits – especially Sam and Frodo – are concerned? According to a widely held view, the hobbits mediate between the epic elements of *The Lord of the Rings* and the "reader's modern awareness" (Shippey, *Author* 6). This view implies that, on the one hand, the hobbits remain an anachronism within the epic structure of the text and, on the other, that Frodo – and Sam, Bilbo, Merry and Pippin with him – are merely "good average" hobbits (Shippey, *Author* 185), who may thus convincingly represent average readers.

One can attribute the hobbits' apparent 'modernity'[27] to the fact that they are set apart from the rest of Middle-earth. Everything in the Shire feels familiar to the reader, and the hobbits' defining characteristics, their love for good food and drink (cf. *LotR* 2), a "good tilled earth", and "peace and quiet" (*LotR* 1), only reinforce this sentiment. What creates the strongest connection between the hobbits and modern readers appears to be the detachment of the Shire from the larger history of Middle-earth. It is no coincidence that the Shire calendar begins with the crossing of the Brandywine (the river Baranduin), for it marks a time when the hobbits' contacts with the Dúnedain and the farther regions of Middle-earth started to dwindle (cf. *LotR* 4). Even though a certain tie between the hobbits and the rest of the world seems to linger, it remains unclear whether it is based on a legend. The question of whether or not the hobbit bowmen actually took part in the battle of Fornost is answered differently by hobbit traditions and the historical accounts of Men (cf. *LotR* 4). Summarily: "They were, in fact, ruled by their own chieftains and meddled not at all with events in the world outside" (*LotR* 4).[28] Even though the hobbits

---

27 Of course the hobbits' way of life is anything but modern. Yet it seems that the portrayal of the hobbits is perceived almost exclusively as a stereotypical representation of the 'good old times': a reader construction often accompanied by specific ideals, such as pacifist, ecologically responsible, non-expansive behaviour. The hobbits' apparent modernity is thus ultimately based on the construction of a common set of values to which readers subscribe as well. However, it is doubtful that hobbit life has anything in common with that of modern readers: the perceived similarities depend entirely on the hobbits' anti-heroic characteristics (yet in this particular regard the text's main protagonists differ radically from all other hobbits).

28 The 'Battle of Greenfields' arises from contact with the outside world, but that connection has apparently faded from collective memory. Unlike the first Ring-war, this skirmish is not part of an epic war either but merely a defensive action against a marauding band of orcs (cf. *LotR* 4 and 1062).

live a life quite separate from the epic history of Middle-earth, some knowledge about the larger world's inhabitants has survived. In *The Hobbit*, the existence of wizards and dwarves does not surprise Bilbo. He is merely astonished that a wizard and a company of thirteen dwarves have singled him out for a visit (cf. *H* 17f.) and finds it odd that the dwarves should wish to involve him in their affairs. (Modern readers, by contrast, would certainly question their own senses and sanity if visiting dwarves were to knock on their door.)

It seems, however, that in the seventy-seven years between Bilbo's journey and Frodo's departure from Bag End, acceptance of the existence of dwarves, elves and other less-than-ordinary beings has dwindled dramatically in the Shire – if Ted Sandyman can be taken to represent common convictions: "I can hear fireside-tales and children's stories at home, if I want to. [...] I heard tell of [dragons] when I was a youngster, but there's no call to believe in them now" (*LotR* 43). Sam begs to differ: "I daresay there's more truth in some of them than you reckon" (*LotR* 43). While Sam acknowledges the true existence of dragons, elves and walking trees, his social status renders this knowledge problematic. In the words of Sam's father, Gaffer Gamgee: "Elves and Dragons! I says to him. Cabbages and potatos are better for me and you [Sam]. Don't go getting mixed up in the business of your betters, or you'll land in trouble too big for you" (*LotR* 24).

At least two discrepant views concerning the facticity of elves, dragons, and old tales exist in the Shire. Sandyman represents a position that correlates anything epically historical outside the Shire with fabulous and magical elements in children's stories – which renders it impossible for him to accept them as true. His position closely reflects Tolkien's reasoning why fairy-tales became a children's genre in *On Fairy-Stories* (cf. *OFS* 129f.). The Gaffer's argument, on the other hand, allows for the factual content of such tales, yet insists that they should be of no concern for hobbits of his and Sam's social standing. (Once again, one must assume that an enlightened modern reader would identify with Sandyman's view.) Both arguments imply an inherent distance between the speakers' range of experience and the mentioned events or beings, resulting from the Shire's profound isolation.

Sam apparently holds a view that differs from both Sandyman's and the Gaffer's. Convinced that the old stories are true, he resembles Bilbo and Frodo far more than the other participants in the discussion. His belief in elves indeed sets him apart from most other hobbits.[29] On the whole, Sam, Bilbo, and Frodo do not seem to experience any distance towards epically historical events and beings, an attitude disparagingly labelled "cracked" (*LotR* 44) in the Shire. One must therefore conclude that, to the modern reader, hobbits appear more familiar than all other creatures of Middle-earth because they share the reader's ignorance of the wider historical contexts – whereas Bilbo, Frodo and Sam turn out to be significantly less ignorant.[30] That Sam is sometimes perceived as dumb results exclusively from a projection on the reader's part, based on Sam's social status, and neatly reflects the Gaffer's views. Sam's alleged ignorance effectively positions him below the reader, for he appears even less knowledgeable. (The fallacy of such a reading will be discussed in more detail below.)

Gildor is right when he tells Frodo: "But it is not your own Shire, […]. Others dwelt here before hobbits were. […] The wide world is all about you: you can fence yourselves in, but you cannot forever fence it out" (*LotR* 82). The fate of the Shire has always been, and still is, bound up with the history of Middle-earth, even if most hobbits have largely forgotten it. Gandalf and the One Ring then transport the larger context into the Shire. The disclosure that Bilbo's Ring is the One runs parallel with Gandalf's revelation of its history (cf. *LotR* 45f.). While it may seem startling how easily Frodo (and Bilbo) become enmeshed in the history of Sauron, Gil-galad, Elendil und Isildur, Déagol und Sméagol, Gandalf offers a simple explanation:

> It was the strangest event in the whole history of the Ring so far: Bilbo's arrival just at that time, and putting his hand on it, blindly, in the dark. There was more than one power at work […]. Behind that there was something else at work, beyond any design of the Ring-maker. I can put it no plainer than by saying that Bilbo was meant to find the Ring, and not by its maker. In which case you also were meant to have it. And that may be an encouraging thought. (*LotR* 54)

---

29 One may assume that "Mr. Bilbo's tales" (*LotR* 24) trigger a desire in Sam which mirrors Bilbo's upon hearing the dwarves' song: "he wished to go and see" (*H* 25).
30 While readers who anticipate the story's outcome may have a certain advantage of knowledge, they experience the gradual unveiling of epic-historical connections together with the hobbits.

Frodo becomes the Ring-bearer because he is meant to play that part. At this point, one might assume that such a configuration urges the character into the novelistic mould. As Bakhtin states about the novel's hero: "One of the basic internal themes of the novel is precisely the theme of the inadequacy of a hero's fate and situation to the hero himself. The individual is either greater than his fate, or less than his condition as a [hu]man" (37). It seems that Frodo is fully circumscribed by his hobbit 'nature' when he tells Gandalf: "I feel very small, and very uprooted, and well – desperate" (*LotR* 61). If Frodo as a hero is indeed 'too small' for his fate, the resulting discrepancy between the hero and his fate could turn 'serio-comical' (cf. Bakhtin 22), once the epic past collides with the present and burdens the 'small, simple hobbit' with a task that would befit a traditional hero.

Boromir represents this very position: at Elrond's Council he almost bursts out laughing when Bilbo offers to take the Ring to Mordor. But, significantly, no one else seems to detect a comical element in this situation (cf. *LotR* 263). If Boromir's inferences about the hobbits' potential, based on their stature and manner of speech, were correct, one might furthermore expect a specific development: Frodo would have to grow towards 'maturity' to become the kind of hero who masters his fate. Yet no one at the Council shares Boromir's amusement. As readers know (if they take the text seriously), it was Bilbo's fate to reach out his hand in the darkness and touch the One Ring. As a consequence, it is Frodo's fate to be the Ring-bearer. Frodo's desperation does not result from being a 'prisoner' of harsh circumstances that touch his innermost being, but from the tragedy of finding himself "caught in the chains of circumstance" that Tolkien describes.

As mentioned above, Frodo's very existence is defined by the Ring. (Outside his destiny, the epic and tragic hero is nothing.) Boromir in particular ought to be aware that the Ring is inseparably linked with Frodo and thus with all of Middle-earth, as it is he who brings the prophecy –

> *Seek for the Sword that was broken:*
> *In Imladris it dwells;*
> *There shall be counsels taken*
> *Stronger than Morgul-spells.*

> *There shall be shown a token*
> *That Doom is near at hand,*
> *For Isildur's Bane shall waken,*
> *And the Halfling forth shall stand*
> (*LotR* 240)

– to Rivendell.[31]

The approach taken in Gondor towards unriddling these words clearly correlates current events in Middle-earth with the absolute epic past. But Denethor, who is "wise in the lore of Gondor" (*LotR* 240), is not prepared to impart any knowledge beyond geography and descriptive history. It is only in Rivendell that Boromir receives an explanation. Since the house of Elrond operates as a link between the textual present and the epic past, it is at this site that the dream (and the prophecy it contains) can be related to the epically historical dimension and become meaningful for the present (cf. *LotR* 240).

While the broken sword points to the future king of Gondor, one question remains unanswered: what is the Halfling's role? Is he an epic character or a novelistic anachronism? The question cannot be answered on the level of the present in the plot, as the "I myself [the epic individual], in an environment that is distanced, exists not in itself or for itself but for the self's descendents, for the memory such a self anticipates in its descendents. I acknowledge myself, an image that is my own, but on this distanced plane of memory such a consciousness of self is alienated from 'me'" (Bakhtin 34). The Halfling's role in the present – eventually, Frodo's and Sam's role[32] – can only be established by taking a 'detour' through the epic past and thereby obtains its specific significance for all the participants.

If one adopts this position, Sam's and Frodo's conversation on the Stairs of Cirith Ungol gains import. Sam's musings – "Still, I wonder if we shall ever be put into songs or tales. We're in one, of course; but I mean: put into words, you know, told by the fireside, or read out of great big book with red and black letters, years and years afterward" (*LotR* 697) – imply two temporal planes

---

31 With its eight short lines, the prophecy provides Boromir with the complete plot of *The Lord of the Rings* and brings to mind the strategy of 'epic broadening'.
32 As Frodo tells Faramir: "we are the Halflings that the rhyme spoke of" (*LotR* 644).

within the text. In the present, Sam and Frodo find themselves *within* a story (a story that relates to older tales of which it is a part). The textual transmission of Frodo's and Sam's story, on the other hand, does not allow for a shared present of readers and characters. Readers can only partake of Sam and Frodo's story in the past, just as the two hobbits can only recall the story of Beren und Lúthien in the past.[33] The connecting thread between the story of the quest for the Silmaril and the One Ring's destruction binds them to both the epic past and their present, which is *not* the present of the reader. Frodo knows that great tales "never end as tales. [...] But the people in them come, and go when their part's ended" (*LotR* 697).

Bakhtin states: "the individual in the high distanced genres is [...] a fully finished and completed being. [He is] something hopelessly readymade; [...] from beginning to end, he coincides with himself [...]. All his potential, all his possibilities are realized utterly in his external [position], in the whole of his fate, [...] outside of this predetermined fate and [...] position there is nothing" (34). The two hobbits seem to 'contaminate' the absolute past with the present that surrounds them, as they can only access a transient, private fragment of the world (their current situation), and the question of how their story will end remains open. (This does not pertain to the reader!) However, this conclusion is at once countered by the reference to Beren and Lúthien (*LotR* 696). The hobbits do not turn the epic past into a private matter, but act within a present predetermined by an absolute past and its meanings.[34] The underlying epic structure is therefore not dissolved at all; indeed this scene illustrates how an epic comes into existence: through (future) oral and written transmission.

That the most important question concerns the story's eventual ending (*LotR* 696) once again demonstrates that the focus is not on how Sam and Frodo have come to terms with their fate; what their predetermined fate has in store for them

---

33 Yet while the *hobbits' present* can only be interpreted by drawing on the epic past, to which Beren and Lúthien belong, the *reader's present* remains untouched by the epic past. For Sam and Frodo, the tale of Beren and Lúthien is not a mere (fictional) story but a true history (whose truth is substantiated by the phial; cf. *LotR* 367, 696). It is this factor that involves the hobbits with epically historical events and distinguishes their perception of the epic past from the reader's.

34 'Privatising' the epic past transforms the perceived objective totality of life into a subjective fragment of the world. As a result, the epic element is displaced by novelistic structures (cf. Lukács 47).

is the point at issue.³⁵ Sam's allusion to the story of Beren and Lúthien – "a long tale" that "goes on past the happiness and into grief and beyond it" (*LotR* 696) – also points to a specific configuration. Beyond the end of Sam's and Frodo's journey (the individual's doom), a third party (a future narrator) will convey the completed history of a (past) world, suffused with meaning, by drawing on the hobbits' doom. Beren's silmaril is directly connected to Frodo's phial, implicating a congruent relation between the two pairings: "The Silmaril went on and came to Eärendil" (*LotR* 696), and "in this phial [...] is caught the light of Eärendil's star" (*LotR* 367). Within their tale (a history), Beren and Lúthien are thus transformed into an epic couple – as Sam and Frodo are in theirs.

The fact that any ending of their tale will affect all of Middle-earth binds their fate to history and purges it of everything that might be called 'private'. When in later years Sam's and Frodo's story is told by the fireside, they will have emerged from a "national tradition" – that of Middle-earth – "not personal experience and the free thought that grows out of it" (Bakhtin 13); they will be heroes who are firmly located in a "national epic-past[, the] absolute-past" (13).

This epic context has an impact on the construction of authorship in *The Lord of the Rings*. If fictionality generates "a loss of temporal definiteness in favour of temporal indeterminacy"³⁶ (Petersen 14), the principle cannot hold true here. Frodo's and Sam's conversation links textual production with the principle of the 'primary epic situation': "A narrator tells an audience something that has taken place" (Petersen 14).³⁷ The absence of an original author and the "mediated nature of epic description", delivered by a narrator, constitute "the most decisive genre-specific characteristic that distinguishes the epic from all other genres" (Petersen 15).³⁸

In his discussion of Tolkien's literary œuvre, Shippey identifies principles that consistently diverge from the defining characteristics of modernity (cf. *Author*

---

35 In fact, only two endings of the Quest seem conceivable in the present. (Yet within the epic past, established across the reference to Beren and Lúthien, Frodo's and Sam's relationship can reach only a single conclusion: that which is predefined by the story of Beren and Lúthien.)
36 Original quote: "Verlust der temporalen Bestimmtheit zugunsten temporaler Unbestimmtheit."
37 Original quote: "epische Ursituation. [...] Ein Erzähler erzählt einer Hörerschaft etwas, was geschehen ist."
38 Original quote: "Mittelbarkeit epischer Darstellung [durch den Erzähler bilden] das entscheidende gattungsspezifische, das Epische von allen anderen Gattungen [...] trennende Merkmal."

310-16). His conclusion then amounts to a startling contradiction: Tolkien "used 'mythical method' [...] because he believed that the myths were true. [...] He took the ideals of modernism seriously" (*Author* 315). The paradox inherent to this reading – 'true' myth vs. the inherent fictionality of 'mythical method' – is evident. But to what an extent can *The Lord of the Rings* be viewed as a modern text? Shippey's comparison with James Joyce's *Ulysses* clearly highlights the differences, but overlooks the fact that Tolkien refrains from letting the epic collide with the reader's time (which would amount to maximal contact with the present). He abstains from dissolving the genre and does not juxtapose the 'high' and the 'low' to create ironic distance.[39] Instead, the author relocates the hobbits (and Aragorn), by shifting them from the level of maximal contact with the present into the epic past.

When Shippey concludes that the genre of *The Lord of the Rings* can never be fully determined (cf. *Author* 221-22), his assessment is certainly correct. Yet his statement that *The Lord of the Rings* is "in continuous negotiation with, and [...] follows many of the conventions of, the traditional bourgeois novel" (*Author* 223) remains open to dispute. Shippey's contention that Sam "tends to sink towards the *ironic*" (*Author* 222) and that Sam/Frodo[40] resemble the pairing Don Quixote/Sancho Panza calls for a critical reassessment as well. If these observations were true, *The Lord of the Rings* would be a novel, its hero caught in a mismatch "between his surface and his center, between his potential and his reality" (Bakhtin 35). Cervantes' heroes appear comical because their behaviour – which reflects an ethics of events – constantly clashes with a world so complex that it requires highly individualized actions. Don Quixote operates as a comic hero because he falls short of achieving a modern interpretation of the world. Ironic elements (and concomitant laughter) result from the contrast between the characters' shortcomings and the reader's feeling of superiority (cf. Jauss 106f.) This principle does not apply to Sam and Frodo;

---

[39] A primary reason why *The Lord of the Rings* works as a text, even if the reader is not aware of any intertextual relations, is the complete lack of parody, irony or travesty (cf. Bakhtin 7). A novel typically requires an awareness of intertextuality to make sense.

[40] It has already been demonstrated that any interpretation identifying Sam exclusively as an exponent of practical everyday knowledge (cf. Shippey, *Author* 222) does not correspond to the information the text provides about Sam.

neither does it hold for Bilbo (in *The Lord of the Rings*) or Merry and Pippin.[41] They act within a structure that has no contact "with contemporary reality in all its openendedness" (Bakhtin 11). Conversely, the hobbits are conceived to meet the fundamental requirements of an epic narrative.[42]

Assuming that these characters correspond to epic structures must lead to a re-evaluation of the author's most prominent functions. In such a context, the author of Frodo's and Sam's tale (and of the entire story of the Ring-war) does not explain events by referring to the discourses that constitute the modern author (for instance, biography) as external sources of meaning. The modern author – including the discourses attached to him – as a constructed means of generating a 'privatised' fragment of the world for the reader cannot illuminate the totalized world of the text. ('Metaphorical reading', therefore, cannot provide a satisfactory interpretation.) Indeed, the author does not create a bridge between history and an incomplete (open-ended) present, but installs a distance between the contemporary present and the epic past.

3. The dumb hobbit –
The Lord of the Rings as a 'development-novel'?

The epic author differs fundamentally from the author of a modern novel. Epic distance creates a distinct separation of the poet and his audience from the epic hero. For the novel, Bakhtin identifies the opposite approach:

> The shift of the temporal center of artistic orientation, which placed on the same temporally valorized plane the author and his readers (on the one hand) and the world and heroes described by him (on the other), making them contemporaries, possible acquaintances, friends, familiarizing their relations […], permits the author, in all various masks and faces, to move freely onto the field of his represented world, a field that in the epic had been absolutely inaccessible and closed. (27)

---

41 While Don Quixote deludes himself about living as a knight within a world that no longer has any use for knighthood, Sancho Panza is unable to share this delusion (cf. Cervantes): it is this structure that generates the persistent comical element. By contrast, Frodo is the Ring-bearer because he is needed in this particular capacity, and Sam inhabits the same world, largely defined by doom. Even at first glance, the basic configurations and the resulting characters differ immensely.

42 Although a definition of genre based on the diverse stylistic levels (cf. Shippey, *Author* 221ff.) must raise questions, this particular aspect will not be pursued any further.

Within the field of a virtually possible acquaintance, the hero's epic wholeness is no longer central. The lifting of epic distance means that "one can disrespectfully walk around whole objects; therefore, the back and rear portion of an object (and also its innards, not normally accessible for viewing) assume a special importance" (23). Such an approach allows for "the first time [a] truly free investigation of the world, of [hu]man and of human thought" (25).

Since the notion of forming a 'possible acquaintance' with the hero indicates that the author forges a link between the world of the readers and the hero, the hobbits must come to mind again. Can they truly be viewed as devices the author employs to mitigate the text's strangeness (cf. Shippey, *Author* 11), a strangeness that the temporal gap between reader and story necessarily generates? Do they function as mirrors in which readers may recognise their own complex subjectivity?

It must be noted that the hobbits – and Sam in particular – appear anachronistic next to characters like Aragorn and Elrond. Whereas the latter are shown as stable, 'complete' heroes, the hobbits have to make sense of a world that in some respects resembles their own (the Common Speech, measurements of time and distance as well as a common geography are shared with other societies), but which also confronts them with cultural differences. Do these cultural differences have an impact on the hobbits, to the point of triggering a *development*? Do the hobbits in turn represent a contrast to the epic structure which – as Shippey concludes as well (cf. *Author* 222) – characterises, for instance, Aragorn? If the hobbits were located on the plane of the novel (or of irony), one could expect a dissociation of their exterior from their inner being (their subjectivity; cf. Bakhtin 9), indicating a certain mutability. From this point of view, a development of the heroes' (the hobbits') subjectivity ought to follow; indeed, their subjectivity could only arise in the course of such a development. Within the novel, the hero's 'ignorance' appears to be a necessary condition for development. Bakhtin points out: "the Novel, however, speculates in what is unknown. [...] It can be used to complete the image of an individual" (32).

If the hobbits functioned as a novelistic ('modern') element in the text, a similar kind of development would have to be in evidence for them. One might then speak of a 'development novel': a novelistic subgenre focussing on a main character's development, based on detailed descriptions of the character's experiences. Psychological processing and the integration of described events into the character's subjective identity are central to this narrative (cf. Mullan 105f.). The *individual* as the development novel's protagonist "is shaped by social influences, by positioning himself within them, and by opposing them" (Czerwinski 84).[43] Does this observation apply to the character Frodo, or should the notion of 'development' be replaced by an alternative concept? The following examination of several exemplary scenes – Frodo's decision to leave the Shire, his choice at the Council of Elrond, the taming of Sméagol, events in the Tower of Cirith Ungol and at Mount Doom – will pursue these questions.

When Gandalf reveals that Frodo is in possession of the One Ring, the following two questions spring to Frodo's mind: "How on earth did it come to me?" (*LotR* 50) and "Why did it come to me?" (*LotR* 60). Eventually, a single explanation suffices: "Such questions cannot be answered. [...] But you have been chosen" (*LotR* 60). Frodo is confronted with a situation for which he feels ill equipped: "But I have so little of any of these things [power and wisdom]!" (*LotR* 60). Interestingly, Gandalf's explanations at first seem to contradict his assertion that Frodo was 'chosen' for the task: "You may be sure that it was not for any merit that others do not possess: not for power or wisdom, at any rate" (*LotR* 60). Gandalf's view (and readers already familiar with Gandalf's superior knowledge will readily adopt this view) thus presents the image of a small, weak, and helpless individual burdened with a task that far surpasses his abilities.

However, the text immediately unsettles this conclusion. Gandalf refuses to take the Ring, indeed has to refuse, *because* he is powerful and wise. (Later in the events, Galadriel will refuse for the very same reasons.) This turn of events begs the question to what extent we may trust Gandalf's judgement in this case. The portrayal of Frodo as an ignorant individual (presented to the reader) depends on a specific narrative configuration: Frodo is apparently plunged into a situation everyone could make sense of – with the only exception of Frodo

---

[43] Original quote: "wird durch die gesellschaftlichen Einflüsse gebildet, setzt sich an ihnen und gegen sie."

himself (and, by extension, all other hobbits). The opening scene could then serve to launch a process of (self-)reflection, so that eventually – at the end of the story – Frodo will have 'learned his lesson'. By dealing correctly with adverse conditions he could become an improved subject. Gandalf's statement about hobbits – "you can learn all that there is to know about their ways in a month, and yet, after a hundred years they can still surprise you" (*LotR* 61) – seems to support this reading. Apparently, hobbits possess more complex personality structures than one – Gandalf – had expected. Yet an altogether different insight prompts Gandalf's amazed conclusion, for Frodo's decision to leave the Shire is not at all based on an act of 'reflection':

> Frodo gazed fixedly at the red embers on the hearth, until they filled all his vision, and he seemed to be looking down into profound wells of fire. He was thinking of the fabled Cracks of Doom and the terror of the Fiery Mountain. 'Well!' said Gandalf at last. 'What are you thinking about? Have you decided what to do?' 'No!' answered Frodo, coming back to himself out of darkness, and finding to his surprise that is was not dark, and that out of the window he could see the sunlight garden. 'Or perhaps, yes [...]'. (*LotR* 60)

This scene is rich in significance: first of all, it demonstrates that Frodo's temporary abstraction is the very opposite of conscious reflection. Secondly, his vision of the Cracks of Doom does not emerge from the struggle of an 'inner self' grappling with a challenge. Instead it resembles a process that is best described by drawing on Tolkien's definition of 'Faërian drama', in which "you are in a dream that some other mind is weaving" (*OFS* 142). It is entirely in keeping with this scenario when Frodo answers no to the question whether he has made a decision. Since he has not defined his role in relation to the challenge he faces, no decision could be made. Yet the sight of the Fiery Mountain reveals to Frodo the kind of story in which he finds himself. The decision he might have made (himself) is effected by conditions that are entirely 'external'. (Frodo's choice indeed sets the external story plot in motion, but it is not based on individualised intention.) Because the overwhelming danger of the Ring threatens everyone in the Shire, it – and with it Frodo – have to leave. As a consequence, Frodo is not 'desperate' because he doubts his own abilities, but because "the Enemy is so strong and terrible" (*LotR* 61). Frodo's departure can thus be compared to the actions of "men caught in the chains of circumstance."

'Doom' motivates his decision, not "the heroic or tragic story on a strictly human plane" (*BMC* 15).

As demonstrated above, the same principle applies when Frodo takes up the Ring for the second time, at the Council of Elrond. Significantly, recent events seem to have left Frodo unaffected on a psychological level[44] – despite his encounters with the Black Riders and an injury that "strong warriors of the Big People would quickly have been overcome by" (*LotR* 216). Frodo's questions focus exclusively on the context and the logic of events: Who are the Black Riders? What do they intend to do (to him) (*LotR* 216f.)? That Gandalf defers answers until the Council congregates (where these questions will be discussed anyhow; *LotR* 214) again suggests that events and their consequences, rather than psychological, internalised processes and their results, form the proper subject matter. "Thinking and wondering" concerns "things that want explaining" (*LotR* 214). The decision that Frodo shall be the Ring-bearer meets Elrond's approval: "If I understand aright all that I have heard, […] I think that this task is appointed for you, Frodo; and that if you do not find a way, no one will" (*LotR* 264). Frodo's appointment is externally motivated, and so is the confirmation of this appointment. Once again, it is Gandalf who insists that neither Frodo nor anyone else (including himself) truly understands the ramifications of this decision:

> 'That is because you [Pippin] do not understand and cannot imagine what lies ahead,' said Elrond. 'Neither does Frodo,' said Gandalf […]. 'Nor do any of us see clearly. It is true that if these hobbits understood the danger, they would not dare to go. But they would still wish to go, or wish that they dared, and be shamed and unhappy […].' (*LotR* 269)

After the episode with the Black Riders, it seems doubtful that Frodo (and Sam, see further below) truly has no inkling of what lies ahead. Yet the passage quoted above illustrates once more that decisions are made and explained with recourse to external, transpersonal connections, even when subjective explanations seem more obvious (no one would blame Pippin for being afraid and staying behind). Pippin's decision is rooted in his relationships with others (his friendships), not in his relationship with himself (his potential doubts, his inner conflicts, etc.).

---

44 That is, all actual changes are external and cannot be equated with inner psychological development.

External bonds and commitments also dominate in the following two examples. "Do you [Frodo] not see now wherefore your coming is to us as the footstep of Doom? For if you fail, then we are laid bare to the Enemy. Yet if you succeed, then our power is diminished, and Lothlórien will fade, and the tides of Time will sweep it away" (*LotR* 356), Galadriel explains after Frodo has gazed into her mirror and has recognized her as the bearer of Nenya, one of the three Elven-rings. She continues: "For the fate of Lothlórien you are not answerable, but only for the doing of your own task" (*LotR* 356). Frodo learns that the Ring not only defines his own doom but affects all the inhabitants of Middle-earth as well, and that the course of events cannot be altered, for "now we [Galadriel and Frodo] have chosen, and the tides of fate are flowing" (*LotR* 357). Although points of contact between all the involved fates become apparent, every doom must be viewed separately. (While the various characters' paths cross time and again, every protagonist has a specific doom.) At no point does the text generate a complex view of the world in the modern sense (a view that relates everything to everything else and incessantly churns out an infinite number of possible actions and assessments).

Recognition of (one's own and others') doom, instead of an internalised subjective process, enables the characters to define their specific roles and positions – as the 'Taming of Sméagol' shows with particular clarity. One could conclude that Frodo has learnt his lesson about pity when he decides not to kill Gollum in the Emyn Muil: after all, he had hoped for Gollum's death back in the Shire (cf. *LotR* 58). Yet comparison with Bilbo in *The Hobbit* shows that Frodo's pity emerges in a very different manner. Bilbo's response bears a certain resemblance with reflection: "And he [Gollum] was miserable, alone, lost. A sudden understanding, a pity mixed with horror, welled up in Bilbo's heart: a glimpse of endless unmarked days without light or hope of betterment, hard stone, cold fish, sneaking and whispering. All these thoughts passed in a flash of a second" (*H* 90).

While Bilbo contemplates the present situation, Frodo recalls a conversation with Gandalf in the Shire: "Many that live deserve death. And some die that deserve life. Can you give that to them? Then be not too eager to deal out death in the name of justice, fearing for your own safety. Even the wise cannot see all ends" (*LotR* 601). In the Emyn Muil, Frodo is able to apply Gandalf's words to his current situation. His fear for his own safety[45] conflicts with his ignorance of Gollum's doom. As Gandalf points out early in the events, Gollum "has some part to play yet, for good or ill, before the end" (*LotR* 58). Frodo understands (or applies the received knowledge) that he, like Gollum and every other actor within the tale, will "come, and go when their part's ended" (*LotR* 697), so that his (as well as Gandalf's and Aragorn's) pity for Gollum may well result from the insight that everyone plays a predetermined role. The narrative structure that ascribes a specific doom to each character also explains why Frodo, after Sam has rescued him in the Tower of Cirith Ungol, insists that the Ring must be returned to him: "I must carry the burden to the end. It can't be altered. You [Sam] can't come between me and this doom" (*LotR* 891). Loss of the Ring would equal the loss of his doom – and thus the loss of his identity within the epic.

Events after the Ring's destruction demonstrate that identity is indeed bestowed by doom (not by subjective experiences). Frodo says: "Well, this is the end. […] Now all is over. I am glad you [Sam] are here with me. Here at the end of all things" (*LotR* 926). Developments prior to, and during, the destruction of the Ring bear out this assessment. Frodo's self-awareness as a hobbit wanes the more that he and Sam approach the end (of their quest and the story). His memories are lost to him (as Frodo cannot personally relate to them any more): "At least, I know that such things happened, but I cannot see them. No taste of food, no feel of water, no sound of wind, no memory of tree or grass or flower, no image of moon or star are left to me. I am naked in the dark […], and there is no veil between me and the wheel of fire" (*LotR* 916). He loses control of his body: "Help me, Sam! Hold my hand! I can't stop it" (*LotR* 921). Immediately afterwards, Sam perceives Frodo with 'other vision': "Stern, untouchable now by pity, a figure robed in white, but at its breast it held a wheel of fire" (*LotR* 922). At the culmination of his doom (quite fittingly on Mount Doom), Frodo is bereft of everything that does not pertain to his identity as Ring-bearer. Apparently, a narrative mechanism eventually

---

45 Frodo adds "fearing for your own safety" to Gandalf's words, thereby pointing out the difference between his and Bilbo's first encounter with Gollum. Bilbo's pity is based on the fact that "Gollum had not actually threatened to kill him, or tried to yet" (*H* 90) – an attitude Gollum does not display towards Frodo and Sam in the Emyn Muil (to say nothing of later events). Frodo's response, furthermore, demonstrates his ability to apply generalized (even theoretical) advice to a concrete situation.

strips the hero of all qualities, except for his doom. As a protagonist, Frodo was never defined by his inner values; now his individual qualities as a hobbit have been shed, so that only the task of bearing the doom of Middle-earth remains. In this respect, Frodo errs (since he lacks knowledge of all the relevant facts) when he announces at the Cracks of Doom: "I have come […], but I do not choose now to do what I came to do" (*LotR* 924). What he had to do, he has indeed done. It was his doom to carry the Ring to Orodruin, where it will be Gollum's doom in turn to destroy it, as foreshadowed in the text.[46] Once the Ring is no more (and the doom fulfilled), the narrative mechanism has run its course and Frodo can be "himself again" (*LotR* 926). With the completion of his task, Frodo's part in the story ends – and "people […] go when their part's ended" (*LotR* 697).

Randel Helms writes: "In Middle-earth, the result of an action is the product of its intent. Here is perhaps the basic difference between the […] structures of Tolkien's world and our own. We know that intention has nothing to do with result" (75). Yet it seems that this intention within the text does not result from psychologically processed choices; it is the product of exigencies predetermined by fate. Frodo's identity does not grow from a conflict between social norms and subjective aspirations, but results from a single decision: to be the Ring-bearer. The freedom that allows for such a choice – and this particular choice only – is circumscribed by an all-encompassing doom. (Obviously, this kind of freedom depends on structures that differ substantially from the modern individual's subjective freedom.) Czerwinski states: "The epic hero can be dumb. But this merely signifies that he is not yet able to perceive and realise the social constraints that make up his identity and which apparently exert their power independently from his own actions" (83).[47] These observations can well be applied to Frodo. The central fact that the text reveals about Frodo is that his identity is bound up with the Ring and thereby with the doom of everyone

---

46 This context stands against the conclusion that Frodo failed in his Quest and counters a reading of the Ring as "addictive" (cf. Shippey, *Author* 119): that an epic hero cannot exist without his fate explains why Gollum so desperately desires the Ring. Only the Ring will accord him the subject status achieved with a fulfilled doom.
47 Original quote: "Daß der epische Heroe tump sein kann, heißt lediglich, dass er soziale Zusammenhänge, die seine Identität festlegen, und zwar von seinem eigenen Handeln […] scheinbar gänzlich unbeeinflussbar festlegen, noch nicht wahrnimmt und zu realisieren vermag."

in Middle-earth.[48] As a consequence, Frodo's character cannot develop: no dichotomy between social and individual intentions (cf. Czerwinski 84) exists in Middle-earth – they are identical. It seems safe to describe this fundamental condition as epic wholeness.[49]

One of the most misunderstood characters in *The Lord of the Rings*, Sam Gamgee, must now move into view. Sam is frequently interpreted as the least insightful character in the text, yet there are good reasons to doubt that he really "is as obtuse as his father" (Shippey, *Road* 108). While the introductory scene has already been discussed, the question remains whether Sam's character undergoes a development in the course of events. If there is evidence for change, it can be found at an early stage, immediately after the hobbits' first encounter with the elves:

> Frodo looked at Sam rather startled, half expecting to see some outward sign of the odd change that seemed to have come over him. It did not sound like the voice of the old Sam Gamgee that he thought he knew. But it looked like the old Sam Gamgee sitting there, except that his face was unusually thoughtful. (*LotR* 85)

Sam confirms Frodo's impression:

> I know we are going to take a very long road, into darkness; but I know I can't turn back. It isn't to see Elves now, nor dragons, nor mountains that I want – I don't rightly know what I want: but I have something to do before the end, and it lies ahead, not in the Shire. I must see it through. (*LotR* 85)

At this very early point Sam is already aware of his fate, and he is the first to point out that the hobbits' journey surely will not end in Rivendell, but will lead them to Mordor: "I never thought I should be going that way [to Mordor] myself" (*LotR* 182). He is also the first to claim a place as Frodo's companion in the Fellowship (cf. *LotR* 264) and insists on it after his look into Galadriel's mirror ("I'll go home by the long road with Mr. Frodo, or not at all"; *LotR* 354) and again at the Breaking of the Fellowship ("I know

---

48 The other major factor that defines Frodo's identity – his love for Sam – is inextricably linked with his doom as Ring-bearer.
49 Another argument against the notion of 'development' in the story is that the exterior plot drives all actions in *The Lord of the Rings*. The episodes obey only the rules of dramaturgy (Théoden has to be healed before he can die on the Pelennor Fields; Frodo has to be imprisoned, so that Sam can free him). They do not reflect a tension created by the hero's development. (Readers need never ask what somebody will *do* next, but only what will *happen* to somebody next.)

that well enough, Mr. Frodo. Of course you are [going to Mordor]. And I'm coming with you"; *LotR* 397). The extent to which Sam's social and individual identity are one and the same is rendered obvious when circumstances threaten to break it apart.⁵⁰

After Frodo's apparent death, thrown back on his own devices, Sam faces the challenge to reach a decision that depends on him alone: "Why am I left all alone to make up my mind?" (*LotR* 715). The situation seems to offer the perfect (literary) setting for a conflict of social demands (destruction of the Ring) with personal needs (Sam's love for Frodo), yet it is resolved in an entirely different, unexpected manner. His initial decision to meet society's demands leaves Sam "motionless in intolerable doubt" (*LotR* 716). It is only when he has changed his mind and decided to stay with Frodo that "he flung [...] away [...] fear and doubt" (*LotR* 718). The following developments show that this choice does not result in a split of inner (subjective) and outer (objective) events – as one might expect in the context of a modern novel. It is not Sam's doom to carry the Ring but to "carry [Frodo] and it as well" (*LotR* 919). Sam's tenacity and willingness to remain faithful to his doom – and thereby within epic wholeness – allows the story to come to a good end.

Throughout the Quest Sam is at one with himself and doom's demands on him. That his speech-patterns (perhaps) lean towards a lower linguistic register has no bearing on the structures that shape the character's epic wholeness. When Shippey contrasts Sam's supposed "blindness" with his "thoughtless courage", culminating in an "Anglo-hobbitic inability to know when they're beaten" (*Road* 108), he implies a discrepancy between comprehension and action (or an inner orientation at variance with an external doom) which ultimately serves to generate irony. Yet there is no evidence for such a discrepancy – and hence for irony – in the text.

---

50 Sam's 'social' identity, prior to his departure from the Shire, is marked by a certain tension. That Sam is convinced of the reality of elves, Ents, and dragons (as described above; cf. *LotR* 43f.), while the majority of hobbits consider these beings the stuff of 'fireside-tales', seems to evidence a certain conflict. Like Don Quixote, Sam believes in the existence of things long discarded and denied by the social system. The major difference between Sam and Cervantes' hero, however, is that Don Quixote's beliefs are exposed as illusory, whereas the beings Sam believes in truly exist. The discrepancy between Sam's convictions and the beliefs of his community ends with his departure on the Quest – an opportunity Sam is happy to embrace (*LotR* 63).

The hobbits' story does not end on Mount Doom, however. The remaining part of Frodo's tale follows a clear logic: once his role within the epic narrative has come to an end, Middle-earth no longer holds a place for him. (Neither does it provide one for Gandalf; Aragorn – who has meanwhile become king – is a different case.) Frodo's journey to Valinor is therefore inevitable. Matters are more complicated in Sam's case. What does it mean when Frodo says "You will have to be one and whole" (*LotR* 1006)? Frodo provides the explanation himself:

> You will be the Mayor, [...] and the most famous gardener in history; and you will read things out of the Red Book, and keep alive the memory of the age that is gone, so that people will remember [...]. And that will keep you as busy and as happy as anyone can be, as long as your part of the Story goes on. (*LotR* 1006)

It seems obvious that Sam's state of being 'torn in two' could only set in with the hobbits' return to the Shire, where the larger world's history is of little interest: "Sam was as busy and as full of delight as even a hobbit could wish. Nothing for him marred that whole year, except for some vague anxiety about his master. [...] Sam was pained to notice how little honour he had in his own country" (*LotR* 1002).[51] Thus it becomes Sam's task to change this deficient situation and to prevent that the story of the Ring-war is forgotten – through political, genealogical and literary activities. Only when a solid tradition had been established (by means of sustained relations with Gondor, the naming of his children and, most importantly, the completion of the Red Book which is finally given into Elanor's keeping; cf. *LotR* 1072, 1077) will his own story be complete, and only then may he join Frodo in Valinor.

Yet Sam's position in the Shire, after their return, is not the result of an inner development. It is completely determined by his relationship with Frodo (although its shape does change, it is always one of love). His 'social advancement' as Frodo's heir is a case in point (cf. *LotR* 1006). It is furthermore conceivable that Sam's literary skills – he is able to read (*LotR* 24), compose (*LotR* 201, 351), and recite poetry (*LotR* 181) – render him predestined to preserve the memory of a now absolute past and afford him a privileged understanding of his own role in the story. His conversation with Frodo on the Stairs of Cirith

---

51 After the end of the Quest, with the resolution of doom, Frodo's identity can only be established by being transformed into history. The hobbits' general disinterest in all the relevant (historical) events corresponds to Ted Sandyman's disbelief at the beginning of the story.

Ungol – which almost qualifies as literary theory – seems to indicate such an awareness. Sam's state of being 'torn in two' then does not result from psychologically explicable inner tensions: it emerges logically from the juxtaposition of his bond with Frodo (urging him towards Valinor) and his task of preserving the history of their deeds (located in Middle-earth).

Unlike the protagonists in a novel, Sam and Frodo lack the division of 'interior' and 'exterior'. As characters, they are not constructed to invite and suggest the reader's 'possible acquaintance' with them. Instead of casting the hobbits in the role of 'everymen' (which would abolish the distance between readers and characters), the text presents them as epic heroes. Of course *The Lord of the Rings* – like any other text – allows readers to identify with the hero. Yet this does not imply that the hero's actions are designed to relate immediately to the reader's reality and experiences. All the heroes within the text (with the only possible exception of the hobbits who never left the Shire) receive an exclusive fate because no mediating author closes the gap between them and the reader.[52] Readings of the text based solely on identification with its protagonists must therefore be problematic.

4. One author, or two, or more

Examination of Sam's role in the transmission of the story begs the question how authorship is conceived in *The Lord of the Rings*. An explanation of its genesis is given early in the text:

> At the end of the Third Age the part played by the hobbits in the great events that led to the inclusion of the Shire in the Reunited Kingdom awakened among them a more widespread interest in their own history; and many of their traditions, up to that time still mainly oral, were collected and written down. (*LotR* 13)

Paul Kocher comments:

> Fundamental to Tolkien's method in *The Lord of the Rings* is a standard literary pose which he assumes in the Prologue and never thereafter relinquishes [...]: that he did not himself invent the subject matter of the epic but is only a

---

52 'Exclusive fate', in this specific context, implies an absolute separation of the text's characters from the readers, i.e. *excludes* them: no direct connection between the characters' fate and the reader exists; nor is there a 'similar fate' for the reader.

modern scholar who is compiling, editing, and eventually translating copies of very ancient records of Middle-earth which have come into his hands, he does not say how. (2)

The sources Tolkien (allegedly) used are introduced in minute detail (cf. *LotR* 13-15): three large collections of texts were kept in the Shire, at Undertowers, Great Smials and Brandy Hall. The text of *The Lord of the Rings* purports to derive mainly from the Red Book of Westmarch, based on Bilbo's private diary and expanded by Frodo, Sam, and at least one other unknown writer, who added "a fifth [volume] containing commentaries, genealogies, and various other matter concerning the hobbit members of the Fellowship" (*LotR* 14). The loss of the original Red Book, of which only copies survive, complicates the situation – all the more so if one takes into account that the most important copy was produced in Gondor, 170 years after the reported events, by a certain "Findegil, King's Writer", a copy not found at Undertowers (where the original of the Red Book was kept) but at Great Smials. This transcript stands out because it "alone contains the whole of Bilbo's 'Translations from the Elvish'" (*LotR* 14), which, however, cannot provide any information about the events described in *The Lord of the Rings* as they cover only those oral and written sources that were already in existence before the year 1418 (Shire Reckoning).

Taken seriously, this construct of sources and origins must have far-reaching effects for the overall perception of *The Lord of the Rings*. To begin with, the text appears as a conglomerate of various genres that must be ascribed to different authors (within the text). A first group consists of the songs sung by the hobbits, especially Bilbo and Sam. The 'Troll Song' (*LotR* 201) and the stanza about Gandalf's fireworks in the 'Lament for Gandalf' (*LotR* 351) can be easily attributed to a specific author (Sam in this case), yet the origins of several other songs are decidedly less clear. Initially, the hobbits attribute the verses about Aragorn, beginning with "All that is gold does not glitter" (*LotR* 167), to Gandalf (cf. *LotR* 168); later on, Bilbo claims to have authored these lines himself (*LotR* 241). The text leaves the reader in the dark as to what is correct. Although it seems unlikely that Bilbo composed these lines – the introduction "those verses go with the name [Aragorn]" (*LotR* 168) suggests that they are significantly older than Bilbo – his claim "I made that up myself […] for the

Dúnadan, a long time ago" (*LotR* 241) stands uncontested and does not lack plausibility.

The author's identity is even less certain in the case of the dirge for Boromir (*LotR* 497). Did Aragorn and Legolas invent it on the spur of the moment, or was it newly assembled from traditional materials, based on formalised rules, and adapted to the specific occasion? Or did they merely change the names and references in a pre-existing, traditional text? Other songs in *The Lord of the Rings* have been transmitted anonymously, such as the song of Beren and Lúthien (*LotR* 187) and that of Gil-galad (*LotR* 181). Characteristically, Sam initially believes that Bilbo is the latter song's author, yet it turns out that Bilbo merely translated it.[53]

Another text that features prominently is not only anonymous but in fact incomprehensible for most readers (save for those fluent in Sindarin): "A Elbereth Gilthoniel, silivren penna míriel" (and its variants) remains untranslated – even though it appears to be a key text for *The Lord of the Rings*. This particular song accompanies the main stages of the Quest-story. It is sung at the eve of Elrond's Council (*LotR* 231); at Weathertop, Frodo calls out *O Elbereth! Gilthoniel!* in desperation (*LotR* 191), and he invokes Elbereth again by the Ford of Bruinen (*LotR* 209). The reader, however, discovers only fragments of the song's meaning.[54] Sam cries out (slightly modified) verses of the same song as he prepares to fight Shelob, even though he does not speak Sindarin (*LotR* 712). The song appears for the last time when Frodo and Sam set out towards the Grey Havens (*LotR* 1005).

Another (necessarily) authorless genre in *The Lord of the Rings* is the prophecy. It remains entirely unclear who authored the verses of Boromir's dream (cf. *LotR*

---

53 Translation, in this context, does not imply the modern philological concept: that is, the exact transposition of a text into another language which does not allow for creative changes or additions on the translator's part. Bilbo, by contrast, has apparently created something new (though not original) on the foundation of an already existing text. When Aragorn says "I never knew that" (*LotR* 182), even though he is aware of Bilbo's sources, he is apparently familiar with the content but not with the specific form.

54 The song is introduced – in English – during the hobbits' first encounter with Elves in the Woody End (*LotR* 78). Yet it is difficult for readers to identify this song with the later (Sindarin) variants, all the more so because the opening lines vary (the translated song starts with "Snow-white! Snow-white", whereas later versions always begin with "A Elbereth Gilthoriel"). Readers unfamiliar with Sindarin cannot be sure whether this is exactly the same song (which it is not). Not least, the three variants also differ in content, rendering it impossible to make sense of them without detailed linguistic knowledge.

240) or the prophecy concerning the Paths of Dead ("Over the land there lies a long shadow"; *LotR* 764). While the list could easily be extended, a few more examples may serve to illustrate the point. In Moria, Gimli recites the verses of an unknown poet: "The world was young, the mountains green" (*LotR* 308). Traditional songs are equally present among the Rohirrim ("Where now the horse and the rider"; *LotR* 497), and the Ents' entire cosmology seems to be contained in a single song ("Learn now the lore of Living Creatures!" *LotR* 453). This song, it seems, is also forever changing and expanding: Merry and Pippin can only successfully enter Treebeard's world by adding the line "Half-grown hobbits, the hole-dwellers" (*LotR* 454). In this context, oral reports – colloquial in style, lacking rhyme and metre – must not be overlooked either. These authorless reports serve to transmit knowledge about the history of Middle-earth and are most often delivered for the hobbits' benefit.

The fiction of (historical) sources and authors can be traced to the level of linguistic variety as well: the solemn Elvish style, Old English elements (in the patterns of naming, metre and poetic allusions) that define Rohan's culture, and the hobbits' particular mode of speech support the impression of ancient traditions authored and transmitted by different (often unknown) poets. Relevant historical knowledge is evidently established and communicated by means of refashioning previous (oral and written) texts: although the wording may vary, the original significance is retained. The shift from colloquial language to the stylised form and diction of lays, songs or poems, furthermore, serves to underline the pertinence of the incorporated knowledge.[55]

If the sheer variety and number of texts and genres that exist in *The Lord of the Rings* were found in, say, a medieval chronicle, its attribution to a single author would be hard to defend. It could be argued that the plurality of authors in the text is employed as a means of novelisation, since "parodic stylizations of canonized genres and styles occupy an essential place in the [modern] novel" (Bakhtin 6). However, processes quite different from 'parodic stylization' are at work in *The Lord of the Rings*. Holle Nester states:

---

55 This concurs with Bumke's description of the oral epic as a text that does not depend on (the preservation of) exact wording. Instead, the epic is defined as an inconstant, variable structure, retold and newly told time and again (cf. Bumke 610).

> He [Tolkien] utilises the form of the chronicle, links it with [...] oral means of transmission and has the text [...] put on parchment by the quill of a chronicler, who took part [...] in the events. His historiography is not scientific, non-analytic but exclusively narrative. All elements that characterise modern historiography, [...] a shift to economical or sociological elements, are missing [...] completely. Tolkien presents history in an old form 'as detailed as an old dim chronicle'. (12)[56]

The purpose of this practice can be determined by drawing on Tolkien's explanations in *On Fairy-Stories*:

> What really happens is that the story-maker proves a successful 'sub-creator'. He makes a Secondary World, which your mind can enter. Inside it, what he relates is 'true': it accords with the laws of that world. You therefore believe it, while you are, as it were, inside. The moment disbelief arises, the spell is broken; the magic, or rather art, has failed. (*OFS* 132)

The preconditions for an effective 'sub-creation' outlined here categorically preclude one factor: the *original author*.[57] This specific perception of the author – distinguished by an "individual's 'profundity' or 'creative' power, his intentions or the original inspiration" (Foucault, "Author" 127) – not only dominates modernity but is also inextricably bound up with the concept of literary fictionality. The novel (as the predominant literary genre of modernity) is often characterised by a "process of active, mutual cause-and-effect and interillumination" between the reader and the text (Bakhtin 12). The (modern) author functions as the primary vehicle for such a process that inevitably generates an infinite number of possible interpretations, readings and 'truths': a concept diametrically opposed to the unequivocal 'truth' within Tolkien's 'sub-creation'.

In a medieval context, reference to an earlier source often serves to substantiate the truth of a text. While this popular literary topos may have been employed as a mere formula in many cases, the following verses from the Middle High German epic *Herzog Ernst* seriously insist on the story's truthfulness:

---

56 Original quote: "Er [Tolkien] benutzt die Form der Chronik, verbindet sie mit [...] mündlichen Überlieferungsformen und legt seine Erzählung [...] in die Feder eines [...] Chronisten, der unmittelbar am [...] Geschehen beteiligt war. Seine Geschichtsschreibung ist nicht wissenschaftlich, nicht ananlysierend, sondern allein erzählend. Die Faktoren, die die moderne Geschichtswissenschaft kennzeichnen, [...] eine Hinwendung zu wirtschaftlichen oder soziologischen Elementen, fehlen [...] gänzlich. Tolkien präsentiert Geschichte in alter Form 'as detailed as an old dim chronicle'."

57 The concept of the '*sub*-creator' differs fundamentally from the modern conception of the original author since his work is *derivative*, based on a previous order of (divine) creation, and therefore not at all 'original'.

> The tale will therefore tell us the truth
> [verbatim: the book therefore does not lie to us].
> If there is anyone here
> who thinks this poem
> is a work of lies,
> he should come to Bamberg.
> There the master who composed it
> will prove him wrong without duplicity.
> It is also written in Latin.
> Thus it is without falsehood,
> an entirely true poem.[58]

Invocation of a (written) source supports the claim that the reported events are true (cf. Knapp 26f.). Fictitious or not, such a reference does not produce a form of 'interillumination', but serves to prove the truth and, consequently, the (social, historical) pertinence of the text.

If one applies the same principle to *The Lord of the Rings*, it becomes more apparent what Tolkien means when he invokes the possibility that a 'fairy-story' might be "found to be 'primarily' true, its narrative to be history" (*OFS* 156). Instead of presupposing the modern concept of descriptive historiography as a collection of 'facts', *The Lord of the Rings* rests on a pre-modern framework that defines history as (truthful) narrative. While the described events belong to a distant past that is no longer accessible, the story's truth is derived from the authority of (accessible) sources and traditions. Fictional sources and the large number of authors in Tolkien's text therefore serve to engender a world that is just as 'real' as the events in it, but which exists only in a remote past (cf. Nester 15). In this context, it is significant that the narrated events were concluded by the time the Red Book was completed (allusions to the reunited kingdom, Frodo's co-editorship and the date – 172, Fourth Age – reveal as much). The completeness of the reported (hi)story indicates that its focus is not on "what happened, but how it happened" (Nester 15).[59] With the beginning of the Fourth Age, the departure of the Elves and the onset of an epoch dominated by Men (cf. Nester 17), a connection between the sub-creation and our

---

58 V. 4466-4476 (translated by Siobhan Groitl, based on the modern German translation by Bernhard Sowinski): *von diu liuget uns daz buoch niht. | ist aber hie dehein man | der dise rede welle hân | vür ein lügenlîchez werc, | der kome hin ze Babenberc: dâ vindet ers ein ende | ân alle missewende | von dem meister derz getihtet hât. | ze latîne ez noch geschriben stât: | dâ von ez âne valschen list | ein vil wârez liet ist.*
59 Original quote: "was geschehen ist, sondern [darauf] wie es geschah."

primary world is established as well: "Middle-earth henceforth only belongs to the humans and as such is acceptable [...] as real" (17). Against this backdrop, the presence of an original modern author would indeed mark "the moment disbelief arises" – which would in turn collapse the story's 'truth'.

5. But they could be betrayed... (for another author was made)

How does one approach a 20th-century text that presents so many challenges? Its protagonists do not function like the characters in a novel; it incorporates fictional sources comprising not only diverse genres but also texts in various languages (some of which the reader cannot understand) – and yet, readers may be expected to experience the story as 'primarily true', in the sense described above. What does the author's description of the text's genesis imply? Tolkien writes: "The mere stories were the thing. They arose in my mind as 'given' things, and as they came, separately, so too the links grew. [...]: yet always I had the sense of recording what was already 'there', somewhere: not of 'inventing'" (*L* 145). Does this configuration leave any room for the modern concept of authorship, and how does it affect interpretation of *The Lord of the Rings*?

To begin with, one may reconsider Foucault's definition of the author as a function that "explains the presence of certain events within a text, as well as their transformations [...]. The author serves to neutralize the contradictions that are found in [...] texts" ("Author" 128). This concept of authorship does not sit easily with *The Lord of the Rings*. The text purports to have either many authors or no author at all; its writer claims that he merely "record[ed] what was already 'there'." As a result, it is well nigh impossible to detect "a particular level of an author's thought, of his conscious or unconscious desire – a point where contradictions are resolved" (Foucault, "Author" 128). Where no 'inventing' takes place, such a point must remain elusive.

This observation must lead back to the question of 'mythical method' which Shippey identifies as an essential constituent of modernity. Haug's remarks about the poet of the German *Nibelungenlied* – vis-à-vis the (post-)modern author – may shed some light on the matter:

> The late- and post-modern author withdraws from his role as creator of his account, to invite instead a multitude of voices, allowing them to exist side by side or to intermingle in complete freedom. Touching upon pre-existing structures and motives – one need only think of ›Ulysses‹ – an intertextual play in its own right is triggered. [...] The *Nibelungenlied* poet, however, is bound to a concrete textual tradition. This tradition, in fact, offers itself to him in its many voices, and he foregoes an authoritarian attitude that would enable him to suppress all but one voice and thereby achieve coherence. (334)[60]

This model could be of interest for a different reading of *The Lord of the Rings*. Commenting on *Beowulf*, Tolkien discusses a poetic principle that can be applied to his own text as well:

> The whole must have succeeded admirably in creating in the minds of the poet's contemporaries the illusion of surveying a past, pagan but noble and fraught with a deep significance – a past that itself had depth and reached backward into a dark antiquity of sorrow. This impression of depth is an effect and a justification of the use of episodes and allusions to old tales, mostly darker, more pagan, and desperate than the foreground. (*BMC* 27)

It has often been noted that Tolkien's texts create just such an impression of depth, yet it is equally important to point out that this effect depends on a concert of many voices. The polyphony of voices and of diverse systems of thought and social organisation in *The Lord of the Rings* embraces the epic heroes' different linguistic styles, varied concepts of social order (kingship in Gondor and Rohan vs. the office of an elected Mayor in the Shire), diverging temporal planes in Lórien and Shelob's Lair (cf. Klinger) vis-à-vis the passage of ordinary time in the realms of Men, different textual genres, various languages and the multitude of poets and variations of texts (such as "A Elbereth Gilthoniel"; cf. *LotR* 231, 712, 1005). This complex interplay does not require an intertextual interpretation[61] to add up to a seamless whole. Instead of employing 'mythical method', Tolkien tells a 'true' mythic story (in epic form). His mode of storytell-

---

60 Original quote: "Der spät- und postmoderne Autor zieht sich als Schöpfer aus seiner Darstellung zurück, um in völlig freier Wahl eine Vielzahl von Stimmen hereinzuholen und sie nebeneinander oder durcheinander stehen zu lassen. In Anlehnung an vorgegebene Strukturen und Motive – man denke z.B. an ›Ulysses‹ – kommt es zu einem souveränen intertextuellen Spiel. [...] Der Nibelungendichter hingegen ist einer konkreten Stofftradition verpflichtet, und sie selbst ist es, die sich ihm vielstimmig anbietet und der gegenüber er auf einen autoritären Zugriff verzichtet, durch die er sie hätte einstimmig, stimmig machen können."
61 The various texts do not enter a dialogue of interillumination, reciprocal challenge or parody (cf. Barthes 49f.).

ing thus follows 'narrative method' which, according to Shippey, was replaced by 'mythical method' in modernity (cf. *Author* 313).

If the polyphony in *The Lord of the Rings* is indeed the result of a concrete literary tradition, not of intertextuality, contradictions within the text cannot be resolved with recourse to the modern author.[62] Instead, the author functions as a device for the collation and framing of contradictions created by "episodes and allusions to old tales, mostly darker, more pagan, and more desperate than the foreground. While the author in *The Lord of the Rings* introduces comparable contradictions to the text, they do not amount to anachronisms (nor do they generate intertextuality[63]), even when they remain incomprehensible. Foucault points out that

> the 'author-function' is not universal or constant in all discourse. Even within our civilization, the same types of texts have not always required authors; there was a time when those texts which we now call 'literary' (stories, folk tales, epics [...]) were accepted, circulated, and valorized without any question about the identity of their author [...] because their real or supposed age was a sufficient guarantee of their authenticity. ("Author" 125)

If the author of *The Lord of the Rings* functions – or chooses to function[64] – in this manner, he cannot provide the discourses that will unlock the text. Only the text itself can deliver the key.

Consequently, one may question the benefit of interpretations drawing on (extra-textual) discourses and concepts such as 'trauma', in order to analyze a text peopled with exponents of epic wholeness. One may perhaps conclude that

---

62 Shippey, for example, explains Frodo's failure to destroy the Ring as well as the anachronistic conceptions of evil in *The Lord of the Rings* with recourse to the Lord's Prayer (cf. *Author* 141) and – since this explanation still involves an anachronism – ultimately invokes the "relevance to the real world of war and politics from which Tolkien's experience of evil so clearly originated" (*Author* 143). It must be stressed that this intertextual connection is not suggested by the text itself but results from interpretation – albeit one that Tolkien himself proposed (cf. *L* 233, 252; Shippey, *Author* 141). Only this interpretation allows for a reading that involves the notion of 'guilt'. As demonstrated above, such a reading disregards the central position 'doom' occupies in the text.
63 Intertextuality in *The Lord of the Rings* does not operate in the specifically modern sense; that is, allusions to other texts, their incorporation and re-interpretation, do not generate new, different, additional and competing meanings, once the reader engages with the texts and the texts alluded to. Within *The Lord of the Rings*, the different texts and various genres complement each other to constitute a single contained understanding of the world.
64 Contrary to the modern 'original author', Tolkien writes a text that requires no author – as he well knows. This awareness of being able to abandon his author-role may be the only substantially 'modern' notion one may identify with regard to his writing.

inquiries focussing on an ironic element will yield no results for the same reasons. Can a world that largely depends on male bonds and friendships among warriors be rendered comprehensible through the lens of (heteronormative) sexuality? Can a text riddled with "allusions to old tales, mostly darker, more pagan" be read as seamlessly Catholic? Conversely, would a focus on discourses beyond the author not lead to different, more convincing results? Is it not conceivable that obsession with the One Author deprives Tolkien studies of a wealth of diverse (possibly more productive) readings?

One could, for instance, identify historical discourses that explain the relationship between Sam and Frodo without recourse to the Officer-and-Batman model. When Tolkien argues against an allegorical reading of his text (cf. *LotR* xvii), it seems probable that "read[ing] metaphorically" (Shippey, *Author* 328) falls under the same verdict. It is, after all, impossible to encounter Ringwraiths (they were destroyed), and nobody but a hobbit can *be* a hobbit: "The question 'Are you a hobbit?' can only be answered 'No' or 'Yes', according to one's birth. Nobody is a 'hobbit' because he likes a quiet life and abundant food" (*L* 365). Middle-earth is (or was) part of this world but does not directly correspond to anything within it – not any longer (cf. Nester 16; *L* 239).

I will conclude with one final question: Would *The Lord of the Rings* lose its relevance as a text outside modernity? Perhaps its persisting relevance, and that of all other Tolkienian texts, does not depend on their modernity but simply on their success as fairy-stories! And that, Tolkien would surely comment, is the best that can be said about any text.[65]

---

65 Here follows a long list of people I'd like to thank: Siobhan Groitl for her translation and Judith Klinger, Mandy Gänsel, Raphaela & Regina Gehrke and Sandra Schramm for their support.

Works cited

Bakhtin, Mikhail M. "Epic and Novel." Translated by Carlyl Emerson and Michael Holquist. *The Dialogic Imagination. Four Essays by M. M. Bakhtin.* Ed. Michael Holquist. Austin: University of Texas Press, 1981. 3-40.

Barthes, Roland. "The Death of the Author." Translated by Richard Howard. *The Rustle of Language.* Ed. Roland Barthes. Berkeley: University of California Press, 1989. 49-55.

Bauer, Hannspeter. *Die Verfahren der Textbildung in J.R.R. Tolkiens 'The Hobbit'.* Bern, Frankfurt a.M. & New York: Peter Lang, 1983.

Beowulf. Das angelsächsische Heldenepos. Edited and translated by Hans-Jürgen Hube. Altenglisch und Deutsch. Wiesbaden: Marixverlag, 2005.

Beowulf. The Fight at Finnsburh. Ed. Heather O'Donoghue. Verse translation by Kevin Crossley-Holland. Oxford & New York: Oxford University Press, 1999.

Bumke, Joachim. *Höfische Kultur. Literatur und Gesellschaft im hohen Mittelalter.* 8. Auflage. München: DTV, 1997.

Burns, Marjorie J. "Norse and Christian Gods: The Integrative Theology of J.R.R. Tolkien." *Tolkien and the Invention of Myth: A Reader.* Ed. Jane Chance. Lexington: The University Press of Kentucky, 2004. 163-178.

Carpenter, Humphrey. *J.R.R. Tolkien – A Biography.* London: Allen & Unwin, 1977.

Cervantes, Miguel de. *Don Quixote.* Translated by John Rutherford. London & New York: Penguin Classics, 2003.

Czerwinski, Peter. *Der Glanz der Abstraktion. Frühe Formen von Reflexivität im Mittelalter.* Frankfurt & New York: Campus, 1989.

Eco, Umberto. *The Name of the Rose: Including Postscript to the Name of the Rose.* Translated by William Weaver. San Diego & New York: Harvest Books, 1994.

Foucault, Michel. *The History of Sexuality: Vol. I. An Introduction.* Translated by Robert Hurley. London: Penguin Books, 1990.

---. "What Is an Author?" Translated by Donald F. Bouchard and Sherry Simon. *Language, Counter-Memory, Practice. Selected Essays and Interviews by Michel Foucault.* Ed. Donald F. Bouchard. Ithaca & New York: Cornell University Press, 1977. 113-138.

Grimm, Jacob and Wilhelm. *The Complete Grimm's Fairy Tales.* Translated by Margarete Hunt, revised, corrected and completed by James Stern. New York & Toronto: Pantheon, 1976.

Haug, Walter. "Das Nibelungenlied und die Rückkehr des Autors." *Die Wahrheit der Fiktion. Studien zur weltlichen und geistlichen Literatur des Mittelalters und Frühen Neuzeit.* Ed. Walter Haug. Tübingen: Max Niemeyer Verlag, 2003. 330-342.

Helms, Randel. *Myth, Magic and Meaning in Tolkien's World.* Frogmore, St. Albans: Panther Book, 1976.

Herzog Ernst. Ed. Bernhard Sowinski. In der mittelhochdeutschen Fassung B nach der Ausgabe von Karl Bartsch, mit den Bruchstücken der Fassung A. Mittelhochdeutsch und Neuhochdeutsch. Stuttgart: Reclam, 1970.

Hooker, Mark T. "Frodo's Batman." *Tolkien Studies* 1 (2004):125-137.

Klinger, Judith. "Hidden Paths of Time: March 13th and the Riddles of Shelob's Lair." *Tolkien and Modernity.* Vol. 2. Ed. Thomas Honegger and Frank Weinrich. Zurich & Berne: Walking Tree Publishers, 2006. 143-210.

Knapp, Fritz Peter. *Historie und Fiktion in der mittelalterlichen Gattungsepik. Vol.1.* Heidelberg: Universitätsverlag C. Winter, 1997.

Jauss, Hans-Robert. "Über den Grund des Vergnügens am komischen Helden." *Das Komische. Poetik und Hermeneutik VII.* Ed. Wolfgang Preisendanz and Rainer Warning. München: Wilhelm Fink, 1976. 103-133.

Jolles, Andre. *Einfache Formen. Legende, Sage, Mythe, Rätsel, Spruch, Kasus, Memorabile, Märchen, Witz.* Tübingen: Max Niemeyer, 1972.

Kocher, Paul H. *Master of Middle-Earth. The Fiction of J.R.R. Tolkien.* (First Ballantine Books Edition). New York: Del Rey, 1977.

Lacey, Nick. *Narrative and Genre. Key Concepts in Media Studies.* New York: Palgrave, 2000.

Lauer, Gerhard. "Einführung: Autorkonzepte in der Literaturwissenschaft." *Rückkehr des Autors. Zur Erneuerung eines umstrittenen Begriffs.* Ed. Fotis Jannidis et al. Tübingen: Max Niemeyer Verlag, 1999. 159-166.

Lee, Stuart D. and Elizabeth Solopova. *The Keys of Middle-earth. Discovering Medieval Literature through the Fiction of J.R.R. Tolkien.* Houndmills & New York: Palgrave Macmillan, 2005.

Lukács, Georg. *Die Theorie des Romans. Ein geschichtsphilosophischer Versuch über die Formen der großen Epik.* Darmstadt & Neuwied: Luchterhand, 1982.

Meyer, Martin J. *Tolkien als religiöser Sub-Creator.* Münster: LIT, 2004.

Mullan, John. *How Novels Work.* Oxford & New York: Oxford University Press, 2006.

Nester, Holle. *Shadow of the Past. Darstellung und Funktion der geschichtlichen Sekundärwelten in J.R.R. Tolkiens 'The Lord of the Rings', Ursula K. Le Guins 'Earthsaga-Tetralogy' und Patricia McKillips 'Riddle-Master-Trilogy'*. Trier: WVT, 1993.

Papajewski, Helmut. "Tolkiens *The Hobbit* und *The Lord of the Rings*: 'Fairy Tale' und Mythos." *Literatur in Wissenschaft und Untericht* 5 (1972):46-65.

Petersen, Jürgen H. *Erzählsysteme. Eine Poetik epischer Texte*. Stuttgart: Metzler, 1993.

Rosebury, Brian. *Tolkien. A Cultural Phenomenon*. Houndmills & New York: Palgrave Macmillian, 1988.

Sale, Roger. "Modern Ideas of Heroism Are a Cornerstone of *The Lord of the Rings*." *Readings on J. R. R. Tolkien*. Ed. Katie de Koster. San Diego, CA: Greenhaven Press, 2000. 80-85.

Shippey, Tom. *J.R.R. Tolkien, Author of the Century*. London: Harper Collins Publishers, 2001.

---. *The Road to Middle-Earth. How J.R.R. Tolkien Created a New Mythology*. New ed. London: Grafton, 1992.

Tolkien, John Ronald Reuel. *The Hobbit or There and Back Again*. London & Sydney: Unwin Paperbacks, 1987.

---. *The Letters of J. R. R. Tolkien*. Ed. Humphrey Carpenter with the assistance of Christopher Tolkien. New York & Boston: Houghton Mifflin, 2000.

---. *The Lord of the Rings*. One Volume Paperback Edition. London: Harper Collins Pub- lishers, 1995.

---. "Beowulf: The Monsters and the Critics." *The Monster and the Critics and other essays*. Ed. Christopher Tolkien. London: HarperCollins, 2006. 5-48.

---. "On Fairy-Stories." *The Monster and the Critics and Other Essays*. Ed. Christopher Tolkien. London: HarperCollins, 2006. 109-61.

About the author

PATRICK BRÜCKNER is a student of German Medieval Literature, Women's Studies and Sociology at the University of Potsdam. His research focuses on gender aspects in the works of J. R. R. Tolkien. He held joint seminars with Judith Klinger on 'Tolkien and the Middle Ages' at Potsdam University. His publications include: "Zur Konstruktion 'richtiger' Weiblichkeit in J. R. R. Tolkiens Lord of the Rings" (Masquerade and Essence, Death and Desire. The construction of 'correct' femininity in J. R. R. Tolkien's *The Lord of the Rings*) in *Hither Shore* 2 (Yearbook of the German Tolkien Society) and "Tolkien on Love" in *Tolkien and Modernity* (ed. Thomas Honegger & Frank Weinreich).

Cécile Cristofari

The Chronicle Without an Author: History, Myth and Narration in Tolkien's Legendarium

Abstract

In the cycle constituted by *The Silmarillion*, *The Lord of the Rings*, and *The Children of Húrin*, Tolkien's secondary world is represented from a historical perspective. Yet Tolkien did not mean to write a pastiche of a modern history book. His works rather appear as a compilation of documents from various sources, reminiscent of mediaeval narratives of history. However, some of these documents should not have existed, since, according to the text itself, they deal with events that were either never reported, or never written about. The author(s) of the chronicle of Middle-earth remains elusive; there appears to be no mediation between events and legends, facts and their narration. Historical events and written history develop together in a symbiotic growth, paradoxically achieving a great impression of reality: The text points to its own gaps where there could always be more stories, and no definitive interpretation is suggested. Tolkien thus achieves his ideal of fantasy: not simply a narrative, but a secondary creation, as real in its own way as the primary world.

Creating a myth for England: Tolkien's ambition may have seemed unrealisable in the 20th century, at a time when 'myths' couldn't have meant more than 'stories'. His attempt to blend Northern European legends[1] with Christian narratives to reconstruct what might have been the mythical past of the British Isles may have been no more than an intriguing exercise in weaving anthropology and literature together. Instead, Tolkien's endeavour helped codify what became a prominent genre in popular literature: high fantasy.

The concept of 'secondary world' is one of Tolkien's most important contributions to fantasy. While Middle-earth was not the first 'secondary world' ever created, Tolkien was the first author to conceptualise it as such. A 'secondary world' is a world that is created by a work of fiction; its very ambition is to be different from the 'primary world', the real world, the world as we know it.

---

1 Germanic legends inspired some of the best-known elements of Tolkien's legendarium, such as the story of the Rings; but Tolkien also drew inspiration from the Kalevala and Celtic traditions, among others.

Why bother with phrases such as 'primary' and 'secondary', when one could refer to the real world and the fictional world? First, 'real' need not refer to a physical, tangible reality. Fictional worlds exist in their own right, and stories are 'real' in the sense that they can be experienced by their readers. The second problem posed by the word 'real' becomes evident once we examine another concept Tolkien developed in "On Fairy-stories": the idea of 'secondary belief'. The idea is drawn from Coleridge's 'willing suspension of disbelief', although Tolkien distances himself from it, asserting that if a reader has to make an effort of the will to believe in a work of fiction, then the work in question is a failure (*OFS* 38). Belief in the secondary world must be actual belief as long as the reading lasts. This makes it somewhat more complicated to address the notion of 'reality' while attempting to differentiate between primary and secondary world: Can a fictional world be believed in unconditionally (even though that belief should still see the distinction between primary and secondary worlds), and at the same time, not be real?

The secondary world is actually meant to give a strong impression of reality; in the words of critic Rosemary Jackson: "The tale seems to deny the process of its own telling, it is merely reproducing established 'true' versions of what happened" (33). Ideally, the secondary world should feel as real as the primary world: an independent entity, not the creation of an author.

Tolkien's collected papers, first drafts and essays, published after his death, were aptly titled *The History of Middle-earth*. Indeed, this is how readers are given to experience Middle-earth: by following its history, from its creation to shortly after the events in *The Lord of the Rings*. This history spans millennia, with the Elves as protagonists in the *Silmarillion*, followed by Men and Hobbits. Yet there is one character that never appears: a historian, a character who could be the origin of the established 'true' version of the history of Middle-earth. Even Bilbo doesn't have this function: Although he does write an account of his travels, it is clear enough that this account is not *The Lord of the Rings*, and while Tolkien claims that *The Hobbit* is indeed a direct translation from the Red Book, he does not make such an explicit claim regarding *The Lord of the Rings* (*LotR* 1). The Red Book has eighty chapters, whereas there are eighty-one chapters in *The Hobbit* and *The Lord of the Rings*; and it is supposed to include "extracts from the Books of Lore translated by Bilbo in Rivendell"

(*LotR* 1344), yet those extracts are not to be found in *The Lord of the Rings*. Sam remarks that Bilbo never appeared to have finished writing the account of his own adventures (*LotR* 1294), and it is not even clear whether the task will ever be completed, although Sam is entrusted with the task of writing the last chapters. As Besson (188) remarks, *The Hobbit* and *The Lord of the Rings* show Bilbo as he writes his book, suggesting the presence of another narrator beside him, and at any rate distancing Bilbo's book from the book the readers have in their hands. Moreover, after the end of his quest, Frodo leaves Middle-earth to enter Valinor, which no mortal is supposed to have seen, making the relation of his journey most problematic.

The Red Book may indeed have been written; but how it was passed on afterwards, by whom, and what additional sources were used to complete the final version contained in *The Hobbit* and *The Lord of the Rings* remains a mystery. Tolkien poses as a historian, compiling from various sources and traditions (see for instance *S* 189, 136; *MR* 304, 336, 370 etc.); however, what this original material was is never established in his stories. What are *The Silmarillion* and *The Lord of the Rings*, then – real stories, fictional history? And who is this supposed 'missing link' between Tolkien the author and the stories he is supposed to have compiled from earlier sources?

There are many ways of writing history in the primary world, and many reasons to do so. While that may not seem immediately relevant to a secondary world, it must be noted that Tolkien imagined Middle-earth mostly in the context of a chronology, divided into ages and oriented towards successive goals (the recovery of the Silmarils; the departures of the Elves from Middle-earth etc.), as opposed to, for example, focusing on examining the details of its geography, its ethnography and so on. To some extent, the fictional history concerned with Middle-earth can therefore be examined as historiography.

The Christian tradition left its mark on Western narratives of history. From an eschatological perspective, history has a direction, from Creation to the end of times (Le Goff 241). This conception is evident in Tolkien's works. The history of Middle-earth is divided into ages which do not amount to a cyclical return of the past but show an eschatological progression (Melkor is imprisoned at the end of the First Age, the end of the Second Age sees the destruction of Numenor and Sauron's temporary defeat, the Third Age ends with a definitive victory over Sauron, thus ending the direct influence of Melkor or his servants in Middle-earth). There is an implication that Middle-earth is actually an imagined past of the Earth, for example in *The Lord of the Rings* (*LotR* 106), where a description of the constellations of the story of Middle-earth shows that they are identical to the ones to be seen in the sky of the Earth, and in the "Athrabeth Finrod Ah Andreth", where Andreth alludes to a legend among Men that claims that Ilúvatar will one day enter the Earth in person to mend it, a clear allusion to the dogma of the Incarnation (*MR* 321). What this remark in the "Athrabeth" shows is that the progression is not yet complete. Our present is supposed to be a part of it, though it is set apart from the events Tolkien depicts. They are put in a coherent written whole our present is not a part of; but this is, after all, one of the very purposes of historiography: separating the present from the past, dividing the past into meaningful periods (Certeau 16). Tolkien's works[2] are indeed fictional historiography, written from a perspective that is distinctly Western. Furthermore, we might draw parallels between the history of Middle-earth and mediaeval historiography, as I will attempt to show.

Guénée (4) wrote: "During the Middle Ages, historians had to choose between two [...] genres: histories, and chronicles." The distinction between chronicles and histories is irrelevant today, as we tend to sum them up under the notion of mediaeval historiography. However, during the first half of the Middle Ages, histories were considered as the more 'noble' genre (Guénée 6), with Greek historians serving as a model: Histories took the form of a tale, "following the course of time but omitting dates" (Guénée 8). Their ties with literature were significant: While histories were supposed to deal with actual events, they were also largely concerned with the beauty of the story. As embellishing was one of the tasks of the mediaeval historian, events were considered most valuable if they could be turned into meaningful stories (Gauvard and Labory 191). Chronicles, on the other hand, a 'minor' genre until the 12th century (Guénée 9), represented the more technical side of history. They were based on a series of dates, and aimed at representing the past in the driest, most factual way they

---

2 For want of a better word, we will refer to the cycle constituted by *The Lord of the Rings* and *The Silmarillion* as the history of Middle-earth – without italics to distinguish it from the published *History of Middle-earth*.

could. Unlike histories, their initial purpose was the recording of dates and facts, without any literary concern. Indeed, although the authors of chronicles were usually known, Guénée insists that they did not perceive their work as autonomous. The idea that the work of individual historians might be unique, offering an original point of view on the past, was unknown: Historians saw themselves as merely adding their contribution to a universal chronicle, started by Eusebius of Cesarea's original chronicle (Guénée 6). The notion that the more exact and factual form might be considered the minor one, and the more literary, but less scrupulously precise, the major form, may come as a surprise to modern mentalities; however, in the early mediaeval mind, the literary aspect was often more valued than adherence to established facts.

Nonetheless, this picture was not unchanging: In Iceland, Snorri Sturluson took great pains to satisfy his audience of the veracity of his stories (Boyer 133), and it was considered a disgrace for skalds to over-embellish the truth or invent facts, even for the sake of writing a pleasing story (Boyer 124). For Snorri, writing about history involved both respecting the truth and giving it a literary value. Around the same period in the rest of Europe, chronicles gained value in the eyes of historians, who were starting to feel more concerned about precise facts (although literary aesthetics were still a prominent concern). Chronicles recorded dates and places with precision, which made them now especially valuable. After the 12th century, chronicles were no longer considered as a minor genre, but viewed as having an advantage over histories: Besides being good works of literature, they were also reliable documents on the past (Guénée 9). The transition from histories as literary works to history as being mainly documents was thus not completed during the Middle Ages. Gauvard and Labory remark that as late as the 15th century, chronicles could still be works aimed at a popular audience, that meant to entertain (190) or moralise, by deducing a morality from actual events (191). Writing history for the sake of knowing the past was an enterprise limited to lawyers, judges or notaries, who had an immediate, concrete use for it (Autrand 163; Heers 77). Outside these professions, historians were authors of literary works as much as scholars.

After these preliminary notes, examining the history of Middle-earth in the light of mediaeval narratives of history may lead to a number of remarks. First of all, it is quite obvious that if it is history, it is not a pastiche of 20th-century historiography: Dates are very rare, there is no discussion of the sources in the text nor any attempt at placing the author in the position of an interpreter of the facts he writes about, a role that is today understood to be part and parcel of a historian's task. At first glance, the history of Middle-earth seems to have much in common with ancient or mediaeval historiography, writing about the past in a literary form, with few concerns for asserting or proving the factual exactness of the text, and not, like late mediaeval chronicles often did, including a formula giving the name of the author and stating that he compiled his notes from trustworthy sources or first-hand accounts (Marchello-Nizia 14). One could picture *The Silmarillion* as the work of a historian writing shortly after Aragorn's return on the throne of Gondor, retrospectively compiling the events that led to the fall of Sauron, the departure of the Elves and the return of peace after three long ages in Middle-earth. However, the structure of the book itself[3] suggests a counter-argument: *The Silmarillion* is hardly a unified work. The opening sections ('Ainulindalë' and 'Valaquenta') are written in the style of religious texts. The phrasing of the 'Ainulindalë' may remind the reader of the Book of Genesis: short phrases taking the form of statements with few stylistic embellishments, a simple, occasionally archaic vocabulary:

> There was Eru, the One, who in Arda is called Ilúvatar; and he made first the Ainur, the Holy Ones, that were the offspring of his thought, and they were with him before aught else was made. And he spoke to them, propounding to them themes of music; and they sang before him, and he was glad. (*S* 3)

The following section, the 'Valaquenta', opens with a paragraph that reads like a shorter version of the paragraph quoted above,[4] suggesting two different versions of the same text rather than a continuation. The style of the

---

[3] The structure of *The Silmarillion* is mostly a result of the circumstances of its publication: Christopher Tolkien, helped by Guy Gavriel Kay, had to collect his late father's manuscripts and give a publishable form to papers that were largely unrelated to each other. Furthermore, the final form of *The Silmarillion* would have been given if Tolkien had lived long enough to finish it is a matter of conjecture. However, given the nature of the manuscripts that were later collected in *The History of Middle-earth* (isolated stories or essays, often with their own beginning and end, which do not always appear to be part of a larger project), it seems quite plausible that a hypothetical *Silmarillion* written and edited by Tolkien himself would have had a similar form – supposing, of course, that such a project could possibly have seen the light in spite of Tolkien's tendency to rewrite and revise elements of the history of Middle-earth to no end. We might argue, moreover, that the history of Middle-earth contemporary readers are acquainted with is the result of a collective effort (from Tolkien, his son and Kay), and that dismissing Christopher Tolkien and Guy Gavriel Kay's work by speculating on what Tolkien himself would have wanted may be misguided in itself.

[4] "In the beginning Eru, the One, who in the Elvish tongue is called Ilúvatar, made the Ainur of his thought […]" (*S* 15).

Valaquenta is more didactic, and the titles of the subchapters evoke the form of an essay or treatise ('Of the Valar', 'Of the Maiar', 'Of the Enemies'). The chapter itself is a catalogue of the various Powers who came to live inside Arda, and their attributes, possibly evoking Hesiod's *Theogony* and its catalogue of gods and heroes. The following chapters retain a style that is characterised by poetic or archaic structures,[5] reminiscent of an epic style. Some of the chapters feature many characters instead of a single protagonist, use an external focus and span long periods of time (such as the first chapter of the 'Quenta Silmarillion', 'Of the beginning of days'). Others, however, focus on a restricted number of protagonists and function in a way that is much closer to the standards of contemporary fantasy: They are centred on the struggles of individual characters whose thoughts may be revealed, develop during a shorter period of time and come to a conclusion when the protagonists' struggles reach a solution. The stories of Beren and Lúthien, and of Túrin Turambar, are the most notable of those.

There is, then, a great variety of styles and narrative modes inside *The Silmarillion* itself, with occasional repetitions (such as the beginnings of the 'Ainulindalë' and 'Valaquenta'), and breaks of narrative continuity marked by a disruption of the chronology (when the focus shifts from the Noldor in Valinor to the Sindar in Middle-earth, and from the Valar to the first awakening of Men), or by a shift to a story that forms a secondary plot and does not further the main plot of the Silmarils (e.g. the story of Túrin). It is therefore impossible to read it as the work of one fictional historian, all the more if one adds *The Lord of the Rings* and the posthumously published *The Children of Húrin*, which are separate works in their own right, but part of the continuity as well. The necessity of including *The Lord of the Rings* is obvious, as it closes the story of the battle against evil in Middle-earth. *The Children of Húrin* may seem to be a more peripheral tale: Túrin slays an important member of Morgoth's army (the dragon Glaurung), but that killing does not end the war, nor even tip the balance to either side. However, although Túrin's story does not immediately further the plot of the *Silmarillion*, another fragment, that was not included

---

5 "And ere yet there was anything that grew [...]" (S 27); "And when Valinor was fullwrought and the Valar were established, in the midst of the plain beyond the mountains they built their city, Valmar of many bells" (S 31).

in *The Silmarillion* (although it is alluded to (45), and although Tolkien found it important enough to rewrite it several times), casts a new light on his story. It refers to one of Mandos' prophecies, and is the only depiction of the end of times in Tolkien's works. According to it, the end of the world will start with Melkor breaking free, and Túrin coming back to fight him and avenge his family (*LR* 333). If Túrin is given such a crucial role for the history of Middle-earth, then there is no doubt that his story should feature in detail in the story of it. The disparity between his story and the rest of *The Silmarillion*, however, remains noteworthy.

Tolkien once expressed his ambition to write "one long Saga of the Jewels and the Ring" (*S* xiii). By 'saga', he certainly referred to the original Norse definition: a work of prose, the most famous of which depicted the lives of saints, heroes or kings, and which featured as historical works and entertainment (as pointed out earlier, from Snorri's commitment to the truth). This statement needs to be discussed: Unlike some popular mediaeval texts of mainland Europe (such as the Reynard cycle) which were largely anonymous compilations realised by more than one person, or even the Sagas of the Icelanders whose authors are still unknown, the sagas of kings and heroes were generally put in written form by one known author who unified the text. However, the writing of sagas such as the *Heimskringla*, or of course the *Eddas*, relied heavily on earlier sources, including oral traditions; the author who put the text into unified written form may be known, but as was most often the case in mediaeval literature, the subject matter was largely not his creation. Maybe Tolkien's intent, then, was simply to pose as a modern day Snorri, compiling earlier material into one long contemporary saga. However, the resulting work is too diverse to suggest that this ambition was realised: The fictional sources are far from being perfectly unified.

In fact, the one historical genre that required a variety of authors, all augmenting it instead of writing their own version, was the chronicle – the universal chronicle that, according to Guénée, was supposed to constitute one large tapestry, rather than a collection of isolated documents. Moreover, this genre required its authors to be absolutely truthful, which meant that the best chroniclers were supposed to be not mere observers, but actors in their own right (Heers 73). Heers (77) argues that, in Italy, notaries made respected chroniclers, because their status as lawyers meant that their words were trustworthy, but especially because they were direct witnesses of many important events where law or administration might have been concerned. Chronicles were the raw fabric of history, directly composed by actors in the events themselves, instead of being put in literary form by a writer who had not actually been present; this is why the skalds in Iceland were to march with a king's army; to be able to tell first-hand accounts of the king's feats (Boyer 124). And we should note that in the history of Middle-earth, too, there are few casual observers. Maglor, the great poet, is a king in Middle-earth; Daeron takes an active part in the adventures of Beren and Lúthien, even though that part mostly consists in trying to forestall Lúthien's efforts to flee Doriath (S 201); Bilbo and Frodo are the heroes of their own adventures. In Middle-earth, anyone who writes also appears to be a man of action, or at least to have directly experienced or witnessed the events they write about.

Should we stop talking about the history of Middle-earth, and call it the chronicle of Middle-earth instead, viewing it as raw material rather than a completed history?[6] The first problem that arises is that the text is not a collection of first-hand accounts, but clearly a collection of rewritten stories. Even if we choose to understand it as a rewriting (most likely an abridged translation) of a universal chronicle, the question of authorship becomes problematic. Chronicles were not anonymous; quite the opposite, in fact, as showed earlier. If one sought to compare the history of Middle-earth to a fictional 'universal chronicle', one should note that the various parts of that chronicle are anonymous, quite different from what happened in the Middle Ages of the primary world. In *The Silmarillion*, Tolkien makes numerous allusions to the legends that were written about the events he depicts, often introducing a chapter with 'It is said' or 'It is told' (sixty-two times in the 'Quenta Silmarillion' alone), but names of actual writers of these legends are extremely rare. Only three of them are named (Elemmirë, Maglor and one Glirhuin), and they are also never the writers of the text itself, but only its sources (as is quite clear when the text alludes to the lays of Beren and

---

6 I understand 'raw material' independently of any consideration of value, but simply as a means to differentiate between first-hand accounts (the chronicles) and rewritten, embellished and stylised second-hand accounts (histories).

Lúthien, or of Túrin, and points out that it is only giving a shortened prose version of these works; *S* 189, 236). Of the two great minstrels of Beleriand mentioned in the text, only one, Maglor, is credited as a supposed source for the *Silmarillion*; the other one, Daeron, is said to have invented writing, but the use to which he put his writing is never revealed. Who, then, is the author of the universal chronicle of Middle-earth?

In fact, a very large number of factors make that question extremely hard, and perhaps impossible, to answer. First of all, let us consider the question of the point of view. According to the perspective of modern readers on narration, some coherence between the source of the story (the narrator) and the viewpoint is expected. For example, only an external, omniscient narrator (often referred to by narratologists as 'God's viewpoint') is supposed to have access to any and all characters' thoughts or private life. If the narrator is a character in the story, then this character is supposed to be able to relate an eyewitness account of the events he or she took part in, and no others. If the narrator is supposed to have compiled the story from earlier sources, then the same requirements apply to those sources, and besides, there should be at least a plausible explanation as to how the narrator came into the possession of the source material. This is not the case in the history of Middle-earth. *The Lord of the Rings* is supposed to come from Frodo's eyewitness account; yet a good third of the novel relates to events at which Frodo wasn't present, and books IV and VI, although depicting Frodo's journey, nonetheless adopt Sam's point of view in many sections. It could be argued that Frodo may have had long conversations with his companions after the victory. However, even though the Red Book is mentioned and seems to be of some importance to Bilbo and Frodo, and even though the aftermath of the quest is described at length, there is a gap where the conversations between former members of the Fellowship, leading to an exchange of information, are concerned. While it was common practice for mediaeval historians to quote the names of the eyewitnesses from whom they learned the information they used in their books, as a guarantee of their sources' reliability in a context where facts could be difficult to ascertain, Frodo's process of research in *The Lord of the Rings* is obscured – even though it would probably have been more crucial to the writing of the book than his conversations with Bilbo which are described at length. Instead, it seems that Tolkien purposefully left an open gap between events and story.[7]

The same inconsistency can be observed between the viewpoint and the supposed sources in *The Silmarillion*. Private conversations between Melian and Galadriel in Doriath are reported in detail (*S* 145-46), even though the Sindar of Doriath are supposed to have little taste for writing, except when events of the utmost importance are concerned. The private feelings of Eöl as he chases after Aredhel and Maeglin are also exposed, even though Eöl was put to death very shortly afterwards, and could not possibly have told anyone about his journey (*S* 157). The land of Dungortheb, which Beren crosses to reach Doriath, is described in detail, even though no Men or Elves ever inhabited it, and Beren supposedly never spoke about his journey (*S* 192). In the case of the story of Fingolfin's death it becomes even more striking: The text states that no songs were ever written about it (*S* 179), yet describes the event in great detail. How could a hypothetical compiler of the story have come across such a detailed account, if no documents exist?

Of course, if we were dealing with actual mediaeval historiography rather than contemporary fiction, this would be quite easy to explain. After all, mediaeval historians did not hesitate to embellish their stories, and could quite simply have invented feelings and thoughts for their protagonists, to strengthen the emotional impact of their tales. This would not be an altogether unacceptable explanation for the discrepancy between supposed narrator and viewpoint in *The Silmarillion*. However, a problem remains: The fact that *The Silmarillion* consists of one book, telling the story of the world from its creation to the end of the Third Age, implies that there was one person, at least, who was in a position to collect all the different stories and compile them into a single book. But examination of the few known authors of the different sources for the book shows that this would hardly have been possible. One of the authors mentioned is one Elemmirë of the Vanyar, a people that went to Valinor and

---

[7] It is worth noting that in the unpublished epilogue to *The Lord of the Rings*, Tolkien indeed shows Sam as he researches and collects details of the adventures of his former companions, before completing the Red Book. There exist different versions of this epilogue, showing that Tolkien gave it a lot of consideration. Nevertheless he ultimately chose not to include it, even though it answered some important questions about the evolution of the story.

never came back to Middle-earth (*S* 80). Another one is Maglor, one of the sons of Fëanor who wrote his songs after spending a long time in Middle-earth after the flight of the Noldor. The other two major ones, of course, are Bilbo and Frodo. Our hypothetical compiler, then, must have been in a position to have access to documents in Valinor, and in Middle-earth at the beginning of the Fourth Age, where they had access to both the Elves' songs and documents in the Shire. Frodo is ruled out, given that *The Lord of the Rings* ends after his departure, and so are Gandalf and Elrond, the two characters most likely to have had access to Bilbo's Red Book. In fact, only an Elf leaving Middle-earth after Aragorn's death would have been in a position to gather the documents relating the history of Middle-earth.

This leaves Legolas as the only possible candidate, since, according to Appendix B at the end of *The Lord of the Rings*, he did not leave Middle-earth until after Aragorn's death. Of course, presenting Legolas as the hidden author of the history of Middle-earth would sound farfetched to many readers, and not only because the text shows him as a warrior rather than a writer. The main problem is that the text hardly shows any trace of unification, which means that no discussion about the character who might have written it could yield a truly satisfactory result. One could go as far as to argue that Tolkien may have deliberately erased any traces of a possible universal historian, not by placing all of his characters in a position where none of them could possibly have compiled all the information contained in the various books (technically, Legolas could have, and perhaps a few other unnamed Elves as well), but by making the very idea of a universal historian unlikely by the sheer diversity and scope of the text.

It should be noted that Tolkien, in his very first versions of the myths of Middle-earth, apparently thought of this problem. The character of Ælfwine, who went to Valinor long after the Elves had departed, satisfyingly fulfilled the part of the historian. But that character does not appear in later versions, and since the later *Silmarillion* tells that as the Earth became round, Valinor was sundered from it, and there only remained a path that was not actually physical, and that none but the Elves could use, this story does not fit well into the final version of the history of Middle-earth.⁸ In any case, it is not consistent with the body of myths gathered in *The Silmarillion*.

The legends remain, then, a hybrid compilation: too diverse to pass as the work of one author alone, but impossible to explain in the contemporary terms of narratology except with the vague notion of a fluid, shifting narrative voice. But legends are not the only narratives present in the history of Middle-earth. Prophecies are quite frequent, too: not omens, but explicitly voiced prophecies, by divine or heroic characters. The prophecies of Mandos are the most important (Mandos foretells Finwë's death and the ruin of the Noldor in Middle-earth, for example), but other characters, such as Finrod, also seem to possess a limited capacity to foretell events (Finrod told Galadriel about the oath he would have to take that would result in his death, long before he even became acquainted with Beren's ancestors; *S* 150). In a way, then, stories appear before the events themselves.

Flieger (xxi) stated that "Tolkien's fictive assumption, the very foundation and basis of his invented world, [is] that language creates the reality it describes and that myth and language work reciprocally on each other." She did have a point in this, although the notion that 'language creates the reality it describes' might be debated. There is indeed a reciprocal relationship in Tolkien's works between language and myths, stories and events, which may become more evident with a brief explanation of what 'myth' could mean. Myths are tales; but there is more to them. Myths are events told in a way that puts the emphasis on their meaning and unity. They are the opposite of anecdotes: Instead of simply narrating events, they construct them as meaningful stories; or even, as Barthes argued, as signs, where the story becomes a signifier with a whole new signification (228). Barthes' theory of myths was primarily intended as a sociological tool,

---

8   The character seemed to reappear sporadically in Tolkien's texts. In *The Notion Club Papers*, an abandoned novel dating from the 1940s, where a group of academics explores the past through their dreams, one member of the group, named Arundel Lowdham, accesses the consciousness of an Anglo-Saxon character called Ælfwine, and has visions of Númenor and Valinor. In some versions of the *Narn i Hîn Húrin*, the text is introduced by "Here begins that tale which Ælfwine made from the *Húrinien*" (*WJ* 311). The identity of Ælfwine in that text is not elaborated on, however, and *The Notion Club Papers* was never finished, nor does it explicitly claim that the whole history of Middle-earth was written by that selfsame Ælfwine who claimed to have confused visions of Númenor. See Honegger for a concise summary of the 'Ælfwine question'.

but it can apply to literature as well: In a literary work, then, a myth would be a narrative told in the form of a tale that is suffused with meaning.

In the context of the fictional history of Middle-earth, myths would be events written into meaningful tales, and the telling of those tales has a particular place in Tolkien's works. In *The Notion Club Papers*, the characters, who receive visions of the past in their dreams, make just such a distinction: What they look for in the past is not raw facts, but meaningful stories. Yet they recognise that these stories would necessarily exist with "uncompleted passages, weak joints, gaps". The gaze that sees events as if they were happening before it may see a complete picture, but this picture would be impossible to understand; the gaze that perceives meaning has to be content with a partial picture, in which there will always remain gaps to be filled, different points of view to adopt, different stories to emphasise (*SD* 230).

I attempted to establish that if one examines the changes in point of view through *The Silmarillion* and *The Lord of the Rings*, authorship in the history of Middle-earth becomes impossible to trace. The stories are there, but no hypothesis concerning their source seems satisfying. Given the fact that a number of narratives actually start as prophecies, it may be possible to formulate another hypothesis. There is in fact no author; stories and events function in a kind of symbiosis. Outwardly, the history of Middle-earth seems to be inspired by mediaeval historical narratives, drawing elements from both histories and chronicles: The past is rewritten as legends with a high aesthetic and symbolic value, as in histories, but the text appears as a collection of fragments, taken from direct eyewitness reports and gathered in one long winding thread, as if it represented a sort of universal chronicle. But the relationship between events and stories is actually even closer. The stories may start even before the events they depict have taken place, in the form of prophetic narratives. The legends then grow organically out of history, seemingly without the assistance of an author. Writers are not absent from Middle-earth, but whatever they write is rarely shown, and when it is, it can fluctuate (thus Bilbo's song 'The Road Goes Ever On and On' changes, depending on whether he sings it or Frodo does; *LotR* 46-47, 96). In any case, aside from Bilbo's poetry, the rendition of which is not always to be trusted as it is subject to variations, no actual excerpt from the writing of known Middle-earth authors is featured in the text. Writers and poets are characters among others, and do not have a special place as narrators or author figures. The stories are disconnected from actual authorship.

I hesitate to second Flieger's claim that language creates reality, precisely because of this lack of authors, and because, while the various episodes of Middle-earth history often do start with prophecies, these do not account for everything that comes to pass in *The Silmarillion* or *The Lord of the Rings*. In fact, the end of the whole story is depicted only in a prophecy that describes the last battle at the end of the world, in a way that is more reminiscent of Ragnarok than of Saint John's Apocalypse (*LR* 333); there is no description of those events outside the vision of Mandos. Prophecies, then, are not a systematic way to hint at history being born in language. I am more inclined to point at the symbiotic growth of history and legends, fusing into 'myths': narratives originating in reality, but stylised and embellished (though that does not have to mean transformed) until they become meaningful in themselves. In this context, the question of authorship becomes extremely uncertain, to the point that the traditional role of the author as go-between in the relationship between history and narratives of history seems inexistent. History is embedded in its narrative, and vice-versa.

It is time now to return to the concept of 'secondary world' with which I opened this paper. Tolkien chose to emphasise the complexity of the history of the world he had created to give the readers an impression of its depth. However, there is an important difference between history in the primary world and history in a secondary world. In the primary world, events do not immediatly have meaning. They may be written about in various different ways that may picture them as meaningful unities; but that meaning is far from being fixed, and new versions can always be written. This cannot be the case in a secondary world, as there is no body of archives, no archaeology that the reader could experience, and from which they might draw their own interpretation of what happened. Instead, history is delivered as an already elaborate narrative that cannot be any more scrupulously objective than historiography is in the primary world. The risk, then, is for the author to deliver a one-dimensional view of the history of their secondary world, implying that the events and their interpretation were one, or at best suggesting unsubtle binary interpretations, such as revealing midway through the story that the version of history told until then is propaganda, and the reality of what happened is in fact the opposite.

What Tolkien did, however, was far more intricate. While showing the history of Middle-earth in the form of an already arranged narrative, Tolkien left his readers to draw their own conclusions: Should the text be considered, not as a second-hand tale, but as a faithful reflection of the 'reality' of Middle-earth? Is it an incomplete, unreliable narrative? A perfectly objective one? Or does it create the reality of Middle-earth altogether? But he also avoided suggesting simple interpretations, such as driving his readers to conclude that narratives are always untrustworthy, that secondary worlds are nothing more than a fallacy that must be exposed, or, on the contrary, that the story must be true because of the nature of its authors or the conditions in which it was written. Quite the opposite, in fact: Tolkien draws the readers' attention, not towards the question of the reliability of texts, but rather to the idea that there will always be gaps, stories to be told, other narrative paths to explore. Who the historians were, how they may have interpreted the facts and whether or not they introduced changes that were important enough to be taken into account will not be known. The very elusive quality of authorship (if, indeed, it is possible to talk about authorship when the narration is so difficult to grasp), the mystery that surrounds the exact route taken by the various accounts that were gathered in the final text, even suggests a possible absence of authors, and instead a symbiotic growth of events and legends together. This construction both openly reminds the reader that this is, after all, the only way secondary worlds can develop (since the history of a fictional world in fantasy fiction can only unfold through the texts that give it birth), and makes the most of it instead of making it seem like a limitation. The many uncertainties, near-contradictions and unanswered questions are, after all, part of what makes Middle-earth such a fascinating world for so many readers. Suggesting that by its essence, a secondary world must bring some unanswered questions is perhaps not admitting a weakness of the genre, but on the contrary, reinforcing the impression of reality: only fiction can carry all its answers. Reality must ultimately be left open for interpretations. As for fantasy, it bridges the gap between the two: It begins as fiction, but builds layer upon layer of complexity, until it gains the elusiveness and uncertainty of the real.

Works Cited

Autrand, Françoise. "Les dates, la mémoire et les juges." *Le métier d'historien au Moyen Age*. Ed. Bernard Guénée. Paris: Publications de la Sorbonne, 1977. 157-182.

Barthes, Roland. *Mythologies*. 1957. Paris: Seuil, 2010.

Besson, Anne. *D'Asimov à Tolkien: Cycles et séries dans la littérature de genre*. Paris: CNRS éditions, 2004.

Boyer, Régis. "L'historiographie médiévale islandaise." *La chronique et l'histoire au Moyen Age*. Ed. Daniel Poirion. Conference proceedings. Paris: Presses de l'Université de Paris-Sorbonne, 1982. 123-136.

Certeau, Michel de. *L'écriture de l'histoire*. Paris: Gallimard, 1975.

Gauvard, Claude, and Gillette Labory. "Une chronique rimée écrite en 1409." *Le métier d'historien au Moyen Age*. Ed. Bernard Guénée. Paris: Publications de la Sorbonne, 1977. 183-232.

Guénée, Bernard. "Histoire et chronique: Nouvelles réflexions sur les genres historiques au Moyen Age." *La chronique et l'histoire au Moyen Age*. Ed. Daniel Poirion. Conference proceedings. Paris: Presses de l'Université de Paris-Sorbonne, 1982. 3-12.

Heers, Jacques. "Le notaire dans les villes italiennes, témoin de son temps, mémorialiste et chroniqueur." *La chronique et l'histoire au Moyen Age*. Ed. Daniel Poirion. Conference proceedings. Paris: Presses de l'Université de Paris-Sorbonne, 1982. 73-84.

Honegger, Thomas. "Ælfwine" *J.R.R. Tolkien Encyclopedia. Scholarship and Critcal Assessment*. Ed. Michael Drout. New York and London: Routledge, 2007. 4-5.

Jackson, Rosemary. *Fantasy: The Literature of Subversion*. London: Routledge, 1981.

Le Goff, Jacques. *Histoire et mémoire*. Paris: Gallimard, 1988. Paris: Folio, 1988.

Marchello-Nizia, Christiane. "L'historien et son prologue: Forme littéraire et stratégies discursives." *La chronique et l'histoire au Moyen Age*. Ed. Daniel Poirion. Conference proceedings. Paris: Presses de l'Université de Paris-Sorbonne, 1982. 13-26.

Tolkien, J.R.R. "Athrabeth Finrod Ah Andreth." *Morgoth's Ring: The History of Middle-earth* 10. Ed. Christopher Tolkien. London: HarperCollins, 1994. 301-366.

---. *The Lord of the Rings*. 1954-1955. London: HarperCollins, 2005.

---. *The Silmarillon*. 1977. London: HarperCollins, 1999.

---. "On Fairy-Stories." 1964. *Tree and Leaf.* 1988. London: HarperCollins, 2001.

---. "Myths Transformed." *Morgoth's Ring: The History of Middle-earth* 10. Ed. Christopher Tolkien. London: HarperCollins, 1994. 367-431.

---. *The Lost Road: The History of Middle-earth* 5. Ed. Christopher Tolkien. London: HarperCollins, 1987.

---. "The Epilogue." *Sauron Defeated: The History of Middle-earth* 9. Ed. Christopher Tolkien. 1992. London: HarperCollins, 2002. 114-135.

---. "The Notion Club Papers." *Sauron Defeated: The History of Middle-earth* 9. Ed. Christopher Tolkien. 1992. London: HarperCollins, 2002. 161-330.

---. *The War of the Jewels: The History of Middle-earth* 11. Ed. Christopher Tolkien. London: HarperCollins, 1995.

About the author

CÉCILE CRISTOFARI is currently completing a Ph.D. in English literature at the University of Aix-Marseille. Her research focuses on secondary worlds in science fiction and fantasy, in particular the mechanisms of secondary belief, immersion and identification. Her articles have been published by Inter-Disciplinary Press and the speculative fiction magazine *Strange Horizons*, among others. She teaches English at the Technological Institute in Nice.

Index

A

Abrazân, see Voronwë
The Adventures of Tom Bombadil 97
Ælfwine 10, 48, 65-67, 70, 89, 184, 185 fn.
Aeneid 32 fn.
Achebe, Chinua 123
ahistorical 113
Akallabêth 4
"Ainulindalë" 178-179
Ainur 178
altered consciousness 49, 60, 79, 85, 91, 102
allegory 169
Amendt-Raduege, Amy 83
Americanization 116
Amon Hen/Hill of Sight 81
Andreth 176
Anglo-Saxon 111-113, 120
Annals of Aman 16
Apocalypse 36
   of Saint John 187
Appendices to *The Lord of the Rings* 5, 119, 184
applicability 22-23, 25, 28-29, 31, 37-38
Arabian Nights 3
Aragorn 28, 32, 35, 37, 118-119, 122, 178, 184
Arda 50, 57 fn., 178-179
Aredhel 183
Arnor 117-119
Artemidorus of Daldis 52-54
artificiality 55
Arthurian 111
Arwen 119
astronomy 93
"Athrabeth Finrod Ah Andreth" 176

Atlantis 14-15, 64, 66, 70, 74, 92
Auden, Wystan Hugh 62 fn., 92
   Secondary Worlds 121
authority 45, 47, 58, 84
authorship 1, 3, 11, 44-48, 50-51, 62, 64, 69, 71-72, 74, 78-79, 83, 90-92, 96-102, 108, 123, 128, 131, 147, 164, 166, 181, 186-188
   biographical 92, 97, 100-102
   collective 47, 51, 61-62, 74, 91-92
Avalāi 14

B
Bag End 87, 112
Baggins 112, 122
Bakhtin, Mikhail 136, 148, 150
   'absolute past' 139
Balrog 7, 30, 31, 117-118
Balmung 9, see also Gram
Barad-dûr 36
Baranduin, see Brandywine
Barfield, Owen 34 fn., 73-74, 76
   on poetry 73-74, 76
Barrow-wight 63, 75-76
Barth, John 2-3, 17
   Chimera 2, 4
   Giles Goat-Boy 2, 4 fn.
   Tidewater Tales 2-3
Barthes, Roland 185
The Battle of Hastings 111
The Battle of Maldon 23 fn., 60-61
Beleriand 182
Beorhtnoth 23 fn., 60
Beorhtwold 60-61
Beowulf 6, 8-9, 12, 15, 21, 24, 29, 112, 134, 167
'betweenness' 88, 94, 96, 100
Bifrost 31
Big Folk 110 fn.
Bilbo Baggins 1, 9 fn., 18 fn., 45, 62, 77-79, 84-85, 97, 117, 122, 136, 143, 149, 174-175, 181-184, 186
Black Riders, see Nazgûl/Ringwraiths
Blake, William 8, 34 fn.
   America: A Prophecy 8
Bombadil, Tom 44, 75-76, 80-81, 83-84, 89
Book of Genesis 178

Book of Judges 14
The Book of Lost Tales 47-48
Books of Lore 174
Boromir 28, 29, 30, 31, 78, 80, 138, 162
Bradbury, Ray 33
    Fahrenheit 451 33
Brandywine/Baranduin 141
Bree 139
Britain 173
British Empire 109, 114, 117, 124
Britishness 111, 115, 117
Brown, Peter 49, 52 fn., 58 fn., 60

C
Cain and Abel 8 fn.
Campanella, Thomas 8
    City of the Sun 8
canon (literary) 17
capitalism 25
Caradhras 32 fn.
The Cat and the Fiddle 10, 97
Catholicism 21, 24, 129
Celts 24 fn., 111, 173 fn.
Cerin Amroth 82
Cervantes 148
    Don Quixote 148-149
chaos 27, 32 fn., 38
The Children of Hurin/Narn i Hurin 14, 179, 185 fn.
Christianity 128
Christian dogma 27
Christian symbolism 21, 31
Christian virtues 25, 29, 32, 36-37
chronicles 164, 176-178, 180-182, 186
Circe 34 fn.
Cirith Ungol 63, 82, 85, 87, 90, 133, 145, 151, 155, 159-160
Classical Antiquity 28
Coleridge, Samuel Taylor 174
   'suspension of disbelief' 174
colonialism 114, 116-117, 123
communism 24
Conrad, Joseph 34 fn.
    Heart of Darkness 34 fn.
contextualisation 6

corpus 97, 102
Crickhollow 80
Curry, Patrick 116
Cynewulf 65
   Crist 65

D
Daeron 181-182
David and Goliath 37
death 69, 82, 91
The Death of St. Brendan 66
defeatism 25, 27, 38
Denethor 35, 139 fn., 145
development novel 149, 151
de Santillana, Giorgio 12
   Hamlet's Mill 12
divine inspiration 52, 58
doom 135, 136, 147, 149 fn., 153
Doriath 181, 183
double vision 8
Downfall of the Lord of the Rings 97
dragons 7, 9, 11-12, 131
   see also Smaug
   see also Glaurung
dragon killer 9
dreams
   allegorical dreams 52
   deep dreams 54, 58
   enigmatic dreams 80
   theorematic dreams 52
   theory of dreams 43
   travel in dreams 63, 72, 90
dream threshold 59
The Drowning of Anadûnê 14
Dungortheb 183
Dwarves 117-119
dystopia 33

E
Eärendil/Earendel 65, 67 fn., 69, 77, 85, 86 fn., 90, 97, 112
Eärnur 117
Early Modern English 111
Eco, Umberto 132

Edda 114, 180
   Thrymskvitha 13
   Heimskringla 180
editor 122-123
editorial frame 97, 100
Elbereth 63, 85, 90, 162
'Elder Days' 88
Elendil 64, 67-68, 139
Elemmírë 181, 183
Eliot, Thomas Stearns 26-28, 33, 109, 115, 124
   Four Quartets 109
   'indirection' 26
   The Waste Land 26, 27, 33
Elrond 5, 12, 89, 117, 135, 138, 151, 184
Elves 4, 8 fn., 10, 14-15, 47, 50, 56, 58, 63-65, 70, 76, 78-79, 82, 84, 88, 94, 99-100, 109, 112, 117-118, 121, 174-175, 178, 183-184
   elven-voices 75
   Elvish poetry and music 77, 121, 184
Emyn Muil 86, 154
enchantment 49, 57, 70, 75-77, 79, 81, 94, 99-102
The Enemy, see Sauron
Enlightenment 52
Englishness 110-111, 113-116, 120
Ents 84
Eöl 183
epic 133, 140, 149-150
epic past 139, 146
epistemology 59, 71-72, 74, 89, 91, 93, 94-95, 100, 102
Eriol 10, 47-48
Erebor 117
Eressëan/Elf-latin 63, 68
Errantry 97
Errol, Alboin 63-65, 68, 75
Eru, see Ilúvatar
escapism 25, 37, 124
Esty, Jed 115-116
Etymologies 55
eucatastrophe 14, 24, 95
Eusebius of Cesarea 177
everymen 160
Exeter Book 112

F

Faërie 47-51, 58, 64, 66, 79, 84-85, 88, 89, 91, 94-95, 98-101, 131
'Faërian drama' 152
Fafnir 9
fairies 94, 95 fn.
fairy-stories 1, 7-8, 49, 89, 91, 94-95, 99, 132-133, 165
fairy-tale 7, 14, 91, 142
Faramir 5, 35, 37, 74, 78, 80, 92
fantasy 56, 70, 101, 173, 179, 188
fascism 24
fate 144
Faulkner, William 16
   Absalom, Absalom! 16
Fëanor 184
'feigned history' 107-108, 123
Felagund, Finrod 57 fn.
Fellowship 29, 30, 32 fn., 82, 118-119, 157, 182
The Fellowship of the Ring 75, 79
fiction 173, 188
fictionality 38, 47, 147, 164
fictional history 175, 186
fictional world 174
fictitious editor 1
Findegil 161
Fingolfin 183
Finrod 176, 185
Finwë 185
First Age 80 fn., 88 fn., 92, 109, 112, 175
First World War 22, 23 fn., 30, 36
Flieger, Verlyn 57, 67, 72, 98, 185, 187
folklore 31
Fornost, battle of 141
Forster, Edward Morgan 111 fn., 115
   Howards End 111 fn.
Foucault, Michel 128
Fourth Age 36, 88, 98-100, 165, 184
fragmentation 112-114, 117, 120, 122
frame narrative 2, 5, 10
free dream 53-55
Free Peoples 28
French 111-113
Freud, Sigmund 51-54
Frey (Norse god of fertility) 31

Frodo Baggins 1, 9, 44-47, 50, 62-63, 75-91, 95 fn., 97-100, 117-119, 122, 175, 181-182, 184, 186
   Frodos Dreme 97-100
   journey 44-46, 79, 89, 98-99, 147
   as Ring-bearer 86, 99, 136, 144, 149 fn., 151, 153
   Sting, see swords
The Frog King 134
future 44-46, 52, 59, 68, 82, 84-85, 87, 91

G

Galadriel 28, 154, 183, 185
   mirror 82-83, 87
   Phial 85
   ring (Nenya) 82, 154
Gandalf 28-31, 31 fn., 32-35, 35 fn., 36-37, 57, 80, 83, 86, 117-119, 136, 184
   staff 30, 31, 34
   fireworks 83
   Glamdring, see swords
   wizard 30, 31, 32, 34 fn.
genealogy of texts 50-51, 66, 68, 71
genre 134, 147-148, 149 fn.
Gildor 63, 89
Gil-galad 85, 162
Gilthoniel 63
Gimli 30, 31, 119
Glaurung 179
Glirhuin 181
goblins 8
Goldberry 75-76
Golden Book of Tavrobel 47
Golden Hall, see Meduseld
Gollum/Sméagol 86, 151, 154
Gondolin 15-16, 117
Gondor 117-119, 140, 178
grace/saving grace 22, 24
Gram 9
'grand narrative' 109
Graves, Robert 30, 37, 37 fn.
   Goliath and David (poem) 37, 37 fn.
Great Britain 114
Great Wave 74, 92
Green Dragon 84
Green, Howard 69

Grey Havens 45, 79, 117, 162
Gríma 32-33
Guénée, Bernard 176-177, 180
Guildford, Nicholas 48, 69 fn.
Gwaihir 87

H
Hall of Fire 77
Herodotus 8
    Ecbatana 8
heroic past 2, 16
heroism 23-24, 27, 136, 144
    heroic code 61
    heroic ethics/warrior ethics 29, 32
    heroic will 61-62, 74
Herzog Ernst 164
Hesiod
    Theogony 179
historiography 108, 121, 141, 165, 175-176, 178, 183, 186-187
The History of Middle-earth 16, 47, 174, 176 fn., 178 fn.
Hitler, Adolf 23, 25, 39
hobbits 2, 14, 28-30, 63, 75-77, 79, 83-84, 97, 116, 118, 121-122, 134, 141, 143, 174
    walking-song 79
The Hobbit 9-10, 116, 142, 174-175
The Homecoming of Beorhtnoth 23 fn., 60, 66, 74
Homer 13, 28
    Odyssey 28
horns 31, 99
Hulme, Peter 114

I
Icelandic sagas 35, 180
identity 43, 69, 76, 78, 151, 158
Ilúvatar 1, 35 fn., 176, 178
imagination 44, 51, 53, 56-60, 63, 66, 69-71, 73-74, 77-78, 84-87, 89-91, 93-95, 101
'imagined wonder' 50, 89-90
immortality 15, 57-58, 88
Immortal Lands/Immortal Realm 66, see also Tol Eressëa
Immram Maelduin 66
imperialism 30, 34, 114-115, 117
incarnation 176

indigenous minorities 116
intertextuality 6, 148 fn.
invention 44, 51, 53, 55-58, 63, 68-69, 71-72, 74, 83, 96, 166, 185
Ireland 109, 111, 115, 117
irony 2, 26, 148, 158, 169
Isengard 33, 33 fn., 34
Isildur 118, 122, 138
The Istari 57 fn.
Ithilien 86

J

Jackson, Peter 121
Jeremy, Wilfrid Trewyn 48, 56, 59, 64, 66-67, 70, 72-74, 90
Joyce, James 26, 148
    Ulysses 26, 148

K

Kay, Guy Gavriel 178
Kalevala 11, 173 fn.
Karmë 57 fn.
Khazad-dûm 31, 37
King Sheave 66
knowledge, transmission of 12
kraken 30
Kullervo 11 fn., 15

L

Landroval 87
Lang, Andrew 9
    The Red Fairy Book 9
lay 133
Lay of Leithian 5
legend 1, 4-5, 7-10, 13, 16-18, 141, 173, 185, 187
legendarium 93, 96, 102
Legolas 78, 112, 118-119, 184
Lettvin, Jerome 12
    The Gorgon's Eye 12
Lewis, Clive Staples 23 fn., 25 fn., 34 fn., 110
linearity of time 70, 89, 102
literary tradition 27, 159
literary creation/invention 44, 56, 58, 101
Looney 98

The Lord of the Rings 2, 5-6, 8-10, 14, 21-22, 24, 26, 29, 31, 38, 44-46, 48, 50-51, 62-63, 71, 74-75, 77-81, 83-85, 88-90, 92, 95-97, 98 fn., 99-100, 107-108, 110, 112, 116- 117, 120-123, 129, 132, 134, 149, 165, 174-176, 179, 182, 184, 186-187
    Epilogue 45, 87 fn., 91 fn., 183 fn.
    Foreword 22, 38, 45, 47 fn.
    Prologue 45-46, 50, 96, 110
    Preface 97-98, 100
The Lost Road 10, 48, 63-67, 69, 71, 93
Lothlórien/Lórien 82-83, 88, 117, 119, 139, 154
Lovecraft, Howard Phillips 4-5, 7
Lowdham, Arundel/Arry Alwin 48, 59, 63-64, 67 fn., 185 fn.
Lowdham, Edwin 48 fn., 67 fn., 68
Lukács, Georg 138
Luling, Virginia 116
Lúthien 181

M

MacDonald, George 8
Macrobius 52-54
    oraculum 52, 80
    visio 52
Maeglin 183
Maglor 181-182, 184
Malleus Maleficarum 8
Mandos 180, 185, 187
manuscripts 2, 10-11, 17, 121-122, 178 fn.
Märchen 135
materialist 34
Meduseld 32, 112
Melian 183
Melkor 8, 175-176, 180
memory 59, 62, 67-68, 75-76, 85, 88, 93, 108, 116, 122-123, 145, 159
Men 174, 176, 179, 183
Meneldor 87
Mercia 68, 112
Merry 63, 75-76, 88-89, 89 fn., 149
meta-narrative 29
metaphor 130-131
middenerd 93
Middle Ages 176-177, 181
'Middle Days' 88

Middle-earth 7-8, 16, 21, 36, 46-47, 50, 60, 64, 75, 80-81, 86, 88, 91, 93-94, 100, 109-110, 112-113, 116, 118-120, 122, 141, 173-179, 181-182, 184-188
Milton, John 34 fn., 35 fn., 111
   Paradise Lost 35 fn.
   History of Britain 111
Minas Morgul 117
Minas Tirith 35
Mirkwood 117
mode of imagination 56, 60, 73, 86, 90
modes of perception 58-59, 71, 74, 77
modernity 22, 25-27, 38, 43, 95, 129, 131-133, 141, 147
modernism 115, 131, 133, 148, 149
modern world-view 154
morality 34, 36
Mordor 81, 87, 157
Morgoth 5 fn., 15, 35 fn., 179
Moria 29-30, 32, 117-119
mortality 22, 47, 57-58, 86, 100,
Mount Doom 86, 136, 151, 159
Muspellheim 31
myth 28-29, 31-32, 148, 185-187
   supermyth 10-11
   new myth 24, 27
mythical imagination 63, 74
mythical method 148, 166
mythical past 48, 59, 63
mythical reality 71-73, 85-86
mythological framework 27
mythology for England 2, 10, 110, 113, 116, 120
   invented past 7
   narrated past 11
   pseudo-mythology 5
Mythopoeia 101 fn., 102

N

Nagy, Gergely 5-6, 7 fn., 8-9, 11, 16-17
narrative framework 45-46, 92, 97, 101, 102
narrative framing 48, 51, 96
narrative voice 185
narratives 173, 175, 177, 185-188
narrator 147, 182-183, 187
nationalism 115
Nazgûl/Ringwraiths/Black Riders 29, 81, 153

nazism 24
Navigatio Sancti Brendani 66
Nibelungenlied 13, 166
Nietzsche, Friedrich 108, 123
    Vom Nutzen und Nachteil der Historie für das Leben 108
Nimruzīr, see Elendil
Njal 35
Noldor 179, 184-185
Norman Conquest 111-112, 114, 117, 120
Northern 24, 25
    culture 22
    literature 22
    mythology 7, 13, 24 fn., 31, 32
    courage 21, 22, 26, 35, 37
Nothung
    see Gram
The Notion Club Papers 10, 48-50, 53, 56-60, 63-67, 69-74, 79-81, 89-90, 93, 95-96, 185 fn., 186
Númenor 14, 16, 36, 48-49, 59, 64-68, 70, 74-75, 77, 85, 90, 109, 117, 175, 185 fn.

O

Odysseus/Ulysses 26, 27 fn., 34 fn.
"Of Beren and Lúthien" 5, 85, 128, 146, 162, 179, 181, 183, 185
ofermod 23, 23 fn.
oikoumenē 93
Old English 24, 111-112
Old Man Willow 75, 83-84
Olórin, see Gandalf
On Fairy-stories 9, 25, 49-50, 56, 66, 70, 92, 94-95, 98, 101, 113, 131, 142, 164, 174
orcs 8
Orodrúin
Orthanc 33, 80
Orwell, George 33, 34 fn.
    Nineteen Eighty-Four 33
    Animal Farm 34 fn.
Other Time 53, 57, 63, 69, 72, 77, 80, 91
'other vision' 86, 155
Otherworld 98, 131
Ovid 13
Oxford 2, 112
The Oxford Magazine 97-98

P

paganism 21-22, 24, 28-29, 31-32, 34-36, 38
palantír 35, 35 fn.
parable 34, 36, 36 fn., 37
Path of Dreams 47, 64
Pearl 49
Perseus/*Perseid* 4, 9, 12
Piers Plowman 49
pipe(s) 88, 99
Pippin 62, 75-76, 89 fn., 149, 153
pity 154
Plato 15
    Timaeus 12, 15
point of view 177, 182-183, 186
postcolonial 108, 114-115, 117, 121, 123
postimperial 115
postmodernism 1-3, 13
Pound, Ezra 26, 108, 110
    Near Perigord 108
pre-modern 2, 17, 52-54, 58, 70 fn., 71, 90 fn., 91, 165
present 176
primary reality 92-95, 102, 130
primary world 6, 8, 11, 13-14, 92-95, 121, 123, 173-175, 181, 187
Prince Imrahil 37
propaganda 23
prophecy 140, 145, 162, 185-187
pseudotext 6
pseudo-history 34 fn.

Q

Quenta Silmarillion 14, 16, 179, 181

R

Ragnarök/Ragnarok 31, 187
Ramer, Michael 48, 53-59, 63, 72
reader 2, 4-5, 9-10, 13 fn., 15, 129-130
real history 64, 72, 90
reality 174, 185, 187-188
real world 173-174
reconstruction 56, 72, 74, 96
re-creation 55 fn., 74, 90-91, 96-97
redactor-translator 45, 96
The Red Book of Westmarch 45-46, 90, 97, 122, 159, 161, 174-175, 182, 184

reincarnation 67
reliability 182, 188
retextualisation 6-7
rewriting 180-181, 186
Reynard cycle 180
Riddermark 112
Ring-quest 44, 62-63, 77, 80, 82, 84, 86-87, 158, 175, 182
Rivendell 77, 80-81, 86, 97, 117-118, 121, 139, 145, 157, 174
The Road goes ever on and on 62, 186
Rohan 32-33
Rohirrim 33, 112
romance 132
Roman de la Rose 49
"The Root of the Boot" 97
Rushdie, Salman 3
    Haroun and the Sea of Stories 3

S

Sackville-Bagginses 112
Saint John's Apocalypse 187
salvation 33, 37
Sam 9, 12, 45-47, 63, 75, 79, 82-91, 97, 119, 122, 143, 157, 175, 182
    Troll Song 97, 161
Saruman 30, 32-34
Satan 8, 35 fn.
Sauron 30, 32, 35-37, 154, 176, 178
The Sea-bell 97-100
The Seafarer 66 68
Second Age 88 fn., 92, 175
Secondary Belief 7, 17-18
secondary reality 92, 94-95, 102, 174
secondary world 6-8, 11, 17, 28, 37, 56, 93-94, 121, 173-175, 187-188
Second World War 22, 30
self-referentiality 28
sexuality 129
Shelob 9, 85, 162
Shire 2, 29, 62, 75, 80, 82, 84, 87-88, 98, 116, 119, 141, 143, 184
Shippey, Tom 62, 79, 98
Siegfried/Sigurd 7, 9, 11 fn., 12-13, 15, 18
    sword, see Gram
Silmarils 85, 146, 175, 179
The Silmarillion 5, 8, 17-18, 47, 57 fn., 112, 174-175, 176 fn., 178-187
Sindar 179, 183

Sindarin 56, 63
skalds 177, 181
Smaug 117
Sméagol, see Gollum
Snorri Sturluson 177, 180
Somadeva 2
somatic dreams 52
Songs for the Philologists 97
song 44, 62, 76-77, 79, 83, 85, 90, 97, 121, 133, 137, 143 fn., 145, 161-163, 183-184, 186
source 45, 51, 53, 58, 62, 67-71, 78, 80-81, 83, 85, 132, 161, 163, 165, 175, 178, 180-182, 183, 186
Spenser, Edmund 34 fn.
St. George 9
storytelling 3, 133
Straight Road 48-49, 64-66, 69, 71, 74, 77, 79, 84, 87, 89-91, 93, 102
sub-creation 101, 112, 164
supernatural realm 73, 88
Surt 31
sword
    broken 145
    Glamdring 31, 34, 117
    Gram 9
    Sting 117
symbolism 43, 51-54, 91

T

textual embedding 48, 50, 60, 66
textual genealogy 50-51, 59, 66, 68, 71, 92
Théoden 32-33, 35
Third Age 88, 97, 99-100, 119, 121, 135, 176, 183
Tídwald 23 fn.
time and space 53-54, 57-58, 79-80, 94, 102
time-travel 48, 63, 66-69, 72, 74-75, 89
Tol Eressëa 10, 44-48, 50, 64, 79-80, 91
    Immortal Realm 10, 44-48, 64, 67 fn., 88, 89 fn.
Tolkien, Christopher 1, 10, 17, 55, 96, 178 fn.
Torhthelm 60-61, 63, 74
totalitarianism 22, 30, 33, 34 fn.
totality 136, 138, 149
Tower Hills 80
traditions
    oral 48, 63 fn., 102

scriptural 102
transition 43-44, 49-50, 74-75, 81, 84, 87-88, 93
translation 162 fn.
translator-redactor 45, 90 fn.
transmission 44, 48-49, 51, 58, 61-62, 91, 93, 146, 164
    oral 62, 163
    scriptural 62, 146
Treebeard 163
Tréowine 48, 66-67, 69-70, 86 fn., 89
truth 50-52, 55-56, 84, 164
Túrin Turambar 6, 8-9, 11 fn., 12, 15, 18, 179-180, 182
Two Trees 15

U

Ur-Text 5, 6
unconscious 44, 51, 53, 69, 101
Undying Lands 49, 57 fn.
un-framing 50, 79, 90-92, 95, 100

V

"Valaquenta" 178-179
Valar 14, 28, 179
Valinor 57, 64, 123, 159, 175, 179, 183-184, 185 fn.
Valmar 179 fn.
Vanyar 183
vera historia 50
visionary dream/dream vision 44-47, 49, 52, 59, 71, 73-74, 78-80, 88, 90-92, 95, 100, 186
visionary history 59, 96
visionary journeys 44, 47-48, 64, 66
voice 33, 34 fn., 43, 60-63, 89 fn., 90, 123, 167
Völsunga saga 9, 13
Völuspa 10
von Dechend, Hertha 12
    Hamlet's Mill 12
Voronwë/Abrazān 64

W

waking reality 43, 50, 53, 58, 81
Waldman, Milton 38 fn.
War of the Ring 1, 22, 23 fn., 30, 32, 36 fn., 109, 121-122, 149
Weathertop 63, 81, 85
wheel of fire 81, 86, 155

White Tree 75 fn., 96 fn., 140
Woody End 63, 84
Woolf, Virginia 115
World Wars 109, 114, 128

Y
Yeats, William Butler 115, 117
Yorkshire Poetry 97

Walking Tree Publishers

Walking Tree Publishers was founded in 1997 as a forum for publication of material (books, videos, CDs, etc.) related to Tolkien and Middle-earth studies. Manuscripts and project proposals can be submitted to the board of editors (please include an SAE):

Walking Tree Publishers
CH-3052 Zollikofen
Switzerland
e-mail: info@walking-tree.org
http://www.walking-tree.org

Cormarë Series

The *Cormarë Series* collects papers and studies dedicated exclusively to the exploration of Tolkien's work. It comprises monographs, thematic collections of essays, conference volumes, and reprints of important yet no longer (easily) accessible papers by leading scholars in the field. Manuscripts and project proposals are evaluated by members of an independent board of advisors who support the series editors in their endeavour to provide the readers with qualitatively superior yet accessible studies on Tolkien and his work.

News from the Shire and Beyond. Studies on Tolkien
Peter Buchs and Thomas Honegger (eds.), Zurich and Berne 2004, Reprint, First edition 1997 (Cormarë Series 1), ISBN 978-3-9521424-5-5

Root and Branch. Approaches Towards Understanding Tolkien
Thomas Honegger (ed.), Zurich and Berne 2005, Reprint, First edition 1999 (Cormarë Series 2), ISBN 978-3-905703-01-6

Richard Sturch, *Four Christian Fantasists. A Study of the Fantastic Writings of George MacDonald, Charles Williams, C.S. Lewis and J.R.R. Tolkien*
Zurich and Berne 2007, Reprint, First edition 2001 (Cormarë Series 3), ISBN 978-3-905703-04-7

Tolkien in Translation
Thomas Honegger (ed.), Zurich and Jena 2011, Reprint, First edition 2003 (Cormarë Series 4), ISBN 978-3-905703-15-3

Mark T. Hooker, *Tolkien Through Russian Eyes*
Zurich and Berne 2003 (Cormarë Series 5), ISBN 978-3-9521424-7-9

Translating Tolkien: Text and Film
Thomas Honegger (ed.), Zurich and Jena 2011, Reprint, First edition 2004 (Cormarë Series 6), ISBN 978-3-905703-16-0

Christopher Garbowski, *Recovery and Transcendence for the Contemporary Mythmaker. The Spiritual Dimension in the Works of J.R.R. Tolkien*
Zurich and Berne 2004, Reprint, First Edition by Marie Curie Sklodowska, University Press, Lublin 2000, (Cormarë Series 7), ISBN 978-3-9521424-8-6

Reconsidering Tolkien
Thomas Honegger (ed.), Zurich and Berne 2005 (Cormarë Series 8),
ISBN 978-3-905703-00-9

Tolkien and Modernity 1
Frank Weinreich and Thomas Honegger (eds.), Zurich and Berne 2006 (Cormarë Series 9), ISBN 978-3-905703-02-3

Tolkien and Modernity 2
Thomas Honegger and Frank Weinreich (eds.), Zurich and Berne 2006 (Cormarë Series 10), ISBN 978-3-905703-03-0

Tom Shippey, *Roots and Branches. Selected Papers on Tolkien by Tom Shippey*
Zurich and Berne 2007 (Cormarë Series 11), ISBN 978-3-905703-05-4

Ross Smith, *Inside Language. Linguistic and Aesthetic Theory in Tolkien*
Zurich and Jena 2011, Reprint, First edition 2007 (Cormarë Series 12),
ISBN 978-3-905703-20-7

How We Became Middle-earth. A Collection of Essays on The Lord of the Rings
Adam Lam and Nataliya Oryshchuk (eds.), Zurich and Berne 2007 (Cormarë Series 13), ISBN 978-3-905703-07-8

Myth and Magic. Art According to the Inklings
Eduardo Segura and Thomas Honegger (eds.), Zurich and Berne 2007 (Cormarë Series 14), ISBN 978-3-905703-08-5

The Silmarillion - Thirty Years On
Allan Turner (ed.), Zurich and Berne 2007 (Cormarë Series 15),
ISBN 978-3-905703-10-8

Martin Simonson, *The Lord of the Rings and the Western Narrative Tradition*
Zurich and Jena 2008 (Cormarë Series 16), ISBN 978-3-905703-09-2

Tolkien's Shorter Works. Proceedings of the 4th Seminar of the Deutsche Tolkien Gesellschaft & Walking Tree Publishers Decennial Conference
Margaret Hiley and Frank Weinreich (eds.), Zurich and Jena 2008 (Cormarë Series 17), ISBN 978-3-905703-11-5

Tolkien's The Lord of the Rings: Sources of Inspiration
Stratford Caldecott and Thomas Honegger (eds.), Zurich and Jena 2008 (Cormarë Series 18), ISBN 978-3-905703-12-2

J.S. Ryan, *Tolkien's View: Windows into his World*
Zurich and Jena 2009 (Cormarë Series 19), ISBN 978-3-905703-13-9

Music in Middle-earth
Heidi Steimel and Friedhelm Schneidewind (eds.), Zurich and Jena 2010 (Cormarë Series 20), ISBN 978-3-905703-14-6

Liam Campbell, *The Ecological Augury in the Works of JRR Tolkien*
Zurich and Jena 2011 (Cormarë Series 21), ISBN 978-3-905703-18-4

Margaret Hiley, *The Loss and the Silence. Aspects of Modernism in the Works of C.S. Lewis, J.R.R. Tolkien and Charles Williams*
Zurich and Jena 2011 (Cormarë Series 22), ISBN 978-3-905703-19-1

Rainer Nagel, *Hobbit Place-names. A Linguistic Excursion through the Shire*
Zurich and Jena 2012 (Cormarë Series 23), ISBN 978-3-905703-22-1

Christopher MacLachlan, *Tolkien and Wagner: The Ring and Der Ring*
Zurich and Jena 2012 (Cormarë Series 24), ISBN 978-3-905703-21-4

Renée Vink, *Wagner and Tolkien: Mythmakers*
Zurich and Jena 2012 (Cormarë Series 25), ISBN 978-3-905703-25-2

The Broken Scythe. Death and Immortality in the Works of J.R.R. Tolkien
Roberto Arduini and Claudio Antonio Testi (eds.), Zurich and Jena 2012
(Cormarë Series 26), ISBN 978-3-905703-26-9

Sub-creating Middle-earth: Constructions of Authorship and the Works of J.R.R. Tolkien
Judith Klinger (ed.), Zurich and Jena 2012 (Cormarë Series 27),
ISBN 978-3-905703-27-6

Tolkien's Poetry
Julian Morton Eilmann and Allan Turner (eds.), Zurich and Jena, forthcoming

J.S. Ryan, *In the Nameless Wood* (working title)
Zurich and Jena, forthcoming

Beowulf and the Dragon

The original Old English text of the 'Dragon Episode' of *Beowulf* is set in an authentic font and printed and bound in hardback creating a high quality art book. The text is illustrated by Anke Eissmann and accompanied by John Porter's translation. The introduction is by Tom Shippey. Limited first edition of 500 copies. 84 pages. Selected pages can be previewed on:
www.walking-tree.org/beowulf
Beowulf and the Dragon
Zurich and Jena 2009, ISBN 978-3-905703-17-7

Tales of Yore Series

The *Tales of Yore Series* grew out of the desire to share Kay Woollard's whimsical stories and drawings with a wider audience. The series aims at providing a platform for qualitatively superior fiction with a clear link to Tolkien's world.

Kay Woollard, *The Terror of Tatty Walk. A Frightener*
CD and Booklet, Zurich and Berne 2000, ISBN 978-3-9521424-2-4

Kay Woollard, *Wilmot's Very Strange Stone or What came of building "snobbits"*
CD and booklet, Zurich and Berne 2001, ISBN 978-3-9521424-4-8

Lightning Source UK Ltd.
Milton Keynes UK
UKOW050612171212

203755UK00002B/17/P